RESIDENTIAL CONSUMPTION, ECONOMIC OPPORTUNITY, AND RACE

STUDIES IN POPULATION

Under the Editorship of: H. H. WINSBOROUGH

Department of Sociology
University of Wisconsin
Madison, Wisconsin

Samuel H. Preston, Nathan Keyfitz, and Robert Schoen. Causes of Death: *Life Tables for National Populations.*

Otis Dudley Duncan, David L. Featherman, and Beverly Duncan. Socioeconomic Background and Achievement.

James A. Sweet. Women in the Labor Force.

Tertius Chandler and Gerald Fox. 3000 Years of Urban Growth.

William H. Sewell and Robert M. Hauser. Education, Occupation, and Earnings: *Achievement in the Early Career.*

Otis Dudley Duncan. Introduction to Structural Equation Models.

William H. Sewell, Robert M. Hauser, and David L. Featherman (Eds.). Schooling and Achievement in American Society.

Henry Shryock, Jacob S. Siegel, and Associates. The Methods and Materials of Demography. *Condensed Edition by Edward Stockwell.*

Samuel H. Preston. Mortality Patterns in National Populations: *With Special Reference to Recorded Causes of Death.*

Robert M. Hauser and David L. Featherman. The Process of Stratification: *Trends and Analyses.*

Ronald R. Rindfuss and James A. Sweet. Postwar Fertility Trends and Differentials in the United States.

David L. Featherman and Robert M. Hauser. Opportunity and Change.

Karl E. Taeuber, Larry L. Bumpass, and James A. Sweet (Eds.). Social Demography.

Thomas J. Espenshade and William J. Serow (Eds.). The Economic Consequences of Slowing Population Growth.

Frank D. Bean and W. Parker Frisbie (Eds.). The Demography of Racial and Ethnic Groups.

Joseph A. McFalls, Jr. Psychopathology and Subfecundity.

Franklin D. Wilson. Residential Consumption, Economic Opportunity, and Race.

Maris A. Vinovskis (Ed.). Studies in American Historical Demography.

In preparation

Clifford C. Clogg. Measuring Underemployment: Demographic Indicators for the United States.

RESIDENTIAL CONSUMPTION, ECONOMIC OPPORTUNITY, AND RACE

Franklin D. Wilson

Department of Sociology
University of Wisconsin—Madison
Madison, Wisconsin

ACADEMIC PRESS

A Subsidiary of Harcourt Brace Jovanovich, Publishers
New York   London   Toronto   Sydney   San Francisco

ACADEMIC PRESS, INC.
111 Fifth Avenue, New York, New York 10003

United Kingdom Edition published by
ACADEMIC PRESS, INC. (LONDON) LTD.
24/28 Oval Road, London NW1   7DX

Library of Congress Cataloging in Publication Data

Wilson, Franklin D.
    Residential consumption, economic opportunity,
and race.

    (Studies in population)
    Bibliography: p.
    Includes index.
    1. Discrimination in housing--United States.
2. Afro--Americans--Economic conditions. I. Title.
II. Series.
HD7293.W545   330.9'73   79-51705
ISBN 0-12-757980-X

PRINTED IN THE UNITED STATES OF AMERICA

79 80 81 82   9 8 7 6 5 4 3 2 1

To Mothers

Especially

MARIAH MALONE
EASTER WILSON
MINNIE (GAINE) LEWIS
ELIZABETH SMOOT
GEORGIA ANN MULLINS
HENRIETTA (LEWIS) WILSON
ELIZABETH CARTER
LELA (GARRETT) MALONE
LILA (SMOOT) MULLINS
ALENE (SMOOT) WILSON
ROSA LEE (MALONE) CARTER
OLLIE LEE (CARTER) WILSON
EFFIE (FOREMAN) VILTZ
JULIA (VILTZ) WILSON

Contents

Preface   *ix*

1   **Overview: Residential Consumption,
    Economic Opportunities, and Race**   **1**

    I. Determinants of the Demand for Residential Services   3
    II. A Model for Consumption of Residential Services   7
    III. Metropolitan Location and Economic Opportunity   12

**I   DETERMINANTS OF THE DEMAND
    FOR RESIDENTIAL SERVICES**

2   **Methodology: Demand for Residential Services**   **19**

    I. Data Sources and Samples   19
    II. The *One Percent Public Use Sample of Neighborhood
        Characteristics* (1970 Census Data)   20

3   **The Demand for Housing Services**   **36**

    I. A Preliminary Model and Some Findings   37
    II. Analysis of Demand for Housing Services   40

4   The Demand for Neighborhood Services   **54**

   I. Sources of Residential Differentiation   55
   II. Analysis of the Demand for Neighborhood Services   59

5   Residential Location:
Central City versus Suburbia   **73**

   I. Suburbanization of the Population   74
   II. Analyses of City–Suburb Location Differentials   77

6   Journey to Work   **86**

   I. Models of the Relationship between Residence
   and Workplace Location   87
   II. Recent Evidence on Journey-to-Work Patterns   94

7   Race and Residential Behavior   **105**

   I. Housing Market Discrimination   106
   II. Empirical Evidence for Discrimination   109

8   Implications of Findings for Determinants
of the Demand for Residential Services   **126**

   I. Summary of Findings, Chapters 3–7   127
   II. Implications   131

II INTRAMETROPOLITAN LOCATION
AND ECONOMIC WELL-BEING

9   The Spatial Structure of Economic Opportunity
in Metropolitan Areas   **137**

   I. The Mismatch Hypothesis   139
   II. Further Analysis of the Mismatch Hypothesis   141

10 Wage Differentials:
Race, Residence, and Workplace   **161**

   I. Analyses of Wage Differentials   165

11 Alternatives for the Improvement of
Black Residential Consumption and Employment   **185**

   I. Black Suburbanization   187

References   **197**

Index   **209**

Preface

The availability of large data files from the 1960 and 1970 Censuses and other national surveys (e.g., the Annual Housing Survey conducted by the Bureau of the Census and sponsored by the U.S. Department of Housing and Urban Development and the Current Population Surveys) makes it possible to evaluate empirically a large number of theoretical generalizations that social scientists have previously been able to present only as hypothetical models. Some of these generalizations are not only of major theoretical import, but also have important implications for policymaking that will influence the course of social, economic, and political events affecting our lives.

The rapidly expanding field of urban studies is one area that is particularly rich in theoretical ideas with major policy implications. In this monograph I take advantage of the availability of the rich array of data files now available to explore three related sets of issues. These involve the following: (*a*) the determinants of the demand for residential services in metropolitan areas; (*b*) the effects of intrametropolitan location (with respect to residence and workplace) on economic opportunities; and (*c*) the effects of racial discrimination on black residential consumption and economic well-being, and the relationship between these two problem areas.

Some readers may feel intimidated by the array of statistical techniques—from simple cross-tabulations to sophisticated analytic statistical models—employed in various sections of this volume. The use of different kinds of statistical techniques was in large part influenced by the issues under investigation and the nature of the data available for manipulation. I do not think it necessary for a reader to master the "statistics" before he or she can relate to the empirical results. The discussion of findings and summaries (which are provided throughout the volume) are not overly laden with disciplinary jargon; hence it should be easy for the layperson to comprehend the results.

The fact that I have chosen not to rely upon a theoretical approach reflecting the orientation of a single academic discipline may distract the reader's attention from the interrelated themes that underly the presentation. However, the field of urban studies itself lacks a unified focus, since it draws practitioners from all of the social sciences who enter the field determined to apply their own disciplinary approaches to a particular issue of interest. The interdisciplinary focus of the presentation reflects my own orientation, along with a belief that the communication of ideas, irrespective of their origin, is what the scientific enterprise is all about.

Acknowledgments

This volume has undergone several revisions since its inception during the summer of 1975. I have benefited enormously from discussions with and reviews by various staff members of the Institute for Research on Poverty and the Department of Sociology at the University of Wisconsin—Madison. I am particularly indebted to H. H. Winsborough and Karl E. Taeuber for advice and inspiration provided during the preparation of this volume.

The staff of the Institute for Research on Poverty performed most of the initial typing and editing, and Barbara Weston contributed substantially to the production of this volume in its final form. Most of the computing work was performed by Jay Goldstein and members of the computing staff of the Center for Demography and Ecology at the University of Wisconsin.

The research reported here was supported in part by funds granted to the Institute for Research on Poverty by the Office of Economic Opportunity, pursuant to the provisions of the Economic Opportunities Act of 1964. In addition, the data processing for this project benefited greatly from the population research center grant (No. 5P01-HD-0-5876) awarded to the Center for Demography and Ecology by the Center for Population Research of the National Institute for Child Health and Human Development. The conclusions and interpretations are the sole responsibility of the author.

Overview:
Residential Consumption,
Economic Opportunities, and Race

This volume explores three related sets of issues, involving (*a*) determinants of the demand for residential services in metropolitan areas, (*b*) the effects of intrametropolitan location (with respect to residence and workplace) on economic opportunities, and (*c*) the effects of racial discrimination on black residential consumption and economic well-being, and the relationship between these two problem areas. This chapter is intended as an overview of what is to follow.

In Part I of this monograph, I will develop and apply a microanalytic model of the demand for residential services in urban areas. There are, in the now extensive interdisciplinary urban studies literature, a number of models developed to explain residential demand. I will review several studies based on these models, which involve individual households or heads of household as the basic unit of analysis. The model that I will present for analysis in this monograph is derived not only from the results of these studies, but also from a number of theoretical ideas advanced by other writers, including Berry and Horton (1970), de Leeuw (1973), Nelson (1973), Apps (1973a,b, 1974), Ray (1973), Whitbread and Bird (1973), Kain and Quigley (1975). The basic objective of this modeling and analysis is to suggest ways in which both black and white residential consumption can be understood, beginning with reformulation of existing theoretical models.

The analyses to be presented here differ from those on which they are based in a number of respects. First, the model of demand for residential services that I will present takes into account the behavior of both owner and renter households, using individual level data. Second, it takes account of the consumption of residential goods inherent in individual dwelling units, the attributes of the neighborhood in which the dwelling is situated, and the attributes of the dwelling's intrametropolitan location and its location relative to workplace. Similar arrays of variables were used by Kain and Quigley (1975) in an analysis of residential consumption in St. Louis and by Straszheim (1974) in an analysis of residential consumption in San Francisco. The major analyses to be presented here involve both nationwide samples with data centering on a single year and neighborhood attributes represented by data from units that are similar in size to that of census tracts used in previous analyses.

In Part II I will investigate the relationships among racial discrimination, residential location, and economic opportunity. Reversing the usual order of hypothetical models in this area, I will ask whether intrametropolitan residential location affects economic well-being. In Chapter 9 I will examine whether commuting patterns for black and white workers are different and whether they have changed during the decade of the 1960s. In the following chapter I will then ask whether various residence–workplace combinations (central city versus suburb) affect wages, whether blacks (and whites) who work in the suburbs are paid higher wages than comparable workers in the central city, and how substantial is the component of the known black–white wage differential that can be attributed to racial discrimination.

In the following sections of this chapter I will briefly sketch the basic rationale behind the models and hypotheses to be examined more fully in succeeding chapters, attempting to give an overview of the major questions that will be addressed. A summary of the results of the first set of analyses will be presented in Chapter 8, along with discussion of their implications. Finally, in Chapter 11 I will try to bring out some of the policy implications of the analyses with respect to the demand for residential services among black households in light of the racial differential found in patterns of commuting and wages.

Some readers may feel, after having read this volume, that the presentation lacks a specific focus or an underlying rationale that integrates the discussion on residential consumption and economic opportunities. Actually, Parts I and II can be treated separately if one so desires, although there are several themes that permeate both. A focus on the important role played by the morphological structure of metropolitan areas in influencing the process of residential selection, the consumption of certain kinds of goods and services, and access to various kinds of activities is one major theme that underlies the discussions in both sections. A second major theme is the focus on the extent and character of racial differentials in both residential consumption and economic opportunities. The intent is to empirically demonstrate that discrimination, as a behavior response to group membership, is one major underlying cause of black–white differences in both residential consumption and economic opportunities.

I. DETERMINANTS OF THE DEMAND FOR RESIDENTIAL SERVICES

A. The Family as a Unit of Production and Consumption

A focal point for every American household is its home, be it a small apartment in the heart of the city, a deteriorating four-family flat in an inner suburb, or a rambling ranch house at the suburban fringes. The dwelling is valued not only for the structural services it provides (such as shelter, warmth, and cooling facilities) but also for its architectural qualities, for the private and public amenities it provides or affords access to, and for the people who live in the neighborhood—in short, for the entire residential environment and, possibly, for the social status it symbolizes. Moreover, housing is financially important since, on the average, it absorbs one-fifth of a family's income and in many cases represents the family's principal form of investment. Because of housing's special importance, it is natural for Americans to take a strong interest in their own housing situations, as well as those of others [de Leeuw, Schnare, and Struyk, 1976:119].

In the perspective taken in this monograph, the family is viewed as a unit of production and consumption. Its major activities include reproduction and maintenance of offspring, production of desired life styles, and labor force participation. The behavior of a family as a unit is oriented toward goals that are important for individual family members, the family as a whole, and the larger society. In order to carry out its functions, the family requires the input of various kinds of goods and services which, with the expenditures of time, are used to produce goods that maximize the welfare of its members. The production process, then, involves services provided within the family itself and goods and services from outside the family—from other families, voluntary associations, government, and, perhaps most importantly, from profit-making economic units that produce and distribute goods especially tailored for household consumption. Residential goods belong in the latter category and can be regarded as input into the production and consumption activities of families. The value of residential goods is determined according to the services they provide, the activities they support, and the amount of time they are available for use.

Societies tend to ascribe to their family units certain normative standards with respect to the appropriate set of goods that their residential packages should contain. Morris and Winters (1975) suggest that the norms governing residential behavior are relatively explicit with respect to space, tenure status, structural type, quality, neighborhood, and location relative to other dwellings and commercial areas. I would add to this that these norms vary in importance across families, depending on their major production and consumption activities. In short, most families have a clear idea of what kinds of dwellings and locations are appropriate for them—what they believe they need—given their particular socioeconomic status and family activities.

Some residential services are obtained directly from the technical attributes of dwellings. In this regard, a family must decide whether a particular dwelling is physically suitable, given the family's usual activities. Such attributes as the following are usually major considerations: interior and exterior space, the arrangement of rooms, technological conveniences, privacy from external disturbances, and privacy for individual members within the dwelling (Smith, 1971; Whitbread and Bird, 1973).

Other residential services obtainable from a dwelling unit are social in nature in that part of their economic value derives from the symbolic valuation of activities that take place in and around them (Ray, 1973). A dwelling unit must not only be functional in a technical sense, but it is also desirable that it be of a quality symbolically appropriate to the family's status. A dwelling becomes a display item that is used to validate family social standing. Although it may be useful theoretically to distinguish between technical and social services provided by a dwelling unit, the distribution of these two types of services across dwelling units are not independent of each other. Dwelling units that provide large quantities of technical services are also accorded high prestige. Finally, it should be emphasized that the model employed here focuses on the residential service value of a dwelling, not on the market exchange value (Harvey, 1972). That is, my interest here is in factors influencing individual choice, and the factor of exchange value of a dwelling is only one of many that are important.

Existing data sets do not allow direct analysis of the relationship between the productive activities of families and residential consumption. However, we can assume that the known social and economic attributes of families are important indicators of the types and quantity of goods and services they produce and that variations in these attributes can be used to explain variations in residential behavior. On the basis of these assumptions, a model can be derived that says that if family attributes (A_n) are indicators of production activities (P_n), then A_n can be used in the place of P_n to predict or explain the dependent variable of residential consumption. The focus of this monograph is on models of this type.

B. Family Attributes Determining Demand for Residential Services

There is an extensive literature on intrametropolitan mobility from which can be derived substantial knowledge of the determinants of the demand for residential services. This literature will be briefly summarized here. (For comprehensive reviews elsewhere see Foote *et al.*, 1960; Sabagh *et al.*, 1969; Guest, 1970; Johnston, 1971; Whitbread and Bird, 1973; Goodman, 1974; Roistacher, 1974; Speare *et al.*, 1975.)

One of the most important generalizations that can be drawn from the literature is that intrametropolitan mobility among white families reflects changes in the family life-cycle. As primary families move through stages of formation, maturation, and dissolution, and as they experience shifts in their economic well-being, they have different housing requirements with respect to internal and external space, type of structure, location, and tenure. The family life-cycle is usually divided into seven stages:

1. Marriage, or household formation
2. Prechild (constant size)
3. Childbearing (increasing size)
4. Childrearing (constant size)
5. Child-launching (decreasing size)
6. Postchild (constant size)
7. Widowhood, or family dissolution

During the first two stages, easy access to consumer goods and services and to place of work tend to be important. Thus a central city location (a small apartment, for example) tends to attract young childless families. During the next three stages, families' demands tend to be for ownership, for detached dwellings that provide increased privacy and increased internal and external space, and for locations with a variety of residential services desirable during the childrearing stage (e.g., high-quality school systems, open space for recreation, safe streets, quiet neighborhoods, and easy access to quality pediatric services). This cluster of desired attributes usually steers white families to the suburbs, which offer relatively sharp segregation of residential, commercial, and industrial land uses, low population density, open space available for recreation, and relatively high quantities of the residential goods desired by families with children to rear.

In the last two stages, some families stay in single-family, suburban dwellings, even though they have less need for many of the residential services available to them. Other families opt to return to apartment living, perhaps in central city locations. This move back to apartments is often associated, in the later years, with declining income and health, both of which may make it difficult for these families to maintain large detached dwellings in good condition. (For studies supporting selected aspects of this model of the relationship between residential demand and family life-cycle, see Duncan and Hauser, 1960; Foote *et al.*, 1960; David, 1962; Powers, 1964; Lansing *et al.*, 1969; Guest, 1970; Butler and Kaiser, 1971; Johnston, 1971; Goodman, 1974; Roistacher, 1974; and Speare *et al.*, 1975.)

One would assume that housing choices are not likely to be based on any one feature of a unit but rather on the combination of attributes that couples feel meet their particular needs. There is little empirical evidence that bears directly on this matter, but there are several studies that offer indirect support. Foote *et al.* (1960) present data suggesting that a family's housing choice is a compromise among location, tenure, and dwelling type, size, equipment, and design features. Greenbee's (1969) survey of priorities among homeowners in Madison, Wisconsin, suggests that location tends to be more important than size or dwelling type. However, his sample is small and his findings may be limited by the fact that the sample was drawn from a university town. David's (1962) analysis of the association among income, family composition, and housing revealed that large families substituted quality in housing (measured by expenditure per room) for space because of income constraints. Winger's (1969) analysis of Federal Housing Administration statistics on home purchases suggests that once minimum space standards have been met, middle-income families generally tend to trade additional space for quality in location and other attributes. In addition, Winger found that, within limits set by income, location costs (i.e., the costs of moving) do not influence housing decisions with respect to space, but they have an enormous impact on the purchase of other housing services besides space. This issue of whether families do or do not make trade-offs in various attributes in the course of choosing housing will not be explored further at this point. For the purposes of the models used in this monograph it is only necessary to assume that families with similar production and consumption functions tend to make similar compromises in their purchases of residential goods and that variations in these compromises coincide with the variations in family production and consumption entered as independent variables in the model to be explored.

C. Constraints on Residential Behavior

Families are not the only decision units that participate and have vested interests in the structure and operation of local housing markets. The basic structure of the residential market is the result of the past behavior of builders, lenders, and government units as well as of families in the market for a residence, and the current behavior of this set of decision units tends to restrict the pool of residential packages available to any specific household (Gans, 1967; de Leeuw, 1973). Owners of rental property can decide to improve it or to allow it to deteriorate or even to remove it from the residential stock. Decisions about the number, quality, and price of new units are made by builders, within limits set by federal, state, and local governments (e.g., through zoning ordinances, housing codes, urban renewal and housing subsidization legislation, and property taxes). Lenders make policies that directly affect decisions of families, builders, and owners, and the lenders' policymaking is affected by governmental regulation. Finally, there is the behavior of intermediaries, such as realtors and landlords whose decisions often have major influence on the kinds of residential choices available to families (Aldrich, 1974).

One consequence of this complex set of influences shaping residential markets is that the total bundle of residential services sought by a household may not be available at any price. The particular bundle may, in fact, exist on the market but may not be represented in the array of bundles made available to that household. The family in this situation must either put off its decision to seek a new residence or settle for a package that does not reflect the family's tastes. Families who want to become both investors in and consumers of residential services (e.g., owners) are usually more affected by constraints than renters, because they usually must borrow in order to buy and so are affected by the risk classification to which lenders assign them and, indirectly, by governmental regulation of lenders' behavior. This general topic will be taken up at greater length in Chapter 4, and the specific constraint placed on black participants in residential markets (e.g., racial discrimination) will be examined in Chapter 7.

Residential behavior is also, of course, subject to a family's budget constraints. Tastes for nonresidential consumption give rise in most families to trade-off decisions in the purchase of goods. An infinite variety of compromises is possible, but it is assumed in most analyses (including the present monograph) that households with similar production functions make similar compromises between residential and nonresidential purchases. It is also assumed that the utility or satisfaction with respect to residential consumption is higher under the following circumstances: (*a*) the higher the flow of residential services consumed; (*b*) the more resources left over for nonresidential consumption; and (*c*) the lower the average net residential expenditure after maintenance costs, tax savings, etc., are taken into account (de Leeuw, 1973:11).

II. A MODEL FOR CONSUMPTION OF RESIDENTIAL SERVICES

A. The Basic Model

It is useful to conceive of families as being distributed in social space in terms of attributes of ethnicity, family composition, and socioeconomic status. In the same way it is helpful to conceive of residence as being distributed in residential space in terms of attributes of housing services, neighborhood or site characteristics, and accessibility to nonresidential activities (Berry and Rees, 1969; Nelson, 1973; Apps, 1973a,b, 1974; de Leeuw, 1973; Whitbread and Bird, 1973; Kain and Quigley, 1975). For any given family, social and residential space intersect when the family selects a bundle of residential services consistent with its position in social space.

With respect to the ith family in social space, a residence decision reduces to the selection of that particular combination of residential services that maximizes its utility (e.g., the services facilitate carrying out the productive functions of the family). The matrix of residential services from which the family selects its residential consumption bundle can be defined according to the following identity equation:

$$RS = \mathbf{DS} + \mathbf{N} + \mathbf{A} + T \qquad (1.1)$$

where RS refers to residential services; $\mathbf{DS}$ is a vector of physical characteristics of a dwelling, defining the unit in terms of the flow of housing services it provides: for example, internal and external space, technological features (heating and utility systems, appliances), structural type (detached, multilevel, row, etc.), and design, construction, and architectural characteristics; $\mathbf{N}$ is a vector of characteristics defining the neighborhood in terms of socioeconomic status (SES), racial composition, intensity and differentiation of land use, stability of the population, and physical attributes; $\mathbf{A}$ is a vector of accessibility characteristics defining dwelling location with respect to employment and various public, commercial, and personal services; and T is a zero–one variable indicating whether the household is a pure consumer of residential services (a renter) or a consumer and an investor in residential stocks.

Figure 1-1 presents a fully recursive explanatory model that defines the relationships between the social attributes of families and the attributes of residential space. Straight lines with arrows at one end indicate the direction of influence among the variables. Curved lines with arrows at both ends indicate exogenously determined relations among variables; these will not be analyzed. All second- and third-order directional arrows have been omitted from Figure 1-1 because the model is already complex.

The following assumptions are made about the relations among these variables:

1. It is assumed that residential goods consist of services peculiar to dwelling units, residential sites, neighborhoods, and location within metropolitan areas.
2. Families tend to rank residential goods in terms of priority, with the valuation of lower ranked goods being partially determined by the valuation of higher ranked goods.
3. The demand for residential services associated with dwelling units is exogenous with respect to neighborhood features and location, since the services obtained from the dwelling unit constitute the minimum required by families in order to carry out their most important production functions.
4. Residential services peculiar to location are treated as endogenous to the demand for housing and neighborhood services.

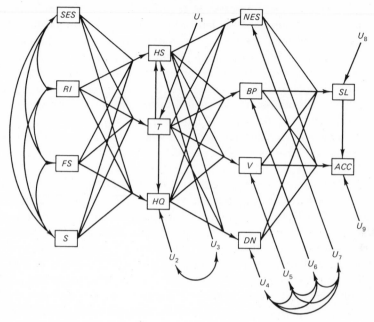

Figure 1-1. Basic model of the demand for residential services.

DEFINITION OF VARIABLES

SES Socioeconomic status
FS   Family status
RI   Relative income
S   Suburbanization of population and
     employment
T   Tenure status
HS   Housing space
HQ   Housing quality

NES Neighborhood socioeconomic status
BP   Racial composition of neighborhood
DN   Residential density
V   Residential stability
SL   Suburban residence
ACC Accessibility of workplace
U_{1-9} Residuals

Assumption 3 requires further elaboration. Families spend the majority of their time and conduct most of their activities within the confines of the dwelling unit. The dimensions of the dwelling unit with respect to space and other attributes are of critical importance if the unit is to support the kinds of activities a given family typically pursues in the course of a day. Further-more, it can be suggested that the insulation of the activities of the family from outside disturbances necessitates more or less the physical separation of families. Thus the dimensions of the dwelling unit probably rank foremost in the residential decision-making process of families. The validity of this assertion is made even more apparent when it is considered that the need to have contact with other decision units is facilitated through the use of personalized means of transportation and communication, which minimizes the effect of physical separation.

The assumption that employment location, in contrast to housing and neighborhood attributes, has the least effect on decisions regarding residential consumption differs significantly from that employed by Kain and Quigley (1975) in their attempt to develop an alternative theory of urban housing markets and spatial structure. Their approach assumes that workplaces are predetermined and that householders decide their place of work before choosing the type and location of their housing (Kain and Quigley, 1975:38). This issue is explored further in Chapter 6, where we report evidence on journey to work and residential mobility, which indicate that the workplace dominance assumption used by Kain and Quigley is without strong empirical support.

It can be observed in the model presented in Figure 1-1 that on the left-hand side are household characteristics of socioeconomic status (SES), relative income (RI), family status (FS), and suburbanization of employment and population within metropolitan areas (S). The direction of influence among the variables goes from left to right; the next set of variables are those that characterize housing services: housing space (HS), tenure or ownership status (T), and housing quality (HQ). Next is a set of neighborhood attributes: neighborhood socioeconomic status (NES), proportion of the neighborhood population that is black (BP), neighborhood stability as represented by dwelling vacancy rate (V), and population density in the neighborhood (DN). Finally, on the right-hand side are the attributes of location within the metropolitan area (central city versus suburbia, or SL) and location relative to workplace (accessibility, or ACC).

The rationale for this model will be expanded in following chapters. It is important to note here, however, that the model does *not* postulate that the social structural attributes of families and the demand for housing services determine the character of residential neighborhoods. There is no evidence that the residential behavior of families acting individually has direct effects on the structure and operation of residential markets, although the collective choices of families do indeed provide residential areas with a degree of continuity in their characteristics. The interrelations among the residual paths (U_{1-9}) leading to the measures of housing services and neighborhood attributes in Figure 1-1 express the fact that these covariations are mainly the consequences of past behavior of residential units (see the preceding discussion).

For example, consider a residential area that consists of only white families at time t_0. At time t_1 a black family, similar to the white families in the neighborhood in all respects except race, moves into the area. Clearly, the average attributes of this area are not appreciably changed by the presence of this single black family. However, its presence may spur whites to move out of the area and other blacks may begin to move into the area—particularly if they find a relatively large number of units available to them in comparison with other similar quality but all-white neighborhoods.

So at time t_{1+n} the area may become predominantly or all black. At this point the socioeconomic character of the neighborhood may have changed, and other characteristics will also change. In other words, the transition from a predominantly white to a predominantly black residential area results not from a single decision, but from the behavior of many units—the sellers and buyers or renters of a variety of dwellings, their intermediaries in these moves, and probably lenders as well.

Tenure status (T), while it is an attribute of households, is treated as endogenous to the other household attributes, because it defines the legal position of households in residential markets with respect to their rights and obligations as participants. Moreover, the choice of owning versus renting has a direct impact on the quantity of residential services consumed. It is assumed that all families participate in residential markets for the purpose of acquiring varying units of residential services and that such participation necessitates the allocation of financial resources to ensure a constant flow of residential services. The primary difference between owners and renters in this regard is that the former choose a legal position in the housing market that minimizes the per unit cost of residential services over time while maximizing the quantity of services that the family can afford to consume.

B. Limitations Inherent in the Basic Model and Its Estimation

Ideally, an analysis of residential behavior should be based on data collected at the point in time when residential decisions are made. Five studies have collected data of this kind (U.S. Department of Housing and Urban Development, 1968; Lansing *et al.*, 1969; McAllister *et al.*, 1971; Morgan *et al.*, 1974; Speare *et al.*, 1975). However, none of these studies used data suitable for the analyses of the type proposed here. Most of the data sets that are suitable are cross-sectional and so yield information mainly on associations between current household attributes and the consequences of past residential decisions. Results from analyses with these data do not allow us to answer some of the important questions of the type raised in this chapter. For example, one can ask whether the elderly live in older housing because it is cheap or conveniently located, or because they have aged with their dwellings, or because cohorts of people age along with the neighborhoods in which they prefer to live. For those aged persons who have changed residence several times in the past it is impossible to answer these questions.

Thus it is necessary to assume in analyses such as those to be presented that the households in the sample are at some equilibrium point with respect to their residential requirements and to what they can afford and are willing to pay for residential services. That is, they can obtain no further utility by changing residence without experiencing some change in their production functions. A household judges the utility of its residence on the basis of whether its attributes facilitate carrying out the activities that the family considers necessary for its well-being. It is assumed that the particular residential package selected by a household is unique in that there are no alternative packages offering better opportunities to the family for the satisfaction of its demands within existing constraints on their choice, or that these constraints would affect selection of alternative packages in the same way as they affected selection of the package currently being consumed (Whitbread and Bird, 1973).

C. Estimation of the Basic Model

In Part I I will present estimations of the basic model presented in Figure 1-1, beginning with consideration of the demand for housing services in Chapter 3. In succeeding chapters, blocks of residential service variables will be added until all variable linkages presented in the model have been empirically evaluated. In Chapter 4 I will present an analysis of the demand for residential services, adding to the housing service variables those variables reflecting neighborhood attributes. In Chapter 5 the central city–suburban differential will be considered. In Chapter 6 the relevance of workplace location to residential consumption will be examined. Up to this point the model will be evaluated in light of data from an exclusively white sample. Once this goal has been accomplished, I will add the variable of race in Chapter 7. The primary objective of this final evaluation is to determine whether black–white differentials in residential consumption reflect differences in income, preferences, race (i.e., racial discrimination), or some combination of these. Accumulated empirical evidence supports the hypothesis that observed black demand for residential services is less responsive to family composition and socioeconomic attributes than white demand. The evidence also suggests very strongly that the explanation for this difference lies in differences in wealth position and external constraints on black residential choice. This latter factor, racial discrimination, is postulated to affect black residential behavior via two channels: (a) the differential treatment of blacks in the labor market, resulting in a relatively low level of black purchasing ability; and (b) differential treatment of blacks in housing markets, which has substantial effects through restriction on tenure choice and residential location and on the character of the residential packages consumed.

III. METROPOLITAN LOCATION AND ECONOMIC OPPORTUNITY

Many of the nation's metropolitan areas have been undergoing suburbanization of their populations and economic activities for at least three-quarters of a century. The literature in urban studies abounds in empirical analysis of this process and in discussion of its impact on the viability of central cities, on the populations involved, and on the structure of municipal services, etc. The factor of white suburban versus central city residential location will be examined in Chapter 5. In Part II of this monograph I will focus on two significant and as yet unresolved issues in this area: (*a*) whether the major metropolitan sectors (e.g., central cities and suburbs) are becoming more economically specialized and (*b*) whether these processes (particularly the suburbanization of employment) are having an adverse effect on the economic well-being of black metropolitan residents.

As human ecologists have pointed out, most metropolitan areas span several counties and are large enough to permit the emergence of functionally specialized subsectors (Schnore, 1963, 1965). At the metropolitan center is the "central city," which specializes in coordination, exchange, and control activities. One finds in the central city such units as the headquarters of large national and multinational corporations and nationally based voluntary associations, state and federal government units (in addition to the major municipal governmental units), transportation and information agencies, financial institutions, and the firms that serve these in legal, public relations, management, advertising, and data-processing capacities.

Analysis of post-World War II trends in suburbanization indicates that the central cities still retain their historical organizational functions of administration, exchange, and control, but they have been losing those activities that consume large amounts of space and require access to expressways and interstate transportation systems (Hawley, 1971; Berry and Cohen, 1973; Christian, 1975; Kasarda, 1976). This observation suggests that specialization by metropolitan sector is increasing. Chapter 9 presents analysis of these trends using data from the 1960 and 1970 censuses, with a focus on decentralization by industry group, region, metropolitan size, and occupation.

This analysis has direct relevance for understanding the determinants of residential consumption and, most importantly for the purposes of this monograph, for understanding the nature of race differentials observed in residential consumption. It is assumed that white families' participation in residential markets is shaped by their assets, income, and preferences, but for black families one must add the factor of racial discrimination, which affects both black demand for residential services and the conditions under which they are supplied. The traditional approach to analyzing the effects of discrimination on residential behavior focuses on isolating those forces leading to differential treatment of black and white households. However, it is argued here that a more appropriate starting point would be to analyze the forces operating in other institutional spheres (most importantly, the labor market) that influence the amount of resources that blacks bring to residential markets.

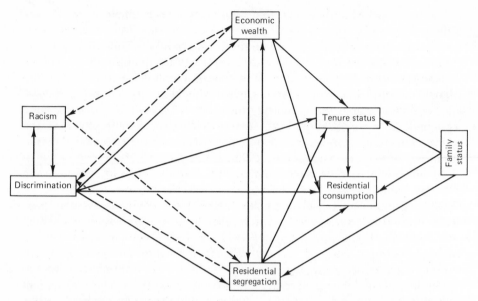

Figure 1-2. A model of the effects of racial discrimination on black residential consumption patterns.

The model presented in Figure 1-2 shows the various ways in which discrimination is hypothesized to affect blacks' residential behavior. There are three direct paths: (*a*) through residential segregation; (*b*) through economic wealth; and (*c*) through tenure status and residential consumption. The latter paths involve both the refusal of owners or their agents to rent or sell particular dwellings to blacks as well as the refusal of lenders to provide mortgages or insurance to blacks. This last type of discrimination involves not only motivation to maintain racial segregation, but also beliefs about what kinds of dwellings and neighborhoods (new versus old, for example) are most appropriate for minority groups.

The discriminatory treatment that results in racial segregation is second only to economic wealth as a major factor, particularly in terms of its long-range effects on black economic well-being. It has been observed that the earning potential of black workers seems to be related to black residential distribution in metropolitan areas (Harrison, 1974a,b). It is thought that residence in the central area of cities restricts the range of opportunities available to blacks in declining or marginally productive industries and in the service industries, which are characterized by low wages and patterns of temporary employment. The effects of this on the black population are to discourage the upgrading of skills in the black labor force (because demand is low), to keep the level and rate of socioeconomic achievement low, and to perpetuate the problem through restriction of the black population to residential areas where access to better paying jobs is limited. More specifically, it has been assumed that since industries with predominantly blue-collar structures are leaving the central cities while the majority of black blue-collar workers are constrained to continue to reside there, the economic condition of the black population not only fails to improve, but it tends to worsen. In Chapters 9 and 10 I will present some analyses of these issues. The goal of these analyses will be, first, to determine whether the incidence of commuting from the central city to the suburbs has increased among black workers between 1960 and 1970. If employment has been decentralizing and the black work force has not, then one would expect increased black commuting to be evident. The second goal will be to determine whether central city versus suburban residence and workplace combinations affect wages. Finally, an analysis will be presented that discusses the impact of labor market discrimination on the wage level of black workers, focusing on the linkage between discrimination and economic wealth presented in Figure 1-2.

In conclusion, I will address some of the policy implications of these analyses, particularly in reference to the value of various strategies designed to improve the economic well-being and housing situation of black central city households. Chapter 11 addresses these issues with reference to the results of the preceding analyses. In addition, this chapter also presents an analysis of post-1970 trends in suburbanization of the black population. The objective of this analysis is to determine whether the historical pattern of black concentration in central cities is changing.

DETERMINANTS OF THE DEMAND FOR RESIDENTIAL SERVICES

In Part I of this monograph I will take advantage of the availability of large data files from the 1960 and 1970 censuses and other national surveys to explore the validity of the model of demand for residential services that was presented in Chapter 1 (Figure 1-1). After describing the data and variables in Chapter 2, I will begin with consideration of the demand for housing services in Chapter 3 (e.g., those services that stem from the physical dwelling itself). In Chapter 4 I will add neighborhood attribute variables and analyze the model with a focus on the demand for neighborhood services. In Chapter 5 the focus will shift to the demand for locational services (e.g., to analysis of the variable of central city versus suburban location). In Chapter 6 the full model for white demand for residential services will be presented with the addition of the variable of workplace location. In Chapter 7 the variable of race will be added and analysis will focus on black–white differentials in residential consumption in an attempt to answer the question of the importance of the factor of racial discrimination in black residential consumption. Finally, in Chapter 8 the results will be summarized with attention to their general implications.

2

Methodology:
Demand for Residential Services

I. DATA SOURCES
AND SAMPLES

The major analyses to be reported in Part I are based on data from the *One Percent Public Use Sample of Neighborhood Characteristics* (U.S. Bureau of the Census, 1972) created from 1970 Census data (referred to hereafter simply as 1970 Census data). In Chapters 5, 6, and 7 use is made of data gathered by the Bureau of the Census for the United States Department of Housing and Urban Development (HUD) during its annual survey of metropolitan housing. In Chapter 6 use is made of data from the Panel Study of Income Dynamics (Morgan, 1974). This study, initiated by the Survey Research Center of the University of Michigan Institute for Social Research, involves a national sample of households interviewed annually since 1968. Data from the period 1972–1974 are used. The data sources and samples for these subsidiary analyses will be described when they are introduced. This chapter will focus on a description of the 1970 Census data, the major source for the analyses presented in Part I.

II. THE *ONE PERCENT PUBLIC USE SAMPLE OF NEIGHBORHOOD CHARACTERISTICS* (1970 CENSUS DATA)

A. Sample

From the total of 2 million households included in the 1970 Census data, a 60% sample of urban black households ($N = 8578$) and a 15% sample of urban white households ($N = 23,612$) were drawn for study. Only primary families were retained in the major analyses (i.e., households in which both husband and wife were present). Rural families were excluded, of course, since the model for analysis concerns specifically urban variables. Other exclusions were (*a*) occupants who did not own their dwelling and did not pay rent; (*b*) part owners of multiple dwellings (cooperatives and condominiums), where individual unit value was unknown; (*c*) occupants of mobile homes or stationary trailers; and (*d*) households with heads reported "not at work" or for whom place of employment was not reported. Thus the final sample consisted of households maintained by married couples (with varying numbers of other persons), who owned or paid rent for nonmobile dwellings, and who were defined by the census as headed by a person with an identified place of employment. (The total sample represented on the census tape was, however, used for calculation of some measures of metropolitan attributes.)

The types of household units studied place some constraints on the generalizability of the results of the analyses to be reported here. The primary reason for imposing these limitations on the sample was to maximize homogeneity among certain variables known to interact with the variables on which the analysis is focused. For example, unmarried or separated individuals tend to differ from married persons on a number of social and economic characteristics, and they also tend to have markedly different living arrangements than primary families (Glick, 1957; David, 1962; Beresford and Rivlin, 1964; Lansing *et al.*, 1969; Sweet, 1972). Thus including other household types in the analysis would necessitate more complex specifications of variable relationships than is possible here.

B. Variables

Table 2-1 offers a summary list of the variables employed in the main analyses in Part I.

1. Household Characteristics

Family status (*FS*), or family life-cycle stage, is represented by two proxy variables: the number of persons in the household (*PR*) and the age of the household head (*AG*).

TABLE 2-1

Variables in the Model of Demand for Residential Services

SES	= family socioeconomic status. High score = high class.
ED	= years of schooling completed.
OC	= occupational status.
I	= expected *family* income (or permanent or normal family income).
FS	= family status (family life-cycle stage).
PR	= number of persons in household.
AG	= age of family head.
RI	= ratio of observed to expected family income.
S	= suburbanization of population and employment in metropolitan area. Low score = low rank = high suburbanization.
SP	= aggregate suburbanization of the population.
SE	= aggregate suburbanization of employment (or the labor force).
T	= tenure status (owner versus renter, 1 = owner).
HS	= housing space (internal and external space).
NR	= number of rooms in a dwelling (internal space).
NU	= single versus multiunit structure (external space).
HQ	= housing quality.
BR	= number of bathrooms in the dwelling.
YB	= year structure built. Low score = old building; age related inversely to score.
NES	= neighborhood socioeconomic status. High score = high class.
MI	= median income level of neighborhood.
PV	= weighted average percentage of owner-occupied units valued at $25,000 or more and percentage of units rented at $150/month or more. High score indicates high average valuation of structures in neighborhood (e.g., high class).
NW	= percentage of units built in 1960 or later. High score = relatively new area = high class.
BP	= Racial composition of neighborhood. High score = black neighborhood.
DN	= neighborhood density (weighted by hedonic estimates).
V	= neighborhood stability, measured by percentage of vacant units at time of census. High score = low stability; stability related inversely to score.
SL	= suburban location (1 = location in suburb).
ACC	= accessibility of workplace.
FW	= devised scale. High score = can walk to work, very accessible.
W	= wife's proportional contribution to expected family income.
RC	= residential consumption in dollars.
R	= race of head of household (1 = black).

Family socioeconomic status (*SES*) is also represented by proxy variables. First, education (*ED*) is defined as number of years of schooling completed. Second, occupational status (*OC*) is estimated from the detailed occupational categories used in the 1970 Census by means of Duncan's socioeconomic index, as suggested by Featherman *et al.* (1975). The final component of *SES* is expected family income (*I*). As many researchers have discovered, measures of current disposable income are not the most reliable measures to use for the study of variables such as housing consumption, since they contain transitory components such as windfalls and extraordinary income discontinuities that would be ignored by most consumers in making long-term housing decisions (Reid, 1962; Lee, 1968; de Leeuw, 1971; Kain and Quigley, 1972; Wilson, 1973). A more reliable measure would be one that reflects expectations for long-run income level—the normal or permanent income level. It is these expectations that are assumed to have the major influence on consumer decisions.

In the present study the expected component of current total family income is defined as the sum of a number of contributory factors. This sum is estimated by regressing 1969 income onto a set of determinants, fitting equations of the form:

$$\text{Income} = f(\mathbf{W} + \mathbf{X} + \mathbf{Y} + \mathbf{Z}) \tag{2.1}$$

where $\mathbf{W}$ is a vector of geographic residence characteristics such as national region and size of the greater urban area; $\mathbf{X}$ is a vector of employment characteristics, including occupation, industry, hours and weeks worked in 1969, and year last worked; $\mathbf{Y}$ is a vector of income characteristics such as wages, salary, business, social security, and welfare; and $\mathbf{Z}$ is a vector of demographic characteristics, including age and years of school completed. Expected income was estimated for heads of households and spouses separately and then combined to yield a measure of total expected family income. (Table 2-A1 in the appendix to this chapter reports the mean vectors and hedonic regression coefficients for each contributory factor, by race and sex, that was used in computing expected income.)

The variable W, the wife's proportional contribution to total expected family income, is also derived from the separate estimates of wife and husband's expected income.

A second basic measure of income used is that of relative income, operationalized as the ratio of current to expected family income (Freedman, 1963; Wolfe, 1977). This variable serves to account for some of the status inconsistency found in residential consumption—that is, for variations reflecting families with incomes below or above the modal income of the socioeconomic group to which they would be assigned on the basis of their residential consumption. Ray (1973) has argued that consumption is shaped by social group membership as well as by income level. Families tend to emulate the consumption patterns of their reference groups. If a family appears to be spending at its reference group's modal spending level, although its income is well above or below this group's modal income level, its behavior can be said to be rational, because it serves to reduce the uncertainty the family might feel at not meeting or at overshooting its own or society's view of the standards it should meet. By treating individual family income in relation to reference group income it is possible to account for variation in consumption patterns that would otherwise be treated as error variance rather than as reflecting factors relevant to residential decision making.

The final household-level variable is race of head (R). Black is coded as 1.

2. Housing Consumption

A variety of measures have been used in the study of housing consumption, and the question of which are most appropriate has been widely discussed in the housing literature (Maisel and Winnick, 1960; Reid, 1962; Winger, 1968; de Leeuw, 1971). For example, Maisel and Winnick (1960:360) describe the issue in these terms:

> What constitutes the appropriate measure of housing consumption whose level and variation we are interested in explaining? Should we concern ourselves with the capital values of occupied dwelling units, or with current consumption flows? With economic measure of consumption or with cash expenditures? With outlays for reproducible shelter or for shelter and environment? With pure shelter or shelter plus various goods and services?

The nature of the problem under investigation should, of course, influence the choice of measures. The model proposed here requires two kinds of measures: (*a*) those that reflect the dollar value of various components of residential packages, as defined by Eq. (1.1), and (*b*) those that reflect the presence or absence of a variety of possible residential services that might be afforded by individual residential packages (e.g., the physical attributes of a dwelling).

The first kind of measure used is that of residential consumption (RC), expressed in monetary terms. Since the models to be set forth in this monograph require that measures be usable for both renters and owners, the concept of residential services was chosen to reflect market valuation of residential packages. Residential stock and residential expenditure are other commonly used concepts in this area. Residential stock can be used only in reference to owners whose legal position with reference to the dwelling they occupy identifies them as both investors in capital stocks and consumers of residential services (Olsen, 1969). Both owners and renters must allocate a certain portion of their annual income in the form of residential expenditures for the residential services consumed. However, Shelton (1968) estimates that renters pay 11.4% more than owners for equivalent bundles of residential services. This difference reflects (*a*) owners' freedom to minimize their consumption costs (unlike those who pay fixed rental amounts) via appreciation and equity, (*b*) the fact that owners who occupy their own dwelling do not have to bear vacancy losses, management costs, and other such expenses that owners of rental units usually pass on to renters, and (*c*) deductions for property taxes and interest paid on capital borrowed to buy residential stock that owners who occupy their own dwellings can claim (Aaron, 1970).

Estimating renters' consumption of residential services can be done very simply, of course, since the rent they pay reflects pure consumption of residential services. Estimation of owners' consumption is not as simple a matter. The approach used here is that of estimating owner consumption expenditures on the basis of rental costs for similar residential packages.

Consider two adjacent dwelling units, D_1 and D_2, representing equivalent residential packages. Dwelling D_1 is owned by O_1 but occupied by R_1 who pays rent to O_1 commensurate with the value of the package. Dwelling D_2, in contrast, is owned and occupied by O_2. Let us assume that the following equations defined the annual housing expenditures of O_1, R_1, and O_2:

$$E_{O_1} = P + a + c \tag{2.2}$$

$$E_{R_1} = P + a + b + c \tag{2.3}$$

$$E_{O_2} = P + b + c \tag{2.4}$$

where E equals annual residential expenditures; P represents annual expenditures by owners, regardless of whether they occupy their dwelling or not; a represents incremental costs incurred by owners who rent their dwelling for occupancy by others, such as vacancy losses and management costs; b represents the opportunity costs incurred by owners who occupy their property or the return on investment to owners who rent their dwelling for occupancy by others; and c represents the costs of occupancy incurred by occupants R_1 and O_2 (costs that may be incurred by O_1 but are passed on to R_1), such as the costs of maintenance and utilities.

If the components of Eq. (2.3) are known, then E_{O_1} and E_{O_2} can be estimated, yielding identical market valuation for the residential services provided by packages D_1 and D_2. However, we provide estimates only of E_{R_1}, not of its components, and no information on E_{O_2}. The census data include information only on the total value of an owner's property when it is a single-unit detached or attached structure. What we do have on the census tape are data on renters' expenditures and on an array of attributes of both owner and renter residential packages. Thus we can only estimate the components of owners' residential packages. This was done here by constructing a hedonic price index.

The following assumptions are made for purposes of the RC estimation procedure:

1. The participation of households in local housing markets is primarily for the consumption of residential services.
2. Such participation necessitates expenditures to ensure a constant flow of residential services of a specific quantity per unit time.
3. Owners may either occupy their units or lease them for occupancy by

others (although the owners in this sample have all chosen to occupy their property).

4. The market value of a residential package is the same whether it is occupied by an owner or a renter household.

The procedure used to estimate a standard measure of consumption of residential services for renter households is as follows:

$$RC = \mathbf{M} + B_i(\mathbf{DS}_i) + B_j(\mathbf{N}_j) + B_k(\mathbf{D}_k) + B_l(\mathbf{R}_l) + e \qquad (2.5)$$

where the dependent variable RC is the annual housing expenditure for an individual household; $\mathbf{M}$ is a vector of characteristics defining the *minimum* residential package consisting of a dwelling unit with the following characteristics: location in the central city of an urban area in the West South Central region of the country and in a neighborhood at least 75% black, less than four rooms, no basement, built before 1940, one half-bath or less, no central heating system or no heating at all, not connected to a public sewer, source of water other than public or private company, and cost of utilities included in rent; $\mathbf{DS}$ is a vector of variables describing the unit in terms of size, quality, technological features, and other physical characteristics; $\mathbf{N}$ is a vector of variables defining the socioeconomic level, racial composition, housing, and population density of the unit's neighborhood; $\mathbf{D}$ is a vector of variables identifying the demand for neighborhood location and dwelling units as reflected in neighborhood vacancy rate, residential mobility, and recency of occupancy by its current resident household; $\mathbf{R}$ is a vector reflecting geographic variations in the price of residential services; and e is an error term. The hedonic regression coefficients and mean vectors used to compute RC are reported, by race, in Table 2-A2 in the appendix to this chapter.

In the final estimation of RC the procedure for owner households required an additional step. Equation (2.5) was applied to the gross annual rent of the renter households that are most similar to owner households, for example, those in detached or single-unit attached structures who paid for at least one utility. This was done separately for white and black owner households and yielded estimated rent figures for use with owners. For the utilities variable, owner households also required an additional step, since the 1970 Census tape did not include the necessary information. All owners were assigned the figures reported for similar renter households for annual per dwelling cost of electricity and (since some households have both) half the sum of the estimated per dwelling cost of gas and heating fuel.

It should be noted here that this estimate is not one of owner expenditures but rather of total residential consumption represented by owner-occupied residential packages. Alternatively, however, it could be interpreted as a measure of expected annual expenditures for residential services that owners would incur if they rented rather than owned their place of residence.

The second kind of measure of housing consumption involves residential services afforded by the purely physical attributes of individual dwellings, or housing services. Measurements of these services were derived from dwelling characteristics such as amount of internal and external space, structural type, and technological features. In Chapter 3, housing space (*HS*) is represented by the number of rooms in the dwelling (*NR*) as a measure of internal space, and whether or not the dwelling is a one-unit structure (*NU*) as a measure of external space. Note that single-family homes, assumed to have the most external space, receive the lowest *NU* score. In Chapters 4–7 *HS* is estimated via a weighted sum of *NR, NU,* and the basement-present variables. The regression coefficients shown in Table 2-A2 were used as weights.

In Chapter 3 housing quality (*HQ*) is represented by the number of bathrooms in the dwelling (*BR*) and the year the structure was built (*YB*). Note that *YB* yields a lower score for older buildings; the lower the score, the lower the structure's quality is assumed to be. In Chapters 4–7 *HQ* is estimated via a weighted sum of *BR, YB,* and utility and heating system variables. The regression coefficients shown in Table 2-A2 were used as weights.

The final housing-related measure is that of tenure status (*T*). Ownership is coded as 1.

3. Neighborhood Attributes

The areas defined as "neighborhoods" in the 1970 Census tape used here form contiguous clusters of households that are approximately the size of a census tract. Note that this definition of a neighborhood is purely statistical and does not conform to any sociologically meaningful conceptualization of the concept of "neighborhood." Nonetheless, the definition of these units captures many gradations in social and economic characteristics relevant to the neighborhood variable in its sociological definition.

The socioeconomic status of a neighborhood (*NES*) is defined by three proxy variables: (*a*) median income of the neighborhood (*MI*); (*b*) valuation of neighborhood dwellings (*PV*), measured by the weighted average of percentage of owner-occupied units valued at $25,000 or more and percentage of units rented at $150 or more a month; and (*c*) percentage of units built in 1960 or later (*NW*).

Population density of each neighborhood (*DN*) is defined as the weighted sum of percentage of units with one or more persons per room and percentage of units in structures with five or more units. The hedonic regression coefficients used as weights are shown in Table 2-A2 in the appendix to this chapter.

Neighborhood stability (*V*) is measured by the proportion of vacant units for rent or sale in the neighborhood at the time of the census among all units in the neighborhood sample.

Finally, neighborhoods are also identified in terms of the percentage of population that is black (*BP*), expressed in log form.

4. Locational Attributes

Four measures of the attributes of the location of residences with reference to the large metropolitan community were used. One was a dummy variable for suburban location (*SL*), given a score of 1, as opposed to location in the central city.

Second, an ordinal scale to measure ease of travel to work was devised (*ACC*). Scale scores were derived from information on location of residence and employment (central city versus the suburbs) and means of transportation to work. Scale values were assigned as follows: four points were given if the head worked at home or could walk to work; three points were given if head could get to work on public transportation; two points were given if the head used private transportation to get to work but at least worked and lived in either the central city or the suburbs; the lowest score, one point, was given for heads who used private transportation and worked and lived in different sectors. This is not a very sensitive measure of accessibility of workplaces in relation to residences, of course. Ideally such a measure would be based on the costs to the individual of getting to work—for example, a sum reflecting distance traveled, mode of travel, time consumed in the journey to and from work, and frequency of the round trip. However, the information necessary to construct the ideal measure is not available on the census tape. Thus the measures used must be viewed as a proxy in which travel by public transportation and travel within the major sectors of the metropolitan area reflect less costly journeys to work than travel by private transportation and travel across sectors.

The last two measures of locational attributes are of degree of suburbanization of population and employment (*SP* and *SE*). Although urban areas vary in absolute size, dispersion of industry and population, and location of centers of industry and residential areas relative to each other, these aggregate attributes are seldom entered into analyses of the demand for residential services. Most individuals are likely to be constrained in some way in terms of where they work and live by the structure of the metropolitan area. In an attempt to control for such constraints, two aggregate measures of suburbanization were computed. These measures were derived by calculating the percentage of the population or labor force residing or employed in establishments located outside the central city for the *i*th size urban area and the *j*th subregion of the United States. There are three size classes and nine major subregions identified in the census, yielding 27 classes of urban areas. Since the distribution of percentages was skewed, they were converted to ranks, with the highest suburbanization ranked 1 and the lowest ranked 27. Thus each household represented on the census tape can be identified in terms of residence in urbanized areas differentiated according to the degree of suburbanization of population and employment opportunity, respectively.

5. A Final Note on Estimation Procedure

A question may be raised, with regard to the estimation procedure, as to whether the approach to estimating DN, HS, and HQ (Chapters 4–7), and RC (Chapter 7) could bias estimates of structural coefficients presented for tenure status (T). An alternative approach that could have been employed would have been to use the regression weights reported for the total rental sample in Table 2-A2. It can be argued that since the major focus in Chapters 3–6 is on residential consumption, the use of different weights for owner and renter households to estimate DN, HS, and HQ may bias the correlations between these variables and tenure status. The assumption underlying this assertion is that the estimates of DN, HS, and HQ generated for owner households results in a different ordering of households than would be obtained if a standardized set of weights had been applied. To check for this possibility, two estimates of DN, HS, and HQ were generated using the two different approaches. The correlations between the two estimates for whites were (.98) for HQ, (.96) for HS, and (.99) for DN. Thus it is unlikely that the results would have changed to any significant extent through the use of the alternative approach.

However, the main reason for not applying the alternative approach to estimating HS, HQ, and DN was to maintain consistency with the manner in which residential consumption (RC) was defined. It will be recalled that renters are defined as pure consumers of residential services, and thus what they pay in rent annually is a good approximation of what they consume. The estimate of RC obtained for owner households was defined as what owners would pay annually if they in fact rented rather than owned their dwelling. In the analysis of black–white differentials in residential consumption (Chapter 7), variations among households reflecting different prices paid for identical residential attributes take on an added significance. In Chapter 7 it will be argued that the price structure confronted by households has a direct effect on the quantity of residential services that can be consumed. Higher prices act to depress the quantity of residential services that can be purchased, which seems to apply particularly to blacks because of their lower purchasing ability.

TABLE 2-A1

Determinants of Total Individual 1968 Income: Means and Coefficients by Race and Sex

Characteristics	Males				Females			
	Whites		Blacks		Whites		Blacks	
	Means	Co-efficients (100's)	Means	Co-efficients (100's)	Means	Co-efficients (100's)	Means	Co-efficients (100's)
1. Age	42.556	$ 1.149	40.782	$ .231	39.912	$ .134	37.697	$ .160
2. Years of Schooling	12.480	6.903	10.451	2.322	12.035	1.212	11.080	1.406
3. Occupation								
Professional-Technical	.192	- 1.806*	.066	19.854	.114	8.508*	.096	21.393
Managers-Officials	.156	19.382	.043	16.682*	.022	9.631	.014	14.306*
Sales	.092	- 5.514	.024	.566*	.0683	- 6.502*	.025	- .844*
Clerical	.079	-31.278	.095	- 3.476*	.3092	- 2.727*	.180	4.247*
Craftsman	.219	-19.489	.169	- .429*	.009	- 3.294*	.009	5.451*
Operatives	.152	-24.053	.303	- 2.794*	.078	- 4.557*	.133	2.151*
Laborers/Private Households	.031	-28.549	.123	- 5.082*	.009	- 4.972*	.091	- .749*
Service Workers	.058	-31.929	.158	-10.539*	.086	- 5.588*	.207	- .791*
Farm owners, Managers, Laborers	-------	-------	-------	-------	-------	-------	-------	-------
4. Industry								
Mining-Construction	.088	25.896	.084	6.839*	.0087	9.225	.003	.973
Manufacturing	.317	15.912	.321	6.851*	.132	12.168	.122	4.217
Transportation, Communications, Utilities	.092	13.083*	.106	5.285*	.032	12.243	.024	2.650
Wholesale-Retail	.184	1.0765*	.153	- 3.976*	.180	5.936*	.112	- 1.571
Finance, Insurance Real Estate	.097	17.197	.066	- .790	.089	8.715	.047	1.065
Personal Services	.016	$-11.614*	.032	$- 8.519*	.031	$ 4.198*	.141	$- 2.888*
Entertainment, Recreation	.008	14.692*	.008	- .688*	.006	9.444	.004	- .432
Professional Services	.104	13.850	.102	3.626*	.189	6.354*	.250	2.894*
Public Administration	.073	10.843*	.102	9.377*	.028	12.514	.052	9.355*
Agriculture	-------[1]	-------	-------	-------	-------[2]	-------	-------	-------

29

TABLE 2-A1 (Continued)

Characteristics	Males				Females			
	Whites		Blacks		Whites		Blacks	
	Means	Co-efficients (100's)	Means	Co-efficients (100's)	Means	Co-efficients (100's)	Means	Co-efficients (100's)
5. Hours Worked (1969)	5.306	4.885	4.993	2.486	1.480	3.085	2.140	1.636
6. Weeks Worked (1969)	5.652	11.699	5.423	5.280	2.040	6.294	2.676	5.331
7. Year Last Worked	NA	NA	NA	NA	3.180	4.043	2.615	1.920
8. Source of Income								
Wages, Salary, etc.	.932	45.775	.963	33.293	.4773	13.772	.611	9.340
Non-Farm, Business	.097	66.848	.042	41.321	.0147	24.471	.011	23.826
Farm	.005	43.293	.002	32.241	.0006	18.028	.033	-11.730
Social Security, Rail Retirement	.023	- 7.499	.022	- 2.501*	.0252	13.971	.022	9.994
Public Assistance Welfare	.005	2.042*	.013	- 1.200*	.0054 3	10.215	.0170	10.402
Other Sources	-----1	-----	-----	-----	-----	-----	-----	-----
9. Size of Urbanized Area by Central City and Suburb								
a. Central City								
Less than 500,000	-----1	$-----	-----	$-----	-----	$-----	-----	$-----
500,000-999,999	.064	1.949*	.107	2.201	.064	.733*	.107	.427*
1,000,000 or more	.191	8.121	.515	5.768	.191	4.233	.515	3.300
b. Suburbs								
Less than 500,000	.113	4.482	.037	5.648	.113	- .496*	.037	.599*
500,000-999,999	.063	9.746	.016	5.224*	.063	.735*	.016	3.496
1,000,000 or more	.390	18.097	.129	12.728	.390	2.318	.129	3.088

10. Regions of the U.S.

West South Central	----[1]	----	----	----	----	----	----	----
New England	.069	6.293	.0190	12.996	.0689	.244*	.019	5.989
Middle Atlantic	.222	6.244	.228	8.643	.222	.788*	.228	3.502
East North Central	.225	9.455	.224	15.751	.225	1.300	.224	4.662
West North Central	.066	1.290*	.035	5.025	.066	-1.410*	.035	.869*
South Atlantic	.113	5.946	.215	1.567*	.113	1.733	.215	2.740
East South Atlantic	.038	4.359*	.064	- .662*	.038	.050*	.064	2.733
Mountain	.034	3.045*	.0111	11.604	.034	- .430*	.011	6.046
Pacific	.151	3.320*	.093	12.244	.151	.732*	.093	3.304
Total N	23,612		8578		23,612		8578	
Mean Income	114.883		67.702		19.705		23.085	
Intercept		-182.531		-59.238		-44.935		-37.495
R^2 (Corrected)		.320		.294		.515		.528

Source: 1970 1% Public Use Sample of Neighborhood Characteristics.

* Indicates that the regression coefficient is not twice the size of its standard error.

[1] Those attributes for which no values are reported were used as reference categories in the regression analysis.

[2] For females this category also includes persons not at work.

[3] For females this category also includes persons who had no income.

TABLE 2-A2

Determinants of Annual Housing Cost for Primary Families Living in Urbanized Areas in 1970: Means and Coefficients by Tenure Status and Race

| | Renters | | | | Owners | | | |
| | Whites | | Blacks | | Whites | | Blacks | |
Characteristics	Means	Coefficients[1]	Means	Coefficients[1]	Means	Coefficients[1]	Means	Coefficients[1]
I. DWELLING SERVICES								
A. Housing Space								
1. Number of Rooms								
3 rooms or less	---[2]	----	---[2]	----	---[2]	----	---[2]	----
4 rooms	.246	$ 175.739	.231	$ 154.501	.271	$ 184.429	.278	$ 142.507
5 rooms	.116	288.288	.122	217.154	.318	298.724	.331	192.6915
6 rooms	.030	341.143	.033	304.805	.170	411.357	.154	263.048
7 rooms	.011	436.093	.012	296.932	.092	480.433	.073	336.778
8 rooms or more	.005	138.831	.006	612.029	.062	187.297	.042	648.756
2. Basement								
No basement	.601	----	.615	----	.609	----	.542	----
With basement	.277	57.780	.257	134.803	.216	14.836*	.265	105.945
Concrete slab		-14.076*		44.268		-5.450		51.751
3. Number of units in Structure	3.047	27.481	3.220	5.055*	.039	-57.674	.126	-68.646
B. Housing Quality								
1. Bathrooms								
1/2 bath or no bath	----	----	----	----	----	----	----	----
1 complete bath	.827	177.571	.888	88.563	.449	148.186	.643	99.765
1-1/2 baths	.070	460.887	.036	194.965	.213	406.544	.181	263.549
2 complete baths	.068	830.316	.023	401.938	.215	573.457	.113	433.261
2-1/2 baths or more	.013	1550.520	.005	501.555	.116	1444.943	.038	325.262

2. Type of Heating System								
central air furnace	----	----	----	----	----	----	----	----
steam or hot water	.342	$ -30.560	.378	$ -41.697	.185	$ 18.383*	.170	$ 17.761*
built-in electric unit	.067	- 3.819*	.049	27.924*	.290	-51.686*	.033	6.317*
floor,wall or pipeless furnace	.101	-53.765	.073	-38.643*	.082	-111.163	.131	40.654*
room heater w/flue	.095	-118.366	.149	-101.590	.038	-191.088	.126	-169.956
room heater w/o flue	.034	-95.678	.084	-121.439	.014	-176.666	.081	-191.839
fireplace,stove,or portable heater	.018	-173.705	.042	-118.651	.009	-218.001	.028	-141.731
3. Year Unit Built								
1969-1970	.037	433.390	.018	174.702	.224	402.536	.131	17.223*
1965-1968	.128	444.296	.058	217.976	.101	393.844	.052	281.325
1960-1964	.127	357.152	.084	160.774	.151	268.274	.099	71.774*
1950-1959	.177	196.795	.163	65.108	.350	109.235	.256	94.846
1940-1949	.134	100.407	.181	31.034	.134	88.410	.189	38.729*
1939 or earlier	----	----	----	----	----	----	----	----
4. Utilities								
water source (public)	.982	-7.356*	.996	96.301*	.946	8.323*	.973	30.950*
sewage	.944	-19.754	.978	-38.169*	.826	6.579*	.928	-13.813*
pay no utilities	----	----	----	----	----	----	----	----
pay electricity[3]	.833	140.713	.775	171.672	NA	94.697*	NA	255.909
pay gas[3]	.629	-37.673	.674	46.661	NA	45.880*	NA	135.873
pay water[3]	.213	121.673	.210	96.289	NA	110.847	NA	123.178
pay fuel[3]	.088	68.311	.096	123.274	NA	72.009	NA	81.141
II. NEIGHBORHOOD CHARACTERISTICS								
A. Neighborhood Quality								
1. Median Income	19.743	52.855	7.457	44.304	12.238	61.530	8.770	31.628
2. Average Percent Units w/Gross Rent of $150 or more and value $25,000 or more	31.927	7.607	12.145	10.082	39.853	4.932	16.870	8.036
3. Percent units built after 1960	24.46	-5.733	13.381	-2.524	30.817	-3.593	17.854	-3.183

TABLE 2-A2 (Continued)

	Renters				Owners			
	Whites		Blacks		Whites		Blacks	
	Means	Coefficients	Means	Coefficients	Means	Coefficients[1]	Means	Coefficients[1]
B. Neighborhood Density								
1. Percent Units One or More Persons per Room	6.508	$ 2.598*	14.405	$ 4.910	5.702	$ 4.037*	12.502	$ 4.256
2. Percent Units in 5-Unit Structures or More	28.160	2.228	35.028	1.843*	10.310	3.416	12.500	1.113*
C. Racial Composition of Neighborhood								
24% Black or less	.922	-54.527*	.179	-35.959	.961	-17.173*	.208	-33.647*
25-49% Black	.052	-88.519*	.157	-70.661	.024	-2.240*	.162	-52.455*
50-74% Black	.019	-22.028*	.181	-42.882	.011	67.029*	.209	-15.939*
75% Black or more	----	----	----	----	----	----	----	----
D. Residential Stability								
1. Percent Same House 5 Years Ago	50.069	-3.444	50.557	-2.232	53.923	-3.660	52.580	-2.730
2. Percent Vacant Dwelling for Sale or Rent	3.122	1.118*	4.861	-2.125*	2.284	9.866	3.860	-9.934
3. Year Household Moved into Units	1.697	-46.295	2.139	-22.451	3.604	-80.874	3.470	-21.762
III. GEOGRAPHIC VARIATION								
A. Central City vs Suburb								
Location by Size								
Central City								
Suburbs	----	----	----	----	----	----	----	----
50,000-499,999	.079	-39.176	.020	-106.01	.125	6.243*	.050	-53.282*
500,000-999,999	.045	-51.531	.010	-64.52	.068	-39.367*	.026	.132*
1,000,000 or more	.295	13.571*	.090	-29.125	.411	118.125	.165	52.691*

B. Regions of the United States

Regions of the United States								
West South Central	----	----	----	----	----	----	----	----
New England	.085	$ 109.445	.029	$ 70.013	.062	$ 196.167	.014	$ 55.786*
Middle Atlantic	.277	98.475	.289	48.738	.201	151.438	.157	119.340
East North Central	.181	36.797*	.217	28.151*	.236	61.228*	.235	81.940
West North Central	.054	24.821	.032	-91.796	.069	31.089*	.041	-74.312*
South Atlantic	.111	-12.196*	.200	3.552*	.116	47.459*	.212	107.892
East South Central	.031	-82.157	.056	-132.303	.039	-62.200*	.075	-62.423*
Mountain	.032	21.256*	.007	126.064	.036	43.014	.014	187.267*
Pacific	.160	74.900	.078	151.043	.157	168.142	.120	186.051
Intercept Value		488.001		381.327		508.112		431.706
Total Sample Size	6,708		4,328		16,904		4,250	
Annual Gross Rent	$1,696		$1,299		$1,731		$1,294	
Multiple R^2 (Corrected)	.599		.493		.652		.549	

Source: 1970 1% Public Use Sample of Neighborhood Characteristics (1970 Census).

* Indicates that the regression coefficient is not twice the size of its standard error.

[1] The hedonic regressions coefficients were obtained from an equation for renter households (N=2260 for whites and 1623 for blacks) whose dwelling units were identical to those of the owner households included in this sample.

[2] Those attributes for which no value is reported were used as reference categories in the regression analysis.

[3] NA indicates that this information not collected for owner households.

3

The Demand for
Housing Services

Chapter 1 described the basic perspective on the family taken in this monograph. Briefly, it was suggested that a useful way of defining the family is to conceive of it as a unit of production and consumption, with its major activities being reproduction, maintenance of offspring, production of a desired life style, and labor force participation. Residential goods can be regarded as inputs into these activities which, when combined with time, are used to produce goods that maximize the welfare of family members. Most families have a clear idea of what kinds of dwellings and residential locations are appropriate for them, given their goals, family composition, socioeconomic status, etc.

In this chapter I will evaluate the basic model (presented in Figure 1-1) developed in terms of its ability to predict the consumption of housing services by white families in various family life-cycle stages—for example, the consumption of services that are obtained directly from the dwelling itself, such as interior and exterior space, technological conveniences, privacy, and the intangible attributes of prestige and display value that stem from the dwelling's apparent quality. First I will describe the results of an earlier modeling attempt, and then I will describe the estimation process and present results from applying a portion of the general model described in Chapter 1 (Figure 1-1) to data on the determinants of the demand for housing services.

I. A PRELIMINARY MODEL AND SOME FINDINGS

In an earlier work (Wilson, 1973) I developed a model for the socioeconomic and demographic determinants of the kinds of housing that white primary households are likely to occupy (see Figure 3-1). The model postulated that the structural characteristics of primary families (marital duration, number of children and others in the household, and age of youngest child) and their socioeconomic characteristics (family income, level of head's education, and head's occupation) are related to the quantity of housing services consumed. The latter were operationally defined in terms of the following: (a) housing space, measured by number of rooms in the dwelling and structural type (single-family unit versus multiunit); (b) housing quality, as indicated by age and condition of dwelling, and the presence of other quality attributes in the dwelling unit; and (c) residential location (suburban versus central city), used as an indicator of residential amenities associated with single-family units. This 1973 model represented an advance over previous models in that the linkages postulated were between unobserved theoretical constructs as represented by relations between their measured indicators.

This early model was evaluated with data on white primary families living in urbanized areas on a 1:1000 public use sample tape derived from 1960 Census data. Owners and renters were examined separately. The linkages were evaluated through multiple–partial canonical correlation coefficients, which are multivariate extensions of univariate multiple–partial correlation coefficients (Rozebloom, 1965, 1968; Wilson, 1975). The theoretical model presented in Figure 3-1 incorporates into one integrated framework indica-

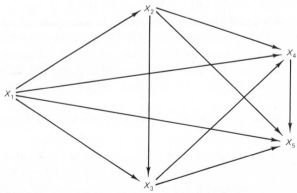

Figure 3-1. Determinants of the dimensions of housing status. X_1 = residence, X_2 = socioeconomic status, X_3 = family status, X_4 = housing quality, X_5 = housing space.

tors of most of the major dimensions of housing services for primary families. The unobserved variable, housing space (X_5), is the primary dependent variable here, followed by housing quality (X_4), family status (X_3), socioeconomic status (X_2), and residence (regional location and size of place) (X_1). The rationale for the postulated variable linkages in this model is as follows:

1. The effect of family size on housing quality was expected to be negative. Large families, with their relatively large total expenses, are least likely to be in a position to spend much on housing, either in absolute amount or in expenditure per room. Given the pressure of numbers, it was expected that large families will tend to substitute quality for quantity in living space. This negative effect for quality could be partially counterbalanced by positive relations among marital duration, income, and preference for relatively high-quality, single-family units. That is, the older the marriage, the larger the family, but also the higher the income the family is likely to have achieved. Also, detached or single-family dwellings are more attractive to families with children and they tend to be more expensive than multiunit dwellings, because they tend to be of higher quality construction and are usually located in relatively high-status neighborhoods—suburbs, for example. Thus the need for more living space for large families may mean that large families must opt for higher quality than the level they would otherwise find suitable.

2. Socioeconomic status was postulated to be negatively related to family size. This relationship has been well documented in the fertility literature, at least for Protestants and several ethnic groups.

3. Socioeconomic status (SES) was also expected to be positively related to level of consumption of housing space and quality. This prediction is based on the positive relationship between income level and SES and on the assumption that consumption of housing services functions as an expression of social class membership.

The only exogenous variables in this model were regional location and size of the urban area in which dwellings were located. As is usual in analyses that employ characteristics of individuals or households as units of analysis, endogenous variables such as size of urbanized area represent composite sources of influence about which little is known. With respect to housing quality and services, the urban size variable represents the combined effects of demand and supply factors in local housing markets. It is known that there are large variations among local housing markets with respect to the character and structure of their inventory, variations that must be controlled before interpreting relationships found among housing attributes and family characteristics. Variations in demand stem from variation in the size, age, and composition of the population, and variations in supply reflect variations in capital and operating inputs (Martin, 1966; de Leeuw and Ekanem, 1971). The variables of regional location and size of urban area capture only some of the variation due to these supply and demand characteristics and thus constitute only partial controls for them.

The results of my 1973 analyses were consistent with the hypothesized unobserved-variable relationships, although not always supportive of the rationale behind the theoretical model. All unobserved-variable relationships were statistically significant, but not as large as expected.

In the analysis of determinants of housing space, as measured by number of rooms in the family dwelling, I found that for renter households, number of rooms was related both to the number of children in the family and their ages and to family income, but not to the other two socioeconomic variables (level of head's occupation and education). In contrast, for owner households number of rooms was only slightly associated with number of children but was strongly related to all three measures of SES. Consistent with prediction, SES was the most important determinant of housing quality for both owner and renter primary families. In short, housing quality, and to a lesser extent, housing space, reflect the social status of occupants of a dwelling.

Housing quality was also found to be positively related to family composition, largely because of the positive association between marital duration and age of dwelling. This finding for family composition was not consistent with predictions from the model. It had been expected, instead, that housing quality would be negatively related to family composition because large families would tend to have less to spend on housing than small families and so would have to substitute quality for quantity in living space.

There are severe limitations on the generalizability of the results from the 1973 study. First, the measurement of physical housing attributes was somewhat limited, given the variety of attributes that probably are of importance in residential decision making (see discussion in Chapter 1). Second, the factor of accessibility to workplace was not included in the analysis. Third, neighborhood characteristics were represented by proxies—that is, the physical attributes of the dwelling itself. These first three deficiencies reflect lack of information in the 1:1000 public use sample data set for 1960.

In addition, the attempt to control for the influence of regional variation and urban size was not successful. As is commonly the case when variables such as these are used to represent composite sources of influence, it is impossible to attach substantive significance to the effects of the variables captured in the analysis.

And finally, the statistical estimation procedure used in my 1973 study lacked the power to evaluate the full implications of the model. In the analysis to be presented in the following section, attempts are made to remedy this problem, as well as the others noted previously.

II. ANALYSIS OF DEMAND FOR HOUSING SERVICES

A. Model

Figure 3-2 presents an unobserved variable model of demand for housing services constructed for use with the 1970 Census data tape described in Chapter 2. This model postulates that the tenure status of primary families and housing space and quality consumed are a function of socioeconomic status (*SES*), family status (*FS*, life-cycle stage), relative income (*RI*), and degree of suburbanization of the surrounding metropolis (*S*). The model presented in Figure 3-2 is a more elaborate version of part of the model presented in Figure 1-1, with the paths depicted in more detail. The rationales for the postulated paths are the same as those advanced for the model presented in Figure 3-1.

The housing space (*HS*) consumed by primary families is indicated by number of rooms (*NR*) and whether the dwelling is a single-unit or a multi-unit (*NU*) structure (one-unit structures are coded as 1). The (*NR*) measure is a proxy for internal space (*IN*), and (*NU*) is a proxy for external space (*EX*), indicating whether a unit is separated from others and provides direct

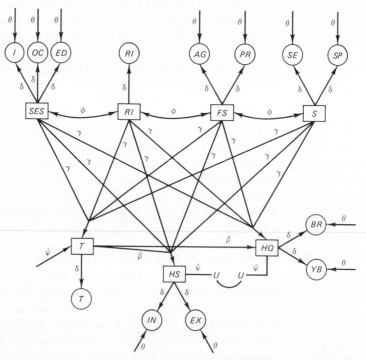

Figure 3-2. A model of the determinants of the demand for housing services.

access to the outside. Housing quality (HQ) is represented by the number of bathrooms in the dwelling (BR) and the year the structure was built (YB)—the younger the building, the higher the score, and the higher the quality is assumed to be. Tenure (T) represents whether the dwelling is owned or rented by its occupants. Socioeconomic status (SES) is indicated by the measure of expected family income (I), years of schooling completed (ED), and occupational status (OC). Relative income (RI) is the ratio of observed to expected income. Family status (FS) is represented by two proxy variables: the number of persons in the household (PR) and age of the household head (AG). Finally, control for variation in the structure of urban areas is represented by suburbanization (S), measured by rank scores reflecting percentages of the metropolitan population resident outside the central city (SP) and percentages of the labor force employed outside the central city (SE). (These variables are defined more fully in Chapter 2.)

The model shown in Figure 3-2 is designed to remedy some of the deficiencies that limited generalizability of my 1973 results. (Other deficiencies will be remedied by supplementary analyses to be reported in subsequent chapters.) In addition there are several other improvements and some minor differences in Figure 3-2 as compared with Figure 3-1. The differences are as follows:

1. Figure 3-2 includes the variable of relative income. As described in the methodology section (Chapter 2), inclusion of this variable makes it possible to account for variation in consumption pattern that fell into the pool of error variance in the earlier model.

2. Age of head of household is substituted for marital duration, which avoids some artifactual scores for persons in other than first marriages.

3. Number of persons in the household is substituted for number of children and relatives present. This difference simply reflects what was available in the 1970 Census tape.

4. In the current model, owners and renters are considered together rather than analyzed separately.

5. The residuals (U) leading to the housing quality and quantity variables in Figure 3-2 are correlated rather than the variables themselves. This reflects the assumption that the correlation between housing quality and space is the result of production characteristics in the housing industry rather than one attribute of housing being the cause of the other.

6. The final difference between the present study and my 1973 work is that the estimation procedures used in the analysis reported here have greater power to test the implications of the model than those used earlier.

B. Estimation of the Model in Figure 3-2

The plausibility of the model in Figure 3-2 was evaluated through the application of Jöreskog's recently developed LISREL program, which estimates the parameters of general theoretical structures (Jöreskog, 1973; see also Burt, 1973; Werts *et al.*, 1973). The postulated relations among the variables in Figure 3-2 can be represented by the following system of structural equations:

$$\beta\eta = \Gamma\xi + \zeta \qquad (3.1)$$

where $\beta(M \times M)$ is a coefficient matrix specifying relations among the unobserved endogenous variables (T, HS, and HQ), $\Gamma(M \times N)$ is a coefficient matrix specifying the relations among the unobserved exogenous variables (SES, RI, FS, and S) and the unobserved endogenous variables (T, HS, and HQ); and ζ is a random vector of residuals for the unobserved endogenous variables.

It is assumed that

$$E(\eta) = E(\xi) = E(\zeta) = 0$$

and Γ and β are nonsingular. Since the elements of vectors η and ξ are not observed, they are postulated to be directly related to observed indicator

TABLE 3-1

Zero-Order Correlations among Measured Variables Used to Estimate Models of the Demand for Residential Services (White Primary Families, N = 23,612)

Variables[a]	T	HS	NR	NU	HQ	YB	BR	BP	V	MI	PV
T	1.000										
HS	.2837	1.000									
NR	.5186	.7076	1.000								
NU	.8037	.1970	.5114	1.000							
HQ	.3496	.3500	.5669	.3051	1.000						
YB	.0868	.0534	.0669	.0372	.5228	1.000					
BR	.3325	.3945	.6012	.2897	.8978	.2947	1.000				
BP	−.1317	−.0463	−.0891	−.1155	−.1233	−.1298	−.0913	1.000			
V	.0164	−.0163	.0225	.0182	.1811	.2915	.1617	.1236	1.000		
MI	.2009	.2336	.3229	.1399	.4333	.1949	.4211	−.2848	−.0742	1.000	
PV	.1059	.2141	.2660	.0488	.3823	.1884	.3764	−.1974	.0528	.6921	1.000
NW	.1156	.0749	.1165	.1097	.3746	.5704	.2650	−.1414	.5758	.2528	.2781
DN	−.1779	−.0313	−.1713	−.2658	−.1164	−.0761	−.0709	.2013	.3258	−.1777	−.0240
SL	.1652	.0971	.1494	.1637	.1796	.1914	.1200	−.1774	−.0681	.2684	.2615
ACC	−.1218	.0031	−.0569	−.1444	−.0959	−.1419	−.0582	.0774	−.0759	−.0154	.0163
SE	.0457	−.0840	−.0299	.1006	.0043	.0982	−.0068	.0800	.2401	−.2329	−.2928
SP	.0268	−.0797	−.0449	.0702	−.0296	.0439	−.0372	.0801	.1436	−.2214	−.2492
ED	.0417	.1965	.2504	.0109	.3520	.2214	.3493	−.0854	.1093	.3106	.2923
I	.2072	.2479	.2997	.1216	.3470	.1117	.3670	−.0970	−.0028	.3708	.3283
OC	.1215	.2345	.2718	.0679	.3432	.1810	.3462	−.0862	.0536	.3115	.2842
PR	.2007	.2523	.3772	.2421	.1669	.0113	.1747	−.0323	−.0257	.0444	.0221
AG	.2798	.1233	.1536	.2093	.0541	−.1981	.1203	.0049	−.0972	.0895	.0702
RI	−.0619	−.0536	−.0878	−.0517	−.0988	−.0436	−.0900	.0145	−.0058	−.0773	−.0402

[a] See text for definitions of variables.

variables y (for T, HS, and HQ) and x (for FS, SES, RI, and S). The relations between these variables are:

$$y = u + \Lambda_y\boldsymbol{\eta} + \mathbf{E} \tag{3.2}$$

$$x = v + \Lambda_x\boldsymbol{\xi} + \boldsymbol{\Delta} \tag{3.3}$$

where the matrices Λ_y ($p \times m$) and Λ_x ($q \times n$) are regression matrices of y on $\boldsymbol{\eta}$ and of x on $\boldsymbol{\xi}$, respectively, and $\mathbf{E}$ and $\boldsymbol{\Delta}$ are vectors of errors of measurement in y and x, respectively.

Table 3-1 reports the zero-order correlations among all the observed variables used to estimate various aspects of the demand by white families for residential services. At this point attention is focused only on those variables displayed in Figure 3-2. The objective of applying the system of linear equations defined by Eqs. (3.1)–(3.3) is to determine whether the relations exhibited in Table 3-1 can be represented by a more parsimonious set of parameters. In matrix form the hypothesis is that

$$S = \begin{bmatrix} Rxx & Rxy \\ & Ryy \end{bmatrix}$$

$$\simeq \Sigma = \begin{bmatrix} \Delta_{xn}\phi_{nn}\Delta'_{xn} + \theta^2_{xx} & \Delta_{xn}(\phi_{nn}\Gamma'_{mn}B'^{-1}_{mm})\Delta'_{ym} \\ \Delta_{ym}(B^{-1}_{mm}\Gamma_{mn}\phi\Gamma'_{mn}B'^{-1}_{mm} + B^{-1}_{mm}\psi^2_{mm}B'^{-1}_{mm})\Delta'_{ym} + \theta^2_{yy} \end{bmatrix}$$

TABLE 3-1 (Continued)

NW	DN	SL	ACC	SE	SP	ED	I	OC	PR	AG	RI
1.000											
.0488	1.000										
.2222	−.1526	1.000									
−.1452	.1535	−.1384	1.000								
.1400	−.1082	−.2917	−.0481	1.000							
.0581	−.1014	−.3157	.0065	.8762	1.000						
.1678	−.0168	.0654	.0249	−.0212	−.0341	1.000					
.0713	.0142	.1349	.0005	−.1347	−.1382	.5178	1.000				
.1338	−.0032	.0542	−.0008	.0261	−.0392	.5695	.5633	1.000			
.0563	−.0695	.0916	−.0350	−.0911	−.0217	.0437	−.0929	.0238	1.000		
−.1436	.0398	−.0283	.0800	−.0548	−.0376	−.2159	.2736	.0001	−.1768	1.000	
−.0325	.0181	.0122	.0330	−.0122	−.0205	.0539	.1634	.0549	−.0979	.0746	1.000

Jöreskog (1973) has shown that Σ can be estimated by means of a maximum-likelihood procedure, which minimizes the function F as

$$F(\Sigma) = \ln|\Sigma| + \text{tr}(\Sigma^{-1}S) - \ln|S| - r \tag{3.4}$$

where ln refers to the natural logarithm, and r refers to the total number of observed variables ($r = x + y$).

That portion of Eq. (3.1) that specifies relations among the exogenous and endogenous unobserved variables depicted in Figure 3-2 can be written in terms of individual structural equations. Thus:

$$T = \gamma_{T,S}S + \gamma_{T,SES}SES + \gamma_{T,FS}FS + \gamma_{T,RI}RI + \psi_T \tag{3.5}$$

$$HS = \gamma_{HS,S}S + \gamma_{HS,SES}SES + \gamma_{HS,FS}FS + \gamma_{HS,RI}RI + \beta_{HS,T}T + \psi_{HS,HQ} \tag{3.6}$$

$$HQ = \gamma_{HQ,S}S + \gamma_{HQ,SES}SES + \gamma_{HQ,FS}FS + \gamma_{HQ,RI}RI + \beta_{HQ,T}T + \psi_{HS,HQ} \tag{3.7}$$

where T, HS, HQ, S, SES, FS, and RI denote unobserved variables; the parameters γ, β, and ψ are elements of the matrices Γ, B, and Ψ, respectively; and $\psi_{HS,HQ}$ indicate correlated residuals. Table 3-2 presents all of the parameter specifications associated with estimating the causal paths indicated in Figure 3-2. The format of Table 3-2 will be used throughout in presenting coefficients derived by applying Eqs. (3.1)–(3.3) to an observed correlation matrix. The rows of Λ_y and Λ_x represent the observed variables whose relations are reported in Table 3-1. The relationships between observed and unobserved variables are estimated by means of the manipulation of the observed variables, and the estimated coefficients are reported as elements of Λ_y and Λ_x.

Values of 0 and 1 indicate that the values of the parameters are fixed and assumed to be equal to some a priori value. In instances where an unobserved variable has more than one indicator, that variable's relationship to one of the indicators was assumed to be equal to 1 in the initial estimation process and was subsequently rescaled to reflect the true relationship. The elements of the matrices should be interpreted by way of their columns, since the columns represent independent variables and rows represent dependent variables. For example, the coefficients $\beta_{HS,T}$ and $\beta_{HQ,T}$ (of the B matrix) indicate that tenure affects consumption of both housing space and quality. On the other hand, the coefficients $\gamma_{T,S}$, $\gamma_{T,SES}$, $\gamma_{T,FS}$, $\gamma_{T,RI}$ in the Γ matrix indicate that tenure status is affected by suburbanization, SES, family status, and relative income. The convention of reporting standardized solutions to equations similar to Eqs. (3.1)–(3.3) is followed throughout this monograph.

Table 3-3 reports the structural coefficients for data from white families used to estimate the model in Figure 3-1, and Table 3-4 reports differences between the information matrix (Σ) and the sample variance–covariance matrix (S) obtained by applying Eqs. (3.1), (3.2), and (3.3) to relevant portions of the observed correlation matrix presented in Table 3-1. The

TABLE 3-2

Parameter Specifications for Figure 3-2, Determinants of the Demand for Housing Services[a]

Λ_y		T	HS	HQ	
	T	1.000	000	000	
	NR	000	1.000	000	
	NU	000	$\lambda_{NU,HS}$	000	
	YR	000	000	1.000	
	BR	000	000	$\lambda_{BR,HQ}$	

Λ_x		S	SES	FS	RI
	SE	1.000	000	000	000
	SP	$\lambda_{SP,S}$	000	000	000
	ED	000	1.000	000	000
	I	000	$\lambda_{IC,SES}$	000	000
	OC	000	$\lambda_{OC,SES}$	000	000
	AG	000	000	1.000	000
	PR	000	000	$\lambda_{P,FS}$	000
	RI	000	000	000	1.000

B		T	HS	HQ	
	T	1.000	000	000	
	HS	$\beta_{HS,T}$	1.000	000	
	HQ	$\beta_{HQ,T}$	000	1.000	

Γ		S	SES	FS	RI
	T	$\gamma_{T,S}$	$\gamma_{T,SES}$	$\gamma_{T,FS}$	$\gamma_{T,RI}$
	HS	$\gamma_{HS,S}$	$\gamma_{HS,SES}$	$\gamma_{HS,FS}$	$\gamma_{HS,RI}$
	HQ	$\gamma_{HQ,S}$	$\gamma_{HQ,SES}$	$\gamma_{HQ,FS}$	$\gamma_{HQ,RI}$

Φ		S	SES	FS	RI
	S	1.000			
	SES	$\phi_{SES,S}$	1.000		
	FS	$\phi_{FS,S}$	$\phi_{FS,SES}$	1.000	
	RI	$\phi_{RI,S}$	$\phi_{RI,SES}$	$\phi_{RI,FS}$	1.000

Ψ		T	HS	HQ
	T	$\psi_{T,T}$		
	HS	000	$\psi_{HS,HS}$	
	HQ		$\psi_{HS,HQ}$	$\psi_{HQ,HQ}$

Θ_E	T	NR	NU	YR	BR			
	000	ϵ_{NR}	ϵ_{NU}	ϵ_{YR}	ϵ_{BR}			

Θ_Δ	SE	SP	ED	I	OC	AG	PR	RI
	δ_{SE}	δ_{SP}	δ_{ED}	δ_I	δ_{OC}	δ_{AG}	δ_{PR}	000

[a] Values of 0 and 1 denote fixed parameters with values established a priori.

45

TABLE 3-3
Structural Coefficients for Figure 3-2: White Primary Families

Λ_y		T	HS	HQ	
	T	1.0000	.0000	.0000	
	NR	.0000	.6830	.0000	
	NU	.0000	.7882	.0000	
	YB	.0000	.0000	.4709	
	BR	.0000	.0000	.8297	

Λ_x		S	SES	FS	RI
	SE	.9727	.0000	.0000	.0000
	SP	.9118	.0000	.0000	.0000
	ED	.0000	.8392	.0000	.0000
	I	.0000	.7662	.0000	.0000
	OC	.0000	.7905	.0000	.0000
	PR	.0000	.0000	.8902	.0000
	AG	.0000	.0000	−.1037	.0000
	RI	.0000	.0000	.0000	1.0000

B		T	HS	HQ
	T	1.0000	.0000	.0000
	HS	.9170	1.0000	.0000
	HQ	.3029	.0000	1.0000

Γ		S	SES	FS	RI
	T	.0708	.2118	.2267	−.0474
	HS	.0345	.1600	.1941	−.0124
	HQ	.0189	.5413	.0786	−.1350

Φ		S	SES	FS	RI
	S	1.0000			
	SES	−.1075	1.0000		
	FS	−.0482	.0163	1.0000	
	RI	−.0200	.1264	−.1348	1.0000

Ψ		T	HS	HQ
	T	.8992		
	HS	.0000	−.0506	
	HQ	.0000	.1278	.5248

ΘE	T	NR	NU	YB	BR
	.0000	.7304	.6155	.8822	.5582

$\Theta\Delta$	SE	SP	ED	I	OC	PR	AG	RI
	.2323	.4106	.5438	.6426	.6124	.4556	.9946	.0000

plausibility of a theoretical model can be evaluated according to whether its specifications are capable of generating an information matrix that gives a reasonable approximation of the parallel variance–covariance matrix. The statistical significance of χ^2 statistics associated with maximum likelihood estimates of the parameters is often used to judge the model's adequacy. However, these statistics will not be used here as the major criteria for

TABLE 3-4

Differences between the Information Matrix (Σ) and the Sample Variance–Covariance Matrix (S), Figure 3-2^a

$\Sigma(YY) = SYY$

	T	NR	NU	YB	BR
T	.1097				
NR	.2561	.1674			
NU	.0565	.0933	.0809		
YB	.1452	.1769	.2335	.1385	
BR	.0536	−.1955	.1608	.1254	.0156

$\Sigma(XY) = SXY$

SE	−.0056	.0617	−.0653	−.1127	−.0174
SP	.0107	.0746	−.0373	−.0574	.0146
ED	.1710	.0027	.2702	.0724	.1396
I	−.0322	−.0913	.1097	.1301	.0353
OC	.0598	−.0560	.1717	.0694	.0705
PR	.0449	−.0743	.0942	.0768	−.0281
AG	−.3056	−.1855	−.2447	.1888	−.1358
RI	.0065	.0382	−.0034	−.0034	.0209

$\Sigma(XX) = SXX$

	SE	SP	ED	I	OC	PR	AG	RI
SE	.0570							
SP	.0565	.0463						
ED	−.0863	−.0661	.4200					
I	.0462	.0557	.3052	.1536				
OC	−.0656	−.0463	.2830	.1382	.1627			
PR	−.0282	−.0233	−.0274	.1063	−.0099	.2620		
AG	.0599	.0424	.2142	−.2750	−.0015	.0715	.0316	
RI	−.0088	.0019	.0726	−.0594	.0529	−.0369	−.0604	.0000

^{a} $\chi^2 = 27{,}720.50$, with 50 df.

accepting or rejecting a model (although they are reported for informational purposes). Chi square is highly sensitive to sample size and, for samples of the size used in this analysis, would be significant in so many cases as to be nondiscriminative. Thus instead of χ^2, I used the relative magnitude of the misappropriations between Σ and S as the basis for evaluating the reasonableness of a model.

1. Revised Model

The pattern of misappropriations reported in Table 3-4 is too large to warrant acceptance of the model in Figure 3-2. Most of them arise from inconsistency within and between indicator correlations. This inconsistency is particularly great for indicators of family status. As can be seen in the Λ_x matrix of Table 3-3, the relationships of family status (FS) to number of persons in the household (PR) and age of head of household (AG) are substantially different. This discrepancy suggests that *PR* and *AG* are not related to the same theoretical construct. It is highly unlikely that neither age of head nor number of persons in the household are appropriate indicators of stages in the family life-cycle. It will be recalled that the sample is one solely of primary families, in which the number of persons in the household is identical to the number of children present for approximately 96% of these families. One of the basic problems with the number of persons variable is that it reflects the number of children present at the time of the census, not the number of children ever present in the family. Hence the negative correlation between *PR* and *AG* simply reflects the fact that the older the head, the fewer the children still living at home.

The model was then modified according to this reasoning by removing the unobserved variable *FS* from the specification and allowing *PR* and *AG* to be directly related to the endogenous variables. Table 3-5 shows the structural coefficients for data from white families used to estimate the revised model. Table 3-6 shows the misappropriations between (Σ) and (S) resulting from the reanalysis.

The revised model is a substantial improvement over the original model, as is shown by comparisons between the misappropriations and associated χ^2 values reported in Tables 3-4 and 3-6. However the revised model, like the original, does not account for all of the covariations among the indicator variables shown in Table 3-1. This problem is common to overidentified models such as those employed here, given the large sample size and the finding that correlations between related indicators of unobserved variables are not as similar as expected. The latter problem can be clearly observed, for example, in the large discrepancies in the size of the coefficients for the correlations between the two indicators of housing quality (*YB* and *BR*) and other variables.

No further effort will be made to refine this model until other aspects of the demand for neighborhood services have been considered. Before going on to describe the substantive significance of the structural coefficients generated from the revised model, I should point out that these coefficients are biased estimates of the true relationships that exist among the variables included. In particular, the revised specifications overstate the effect of tenure (*T*) on housing space (*HS*) and the effects of SES on housing quality (*HQ*).

2. Results

Following the usual convention, significance is attached only to those relationships represented by coefficients in Table 3-5 greater than .09.

The B matrix shows, not unexpectedly, that *T* is strongly and positively related to both *HS* and *HQ*. That is, families who own their own homes choose bigger and higher quality dwellings than renters. More specifically,

TABLE 3-5

Structural Coefficients for the Revised Model (Figure 3-2): White Primary Families

Λ_y		T	HS	HQ		
	T	1.0000	.0000	.0000		
	NR	.0000	.6436	.0000		
	NU	.0000	.7761	.0000		
	YB	.0000	.0000	.4415		
	BR	.0000	.0000	.7884		
Λ_x		S	SES	PR	AG	RI
	SE	.9690	.0000	.0000	.0000	.0000
	SP	.9169	.0000	.0000	.0000	.0000
	ED	.0000	.8445	.0000	.0000	.0000
	I	.0000	.7561	.0000	.0000	.0000
	OC	.0000	.7880	.0000	.0000	.0000
	PR	.0000	.0000	1.0000	.0000	.0000
	AG	.0000	.0000	.0000	1.0000	.0000
	RI	.0000	.0000	.0000	.0000	1.0000
B		T	HS	HQ		
	T	1.0000	.0000	.0000		
	HS	.8672	1.0000	.0000		
	HQ	.2555	.0000	1.0000		
Γ		S	SES	PR	AG	RI
	T	.0826	.1928	.2537	.3372	$-.0792$
	HS	.0445	.1564	.2346	.0602	$-.0287$
	HQ	.0445	.5686	.1295	.0598	$-.1436$
Φ		S	SES	PR	AG	RI
	S	1.0000				
	SES	$-.0908$	1.0000			
	PR	$-.0217$	$-.0008$	1.0000		
	AG	$-.0566$	$-.0193$	$-.1771$	1.0000	
	RI	$-.0174$	.1272	$-.0985$	.0738	1.0000
Ψ		T	HS	HQ		
	T	.8152				
	HS	.0000	.0076			
	HQ	.0000	.1727	.5202		

ΘE	T	NR	NU	YB	BR			
	.0000	.7654	.6307	.8972	.6152			

$\Theta\Delta$	SE	SP	ED	I	OC	PR	AG	RI
	.2472	.3991	.5356	.6545	.6156	.0000	.0000	.0000

TABLE 3-6

Differences between the Information Matrix (Σ) and the Sample Variance–Covariance Matrix (S), Revised Model (Figure 3-2)[a]

$\Sigma(YY) = SYY$

	T	NR	NU	YB	BR
T	.0077				
NR	.1034	.0044			
NU	−.0581	−.0124	−.0075		
YB	.1023	.1333	.2028	.1170	
BR	−.0137	−.2636	.1150	.0724	−.0045

$\Sigma(XY) = SXY$

	T	NR	NU	YB	BR
SE	−.0037	.0677	−.0552	−.0982	.0067
SP	.0128	.0805	−.0275	−.0439	.0371
ED	.1275	−.0611	.2160	.0531	.1133
I	−.0702	−.1464	.0621	.1105	.0076
OC	.0222	−.1110	.1248	.0521	.0467
PR	−.0001	−.1199	.0663	.0739	−.0310
AG	−.0007	.0090	−.0144	.2372	−.0544
RI	.0055	.0381	−.0078	−.0006	.0245

$\Sigma(XX) = SXX$

	SE	SP	ED	I	OC	PR	AG	RI
SE	.0651							
SP	.0651	.0541						
ED	−.0695	−.0513	.4023					
I	.0611	.0690	.2920	.1470				
OC	−.0510	−.0334	.2800	.1245	.1619			
PR	−.0017	.0013	−.0445	.0922	−.0245	.0000		
AG	−.0018	−.0157	.1966	−.2892	−.0165	−.0003	.0000	
RI	−.0062	.0042	.0734	−.0604	.0532	−.0006	−.0007	.0000

[a] $\chi^2 = 22,671.64$, with 46 df; $\chi^2_{(1/0)} = 5048.86$, with 4 $df_{(1/0)}$.

homeowners on the average have more rooms in their dwellings, more privacy from outside disturbances (because they live in detached dwellings), and newer and better quality houses (as indicated by age of dwelling and number of bathrooms) than renters.

The demand for housing space and homeownership is influenced more by attributes of family status than by those of socioeconomic status. In contrast, the demand for better quality housing tends to be influenced more by socioeconomic status than by attributes of family status.

More specifically, as the Γ matrix in Table 3-5 shows, the family status proxy of household size (PR) is a determinant of tenure and housing space, and to a lesser degree, of housing quality. The relationship of PR to tenure and housing space was expected since it was assumed that white families with increased size meet their demand for increased space primarily through a shift in tenure status, from renting to ownership. The relationship of PR to housing quality was not as expected, however, since it has been assumed that large families substitute housing space for quality and cannot demand both because of income restraints. This assumption did not take into account two facts: (*a*) the average size household in this sample is modest (less than five persons); and (*b*) shifts from renter to owner status usually result in an improvement in housing quality. This latter result stems from the fact that owned dwellings tend to be higher quality than rented dwellings because of location and production factors in the construction process. In other words, families with a need to increase their housing space (either because of increased family size or because their children need more space as they grow older) may confront a housing market in which the demand for more space and privacy can only be obtained in residential packages of relatively high quality. Thus families that need more housing space may not be able to substitute space for quality.

In contrast to household size, the other proxy variable for family status, age of the head (*AG*), affects only tenure status. As expected, older heads are most likely to own their dwelling. There was very little effect of age of head on housing space, again as expected. Since age of head serves as a proxy for family life-cycle stage, it would be expected to be curvilinearly related to demand for space (e.g., as a family's space needs first increase and then decrease), with the observed linear effect close to zero.

The small positive effect of age of head on housing quality actually results from an inconsistency in the former's relationship with the indicators of housing quality. Age of head, for example, is negatively related to age of dwelling (newer units are assigned the highest score), but positively related to the number of bathrooms in a dwelling unit. This finding undoubtedly reflects the net effect of the tendency of some people to stay on in dwellings even when they achieve the ability to pay for better dwellings and the tendency of others to move when they can afford more. Also, it should be noted that many older heads (particularly owners, who tend to be older than renters) will have the resources to maintain or improve the quality of their dwellings, so that for these people age of dwelling may not be a negative indicator of quality.

In contrast to the family status variables, SES is a major determinant mainly of housing quality and only to a lesser extent of housing space and tenure. Thus, in line with assumptions about the social status value of housing attributes and SES-related residential consumption norms, white families show upgraded residential consumption through ownership of relatively high quality, large dwellings as they achieve higher income and social status, with the emphasis on quality. Generally in this sample, white families exhibit high levels of homeownership even at low income levels—70% of all white primary families in the 1970 sample. It should also be noted here that the positive effect of SES on housing services probably reflects in part an effect of SES on the average market exchange value of dwelling units available for owner occupancy. That is, residential packages of high use value (yield large quantities of housing services) are built for and can only be afforded by high SES families.

Finally, suburbanization (*S*) and relative income (*RI*) were found to have only minor effects on white demand for housing services. The small negative effect of *RI* on demand for housing quality and tenure supports the permanent income hypothesis (outlined in Chapter 2). That is, white families do not increase their housing consumption as their income rises if they remain in the same socioeconomic class in terms of other indicators. In fact, the negative sign suggests that, if anything, the housing consumption of white families with incomes above that of their reference group average is actually lower than the average consumption level of their reference group.

3. Conclusions

By way of a summary, we may ask what do these results tell us about families' demand for housing services? First, tenure status appears to be far more responsive to the compositional structure (number of persons and age of head) of families than to status characteristics. Part of the explanation for this lies in the fact that white primary families exhibit high levels of homeownership even at low income levels (see Chapter 9). Second, the choice of owning versus renting results in a substantial improvement in available space as well as in the level of quality of housing.

Third, socioeconomic status had significant effects on tenure status as well as the demand for housing services (e.g., space, type, and quality). These findings imply that maximizing the technical and social status value of housing service attributes increases simultaneously the market exchange value of a dwelling unit. Thus, although the relationship between use value and market exchange value may not be perfectly linear, residential packages of high use value are likely to command higher prices; and thus the net income benefits in the long run will probably be appreciably higher.

My original expectations in regard to the effects of family status on the demand for housing services must be revised to take account of the differences in consumption patterns resulting from different effects of the proxy variables for family status on the dependent variables. Age of head affects mainly tenure, whereas number of persons in the household affects tenure, housing space, and housing quality. It should also be pointed out here that the effect of the number of persons per household on the demand for housing services is greater than the direct coefficients in Table 3-5 indicate. This is because part of the influence exerted by family composition on housing services is mediated through tenure, the effects of which are statistically controlled for in the coefficients seen in Table 3-5.

In the next several chapters, the model evaluated in this chapter will be expanded to include other aspects of the demand for residential services as presented in Figure 1-1. As was indicated previously, the flow of services derived from residence in a dwelling unit is not the only factor which exerts influence on the residential behavior of families. The neighborhood and the location of residence in relation to other activities to be found in metropolitan areas are also important.

4

The Demand for
Neighborhood Services

One can observe much regularity in the way in which households distribute themselves spatially in urban areas, with outcomes that give each neighborhood some uniqueness. There are many dimensions of residential differentiation in the urban population, and almost any criterion that distinguishes social groups may also be the basis for their physical separation into different neighborhoods. The basic question addressed here is this: Why do households with similar characteristics tend to be located in similar types of residential environments in a variety of urban areas? There is no simple answer to this question, since the residential location of households in urban areas is as much a product of external forces operating in local housing markets as it is a result of a selection process reflecting consumer choice. Moreover, a number of interrelated factors can be suggested as constituting the underlying basis for residential differentiation. First, households with similar life styles will tend to cluster together to protect themselves from disruptive influences. Second, housing tends to be supplied in tracts differentiated by prices and types. Third, households' demand for various kinds of goods and services may differ, and thus, they may not place the same emphasis on being accessible to various kinds of nonresidential activities. Finally, the behavior of other decision units operating in housing markets may affect the locational decisions of households.

The following section discusses the relevance of each of these factors with respect to the general process of residential differentiation and their impact on the clustering of households with similar characteristics. The issues raised in that discussion are used in turn to extend the model of the demand for residential services presented in Chapter 3 to include consideration of the demand for neighborhood services. An obvious issue that such an elaboration raises is that of the extent to which the demographic and socioeconomic attributes of primary families impact on the demand for neighborhood services directly once choice of tenure and the demand for housing services (with respect to space and quality) have been taken into account.

I. SOURCES OF RESIDENTIAL DIFFERENTIATION

A. Differentiation Resulting from Demand

Families with similar characteristics tend to make similar demands for goods and services as a consequence of their sharing a particular life style. *Life style* is defined here as a set of values, attitudes, beliefs, and behaviors associated with biological, psychological, and social maintenance, reproduction, socialization, status placement, social control, and labor force participation. A number of empirical studies have shown that these life-style differences between groups and individuals affect residential decision making—for example, families with similar life styles tend to cluster together (Strauss, 1961; Gans, 1962; Keller, 1968; Michelson, 1970; Timms, 1971; Suttles, 1972; Popenoe, 1974). Hence, observed differences are perceived as having important implications with respect to behavior, attitudes, value, and the development of nonthreatening associational patterns.

Ethnicity is one factor producing residential segregation and has played an important role, historically, in producing the segregated residential patterns observed today (see Lieberson, 1963). The importance of ethnicity is quite evident in recent estimates of residential dissimilarities between old and new world immigrants, blacks, and persons of hispanic origin (Guest and Weed, 1977; Klaff, 1978). In addition, similarity in occupation, education, and income level also plays a role in producing residential segregation; families generally desire to have neighbors who share their values (Duncan and Duncan, 1955; Tilly, 1961; Uyeki, 1964; Hawley, 1971; Foley, 1973; Marrett, 1973; Erbe, 1975; Farley, 1977; Simkus, 1978). Similarly, in some respects, residential differentiation is simply a component of the much broader phenomenon of social stratification. Some individuals are accorded higher status than others and have life styles considered worthy of emulation because of the prestige, recognition, and deference assigned to their position in society.

The sociological significance of residential areas lies in the opportunities they afford for social contacts. The selection process that results in homogeneous residential areas on the basis of social status and ethnicity, according to Ray (1973:314), is related to three factors. First, segregation by choice is a way of isolating one's family from influences disruptive of their culture and from conflict with other groups that might threaten their status, property, and even their lives. Second, neighborhoods function as sources of friends and companions for the pursuit of common interests, and they aid in the socialization of children into the family's cultural heritage. Third, the segregation of households by life style facilitates the flow of information on socially appropriate patterns and helps families to accommodate to novel ways of behaving and thinking as the greater culture changes.

Suttles' (1972) concept of the "defended neighborhood" is useful here. In Suttles' view, the inhabitants of urban areas share mental maps of their city that involve evaluation of residential areas on the basis of safety and expected social contacts—that is, according to the perceived modal life styles of the inhabitants. Some sections have higher status than others, mirroring the evaluation of life styles according to prestige. Suttles notes that one of the most important attributes of a residential area is its consensually assigned label of snobbish, trashy, tough, exclusive, dangerous, mixed, and so on. The perception of where people stand in the social hierarchy is not only determined by what kind of dwelling they live in, but also by who lives next door, and residential selection processes are strongly influenced by perceived opportunities for social contact in the neighborhood.

The significance of these cognitive maps is that they constitute a shared set of rules that have the effect of regulating and restricting residential mobility. These rules are part of the general social control apparatus of urban areas and perform the functions of separating groups that might come into conflict, decreasing anonymity among individuals through restriction of their type and range of associations, and thrusting people into common networks of social relations, which adds in the maintenance of social cohesion.

B. Metropolitan Growth Patterns

Another factor leading to homogeneity in residential locations stems from the usual growth pattern of urban areas. As one moves from the center of the city toward the perimeter and the suburbs, one finds marked changes in dwelling age, type, size, condition, and tenure characteristics. In some central cities the major structures at the center are replacements for earlier buildings, but by and large the oldest structures in American cities are those built when the central city was relatively new. This geographic distribution of structures has a marked effect on the distribution of occupant types. Guest (1970, 1971, 1972), in a systematic analysis of the spatial distribution of metropolitan population, found that childless couples and singles tended to live close to the central business district, whereas couples with children tended to live away from the central city. This distributional pattern was almost completely explained, statistically, by the relationship of distance from the central city to population density (rooms per dwelling and dwellings per area) and age of dwelling.

The major factor producing these findings is that families in different stages of the family life-cycle tend to have needs for particular types of dwellings, needs that can be met only in certain areas. High-rise apartment buildings are often located near nucleated business centers or major thoroughfares, whereas single-family dwellings with relatively great internal space, yards for children to play in, quiet streets, etc., can usually be found only at the periphery of the city, far from business or industrial districts.

Another major factor at the base of these findings is ease of access to the diverse goods and services provided by the public and private sectors. Many of the activities of households, as producing and consuming units, take place beyond the dwelling. When a residential decision is made, the household is purchasing not only housing services from the physical dwelling, but also a package of public and quasi-public services including schools, police and fire protection, recreation facilities, etc. (Foote *et al.*, 1960; Maisel and Winnick, 1960; Meyerson *et al.*, 1962; Kain and Quigley, 1970). Families at different stages of the family life-cycle have needs for particular kinds of services as well as dwellings, and these services too are distributed in a pattern explained statistically by distance from the central city. For childless couples and singles, residential decisions are likely to be strongly influenced by access to places of employment and to adult social, cultural, and recreational activities. Thus these households are likely to be found in multiunit structures close to the urban centers where such activities are found. In contrast, married couples in the childrearing and child-launching stages need access to activities appropriate for children, which tend to predominate in the suburbs (Michelson, 1970).

Another source of residential clustering related to access factors is that of demand for services that are key elements in specific life styles. Families have located in specific areas because of the presence of a lake, park, scenic view, country club, high-quality or specialized school, and so on. Ethnic groups have tended to cluster in areas with retail outlets, restaurants, recreational facilities, etc., that provide the specialized goods and services required by their life styles. Such clustering provides these groups with the added benefits of economies of scale (Suttles, 1968; Wilson, 1975). Conversely, any feature of the environment that might have a negative effect on residential quality, achievement of desired life styles, family functioning, etc., will repulse residential consumption in the surrounding area. Commercial and industrial activities that generate pollution and traffic congestion tend to have this effect. And finally, household members who are employed in the urban marketplace will value accessibility to place of employment in making residential decisions. (This latter factor will be treated in detail in the following chapter.)

C. The Structure of the Housing Market

Housing tends to be provided in tracts differentiated by price and type of dwelling. Developers have found it to be to their advantage over the years to erect a number of dwelling units—sometimes a very large number—at one time, with only minor variations in design from house to house. It has also proved profitable to provide new areas with ready-made social status—for example, by giving them names with status significance, such as "Country Club Acres." The practices that lead to this kind of initial differentiation of new neighborhoods are supported not only by economies of scale and by the importance of prestige in residential consumption, but also by the tax laws. In addition, municipal zoning ordinances have had a substantial effect on intensifying this differentiation through prohibition of the erection of structures that do not conform to designated or existing land uses for each area.

The net result is the segregation of families into neighborhoods according to ability to pay for residential services. Most locations can be fairly clearly identified in terms of the socioeconomic status of their residents, and the housing services consumed by any given household provide a rough approximation of the average housing consumption of all households in the same location. Conversely, the financial resources that a family can allocate to residential consumption limits the pool of sites that it can choose from. Ray (1973) suggests that:

> Supply factors can reinforce status segregation by virtue of the first filter [income limitation] tending to exclude from consideration all housing/site packages (e.g., neighborhoods) of too low a price and status . . . as inferior goods . . . and by excluding from consideration all housing/site/neighborhoods of too high a price or status [p. 271].

It is not only the families themselves who, from personal preference or as a result of market or geographical factors, restrict the range of residential packages that they will consider. Competition with other purchasers can restrict their choice to some extent. Families seeking residential packages may not be able to compete with other economic units with different land use needs. Although zoning ordinances protect residential packages from being switched to nonresidential land use, at least to some extent, the ordinances are susceptible to change. Some owners or potential buyers desiring to make such a switch often wield greater economic and political power than the residential users of an area.

Financial institutions and real estate brokers are probably the two other decision-making units in the housing market whose activities have the most direct effect on residential decision making. The lending policies of financial units directly affect the behavior of families seeking residential packages, builders, and existing owners of residential properties. For example, a lending institution can influence the course of aging for a whole neighborhood and may have the final say in whether the neighborhood is maintained or is allowed to deteriorate and eventually to be removed from the residential market. To give another example, until recently, the lending policies of financial units (including the federal government) were explicitly designed to promote the development and maintenance of homogeneity in neighborhoods in order to ensure the stability of residential property values (Foley, 1973).

Real estate brokers are considered the gatekeepers of the urban land market and tend to have relatively great influence on the choices made by individual families. Real estate agents often have their own idea of who should buy what and screen buyers according to their perceptions of who is appropriate for what neighborhood (Aldrich, 1974). Agents are influenced not only by their own perceptions of their customers and of the characteristics of local communities, but also by the opinions of their peers and other external forces. An agent's intimate knowledge about the social fabric and physical structure of urban areas is, of course, often invaluable to families who seek specific residential packages. But this knowledge may also be used to steer some families away from the locations that would best suit their needs because the agent does not believe these families belong in these locations or because the agent is under social and economic pressure to maintain specific segregation patterns. (The more general issue of race discrimination as a major determinant of residential differentiation will be taken up in Chapter 7.)

II. ANALYSIS OF THE DEMAND FOR NEIGHBORHOOD SERVICES

A. Models

This section will report a statistical estimation of models of the demand for neighborhood services based on the preceding discussion of the determinants of residential differentiation. The major hypothesis is that SES, family status, and family housing demand affect the type of residential area in which families are located. Socioeconomic status is used here as an indicator of family life style. It is postulated that families with different SES attributes have different life styles, which require different input goods in order to carry out their individual and societal functions, and so affect residential choice. Also, families of differing compositional or demographic structures (who are in different family life-cycle stages) make different demands for neighborhood services as well as different demands for housing services. Finally, it is assumed that the demand for particular types of residential packages limits the range of neighborhoods that a family may choose from.

Figure 4-1 presents a hypothetical model of the demand for neighborhood

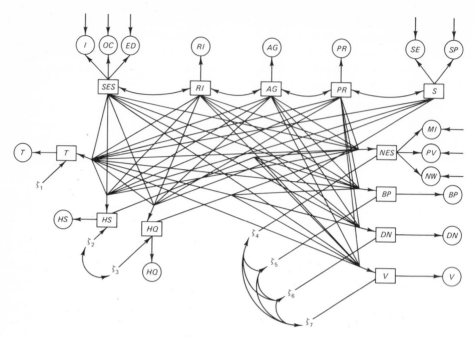

Figure 4-1. Determinants of the demand for neighborhood services.

services. This model is an extension of the model discussed in Chapter 3 and is an elaboration of the causal paths between suburbanization, family status, socioeconomic status, tenure, housing space and quality, and the neighborhood attributes of socioeconomic status, density, stability, and racial composition as presented in Figure 1-1 of Chapter 1. The model as it stands is incomplete, since considerations of intraurban residential location and accessibility to employment are not included. This is because of my previous decision to estimate the model in stages. Moreover, as noted previously, there is a certain degree of indeterminancy in the way in which particular kinds of residential choices are made. Do households, for example, decide upon the type of dwelling unit desired first, and then choose an appropriate neighborhood and location, or is the reverse likely to occur? In an attempt to resolve this dilemma for estimation purposes, I stated a number of assumptions in Chapter 1 with respect to this model, which are reiterated here:

1. Residential goods are composed of three categories: services, housing, and neighborhood and location.
2. Families rank available residential goods, with the evaluation of low-priority goods partially determined by the evaluation of higher-ranking goods.
3. Residential services peculiar to the dwelling's location within the urban

area are treated as endogenous to the demand for housing and neighborhood services.

4. The demand for services peculiar to both neighborhood and location is not as important as determinants of residential demand as is the demand for housing services.

The latter assumption is so for a variety of reasons. The services peculiar to the dwelling itself constitute the minimum required by families in order to carry out their most important functions. Since families spend most of their time and conduct most of their activities within the dwelling, the attributes of the dwelling itself (space, etc.) are of critical importance in the family's residential decision making. Furthermore, because of the physical separation of dwellings from each other, attributes of site and location are not as salient as attributes of the dwelling itself and thus have less power to influence decision making. Also, modern communication and transportation services tend to minimize the importance of the dwelling's location within the greater urban area. These are somewhat arbitrary assumptions, since our knowledge in the area of residential demand does not yet allow us to say with certainty whether families decide first on the type of dwelling desired and then on neighborhood and location or the reverse. For the sake of having a workable model, I have chosen the first alternative, which seems most likely to be true on the basis of present knowledge (see Chapter 6).

1. Variables

The definition of variables *SES, RI, AG, PR, S,* and *T* in Figure 4-1 are given in Chapter 2. The variables of housing space (*HS*) and housing quality (*HQ*), each measured by two proxy variables in the analyses in Chapter 3, are measured by weighted combinations of proxies here. This change was made on the basis of the results, reported in Chapter 3, showing the same pattern of relationships between alternative proxies and other variables in the model. (There were some observed differences in the size of the coefficients, but the pattern and direction were similar.) In addition, since the major focus in this chapter is on demand for neighborhood services, it is not necessary to consider minor differences due to alternative proxies for the major housing services variables. The present operationalization of *HS* and *HQ* includes some variables in the summed measures that were not used in the preceding analyses because of limitations on the number of variables that could be entered. These additional variables, however, were included in hedonic regressions estimating determinants of annual housing costs, and they are used here with the weights resulting from that estimation procedure (see Table 2-A2, pp. 32–35). More specifically, housing space (*HS*) is defined here as the weighted sum of type of structure (*NU*), rooms per dwelling (*NR*), and presence or absence of a basement. Housing quality (*HQ*) is defined here as the weighted sum of the number of bathrooms (BR), year the structure was built (YB), type of utility system, and type of heating unit. The weights used for all components of these composite scores and the categories within each variable can be found in Table 2-A2.

Variables newly introduced in Figure 4-1 represent components of the demand for neighborhood services. The socioeconomic status of the neighborhood (NES) is defined by three proxy variables:

1. Median income of the neighborhood (MI)
2. Valuation of neighborhood dwellings (PV), measured by the weighted average of the percentage of owner-occupied units valued at $25,000 or more and the percentage units rented at $150 or more a month
3. Percentage of units built in 1960 or later (NW)

Neighborhoods are also identified in terms of the percentage of population that is black (BP). Neighborhood stability (V) is defined as the proportion of vacant units for rent or sale among all units in the neighborhood sample. Population density in the neighborhood (DN) is defined as the weighted sum of the percentage of units with one or more persons per room and the percentage of units in structures with five or more units. (A fuller description of these variables can be found in Chapter 2.)

Note that the model in Figure 4-1 postulates residual correlations between the various neighborhood characteristics and between housing space and housing quality. These residual correlations reflect the fact that these factors covary in existing dwellings. That is, in the production of housing, certain neighborhood characteristics tend to occur jointly, and the more space provided, the higher the general quality of the unit. Buyers' and renters' choices are restricted to the available mixes of space and quality, and these may not fully reflect actual demand.

B. Estimation of the Model in Figure 4-1

Tables 4-1 and 4-2 show the misappropriations and the structural coefficients resulting from the preliminary estimation of the model in Figure 4-1, respectively, using the procedure followed in Chapter 3. The differences between the information matrix (Σ) and the sample variance–covariance matrix (S) shown in Table 4-1 were unacceptably large, indicating that the initial set of structural coefficients presented in Table 4-1 were biased estimates of the true relationships among the unobserved variables and suggesting that the model as originally specified warranted rejection.[1] The observed

[1] Estimation of the model in Figure 4-1 required several stages of computation since the LISREL program used can only estimate 80 parameters at a time and there were 86 parameters to be estimated, as Table 4-1 shows. In reducing the number of parameters to 80, I assigned a priori values first to the Φ matrix, estimating the Ψ matrix coefficients, and then to the Ψ matrix, estimating the Φ coefficients. In the first stage the correlations among S, AG, PR, and RI were

TABLE 4-1

Differences between the Information Matrix (Σ) and the Sample Variance–Covariance Matrix (S), Figure 4-1[a]

$\Sigma(YY) = SYY$

	T	HS	HQ	BP	V	MI	PV	NW	DN
T	.0310								
HS	.0420	.0727							
HQ	.0615	.0746	.0807						
BP	.0090	.0081	−.0071	.1073					
V	.0254	.0257	.0136	.1134	.1139				
MI	.0639	.0996	.1199	.0328	.1069	.1380			
PV	.1318	.0850	.1143	−.0288	−.0234	.1100	.0912		
NW	−.0169	.0493	−.1683	.0474	−.5636	.0804	.0210	.0158	
DN	.0169	.0245	.0196	.0990	.1053	.0854	−.0589	−.0832	.0938

$\Sigma(XY) = SXY$

	T	HS	HQ	BP	V	MI	PV	NW	DN
SE	−.0629	−.0998	−.1564	−.0180	−.0896	−.2226	−.1161	−.3098	−.0266
SP	−.0433	−.0971	−.1167	−.0205	.0012	−.2168	−.1440	−.2214	−.0281
ED	.2575	.2567	.2860	−.1262	−.1283	.2765	.2346	.0511	−.0568
I	−.0241	.0295	.0439	−.0325	−.0089	−.0115	−.0057	.0626	−.0592
OC	.0505	.0262	.0241	−.0355	−.0646	.0261	.0188	−.0079	−.0391
PR	−.0101	−.0120	−.0199	−.0029	−.0076	−.0367	−.0152	.0534	.0027
AG	−.0155	−.0157	−.0261	−.0035	−.0126	−.0467	−.0317	.1595	.0003
RI	−.0044	−.0103	−.0148	−.0109	−.0120	−.0202	−.0473	−.0039	−.0025

$\Sigma(XX) = SXX$

	SE	SP	ED	I	OC	PR	AG	RI
SE	.0769							
SP	.0855	.0912						
ED	−.4287	−.3986	.7348					
I	−.1408	−.1267	.0944	.0912				
OC	−.2327	−.2097	.0057	−.2112	.0843			
PR	−.0020	.0005	−.1092	.0527	−.0615	.0000		
AG	−.0022	−.0172	.1314	−.3253	−.0487	−.0002	.0000	
RI	−.0058	.0041	−.0037	−.1327	−.0261	−.0011	−.0005	.0000

[a] $\chi^2 = 38,313,04$, with 73 df.

pattern of relations was, in fact, too complex to be reproduced using the scheme provided by the model in Figure 4-1.

Most of the largest misappropriations are associated with measured variables postulated to be indicators of unobserved variables, rather than with variables for which direct measures are available (such as tenure status). For example, of the three indicators of socioeconomic status, years of schooling (ED) does not show the same pattern of relationships with other measured

set equal to their observed correlations. In the second stage the correlations among the residuals for NES, BP, DN, and V were set equal to the correlations obtained from the first stage, and the relationships among S, AG, PR, and RI were estimated. This procedure was repeated four times for each matrix, at which point the values for the elements in Φ and Ψ converged on stable values.

TABLE 4-2
Structural Coefficients for Figure 4-1: White Primary Families

Λ_y	T	HS	HQ	BP	V	NES	DN
T	1.0000	.0000	.0000	.0000	.0000	.0000	.0000
HS	.0000	1.0000	.0000	.0000	.0000	.0000	.0000
HQ	.0000	.0000	1.0000	.0000	.0000	.0000	.0000
BP	.0000	.0000	.0000	1.0000	.0000	.0000	.0000
V	.0000	.0000	.0000	.0000	1.0000	.0000	.0000
MI	.0000	.0000	.0000	.0000	.0000	.8861	.0000
PV	.0000	.0000	.0000	.0000	.0000	.8122	.0000
NW	.0000	.0000	.0000	.0000	.0000	.3497	.0000
DN	.0000	.0000	.0000	.0000	.0000	.0000	1.0000

Λ_x	S	SES	PR	AG	RI
SE	.9637	.0000	.0000	.0000	.0000
SP	.9207	.0000	.0000	.0000	.0000
ED	.0000	.7592	.0000	.0000	.0000
I	.0000	.5860	.0000	.0000	.0000
OC	.0000	.5523	.0000	.0000	.0000
PR	.0000	.0000	1.0000	.0000	.0000
AG	.0000	.0000	.0000	1.0000	.0000
RI	.0000	.0000	.0000	.0000	1.0000

B	T	HS	HQ	BP	V	NES	DN
T	1.0000	.0000	.0000	.0000	.0000	.0000	.0000
HS	.0639	1.0000	.0000	.0000	.0000	.0000	.0000
HQ	.1259	.0000	1.0000	.0000	.0000	.0000	.0000
BP	−.0534	.1065	.0477	1.0000	.0000	.0000	.0000
V	.0425	.0343	.3349	.0000	1.0000	.0000	.0000
NES	.0601	.0339	.3247	.0000	.0000	1.0000	.0000
DN	−.1299	.0807	.0117	.0000	.0000	.0000	1.0000

Γ	S	SES	PR	AG	RI
T	.2069	.4408	.2774	.3646	−.0834
HS	.0556	.4811	.2789	.1854	−.0669
HQ	.1687	.6789	.1716	.1007	−.1227
BP	−.0523	−.2945	−.0805	−.0408	.0206
V	.0777	−.2415	−.1354	−.1704	.0373
NES	−.3171	.2486	−.0531	.0173	−.0861
DN	−.1876	−.1617	−.0690	.0262	.0089

Φ					
S	1.0000				
SES	−.4499	1.0000			
PR	−.0220	−.0655	1.0000		
AG	−.0570	−.0845	−.1770	1.0000	
RI	−.0170	−.0501	−.0990	.0740	1.0000

Ψ							
T	.7213						
HS	.0000	.6915					
HQ	.0000	.0301	.5183				
BP	.0000	.0000	.0000	.9444			
V	.0000	.0000	.0000	.2018	.9018		
NES	.0000	.0000	.0000	−.1394	.0209	.4726	
DN	.0000	.0000	.0000	.2383	.4174	−.0813	.9408

E	T	HS	HQ	BP	V	MI	PV	NQ	DN
	.0000	.0000	.0000	.0000	.0000	.4634	.5833	.9369	.0000

Δ	SE	SP	ED	IC	OC	PR	AG	RI
	.2672	.3903	.6508	.8103	.8336	.0000	.0000	.0000

variables as do expected income (I) and occupational status (OC). This is also true of the indicators of neighborhood socioeconomic status (NES).

Several alternative specifications of this model were then tested, using the LISREL program (Jöreskog, 1973), but all yielded structural coefficients that were as unsatisfactory as the initial specification. Since many of the misappropriations reflected a lack of consistency in relationships between alternative indicators for single variables, it appeared that a two-stage estimation procedure might yield more conclusive results.

The first stage in this reestimation involved using a confirmatory factor analysis model to determine what the best single measure of each unobserved variable is. This is accomplished with the aid of Jöreskog's (1973) model for analysis of covariance structure. The general equation for this model is:

$$\Sigma = B(\Lambda\Phi\Lambda^1 + \Psi^2)B^1 + \Xi^2 \qquad (4.1)$$

where B is defined as a matrix of factor loadings, Λ is an identity matrix, Φ is a matrix of factor correlations, and Ξ is a vector of communalities. For estimation purposes, the correlations between factors with one indicator are defined a priori as being equal to the correlations among the measured indicators. (This definition is made possible by the fact that the relations between indicators and unobserved variables are exact when there is only one indicator.)

Table 4-3 presents the epistemic and factor correlations and the communalities among the variables in the model in Figure 4-1. Table 4-4 presents the misappropriations resulting from the specifications used to estimate the confirmatory factors model in this first stage. Although the χ^2 value is quite large, the model in Figure 4-1 need not be rejected. As explained previously, the great sensitivity of χ^2 to sample size makes this statistic nondiscriminatory for use with samples as large as that under analysis here. Examination of the misappropriations themselves, in fact, shows that all but two of those with absolute values greater than .09 are associated with the variable of neighborhood age (NW).

The second stage in this reestimation of the model in Figure 4-1 involved applying the LISREL model to the Φ of factor correlations to obtain revised structural coefficients. These are presented in Table 4-5. The Λ_y, Λ_x, and Θ matrices have been omitted, since under current specifications the former two are identity matrices and the latter contains only null vectors.

As noted previously, by applying the confirmatory factor analysis model first, the measured indicators of unobserved variables have been replaced by a single measure derived from the factor analysis. Since the specification involving unobserved variables in Figure 4-1 now constitutes a fully recur-

TABLE 4-3

Confirmatory Factor Analytic Model of the Demand for Neighborhood Services: White Primary Families

B

	T	HS	HQ	BP	V	NES	DN	SL	ACC	S	SES	PR	AG	RI
T	1.000	.000	.000	.000	.000	.000	.000	.000	.000	.000	.000	.000	.000	.000
HS	.000	1.000	.000	.000	.000	.000	.000	.000	.000	.000	.000	.000	.000	.000
HQ	.000	.000	1.000	.000	.000	.000	.000	.000	.000	.000	.000	.000	.000	.000
BP	.000	.000	.000	1.000	.000	.000	.000	.000	.000	.000	.000	.000	.000	.000
V	.000	.000	.000	.000	1.000	.000	.000	.000	.000	.000	.000	.000	.000	.000
MI	.000	.000	.000	.000	.000	.853	.000	.000	.000	.000	.000	.000	.000	.000
PV	.000	.000	.000	.000	.000	.806	.000	.000	.000	.000	.000	.000	.000	.000
NW	.000	.000	.000	.000	.000	.336	.000	.000	.000	.000	.000	.000	.000	.000
DN	.000	.000	.000	.000	.000	.000	1.000	.000	.000	.000	.000	.000	.000	.000
SL	.000	.000	.000	.000	.000	.000	.000	1.000	.000	.000	.000	.000	.000	.000
ACC	.000	.000	.000	.000	.000	.000	.000	.000	1.000	.000	.000	.000	.000	.000
SE	.000	.000	.000	.000	.000	.000	.000	.000	.000	.000	.726	.000	.000	.000
SP	.000	.000	.000	.000	.000	.000	.000	.000	.000	.876	.000	.000	.000	.000
ED	.000	.000	.000	.000	.000	.000	.000	.000	.000	.000	.742	.000	.000	.000
I	.000	.000	.000	.000	.000	.000	.000	.000	.000	.000	.759	.000	.000	.000
OC	.000	.000	.000	.000	.000	.000	.000	.000	.000	.000	.000	.000	.000	.000
PR	.000	.000	.000	.000	.000	.000	.000	.000	.000	.000	.000	1.000	.000	.000
AG	.000	.000	.000	.000	.000	.000	.000	.000	.000	.000	.000	.000	1.000	.000
RI	.000	.000	.000	.000	.000	.000	.000	.000	.000	.000	.000	.000	.000	1.000

Φ

	T	HS	HQ	BP	V	NES	DN	SL	ACC	S	SES	PR	AG	RI
T	1.000													
HS	.284	1.000												
HQ	.350	-.046	1.000											
BP	-.132	-.016	-.123	1.000										
V	.016	.269	.181	.124	1.000									
NES	.197	-.031	.511	-.301	.023	1.000								
DN	-.178	.097	-.116	.201	.326	-.128	1.000							
SL	.165	.003	.180	-.177	-.068	.328	-.153	1.000						
ACC	-.122	-.084	-.096	.077	-.076	-.014	.153	-.138	1.000					
S	.046	.306	.004	.080	.240	-.290	-.108	-.292	-.048	1.000				
SES	.169	.252	.467	-.121	.070	.514	-.002	.114	-.010	.082	1.000			
PR	.201	.167	.253	-.032	-.026	.045	-.069	.092	-.035	.020	-.012	1.000		
AG	.280	.123	.054	.005	-.097	.083	.040	-.027	.080	.055	.033	-.177	1.000	
RI	-.062	-.054	-.099	.014	-.006	-.075	.018	.012	.033	.011	.122	-.098	.074	1.000

66

TABLE 4-4

Differences between the Information Matrix (Σ) and the Sample Variance–Covariance Matrix (S), Confirmatory Factor Analytic Model[a]

Residuals = $S = \Sigma$

	T	HS	HQ	BP	V	MI	PV	NW	DN	SL	ACC	SE	SP	ED	I	OC	PR	AG	RI
T	.000																		
HS	−.000	.000																	
HQ	−.000	.000	.000																
BP	−.000	−.000	.000	.000															
V	−.000	−.000	.000	−.000	.000														
MI	.033	.004	−.003	−.028	−.094	.000													
PV	−.053	−.003	−.030	.045	.034	.005	.000												
NW	.049	−.016	.203	−.040	.568	−.034	.007	−.000											
DN	.000	.000	.000	−.000	.000	−.069	.079	.092	.000										
SL	.000	−.000	.000	.000	.000	−.011	−.003	.112	−.000	.000									
ACC	−.000	−.000	.000	.000	−.000	−.003	.028	−.140	−.000	.000	.000								
SE	−.000	−.000	−.000	.000	−.000	.015	−.059	.238	.000	.000	−.000	−.000							
SP	−.013	−.006	−.033	.010	−.067	−.005	−.045	.144	−.007	−.060	.049	−.000	−.000						
ED	−.081	−.025	.013	.002	.058	−.008	−.008	.042	−.015	−.017	−.017	.038	.018	.000					
I	.082	.021	.000	−.008	−.055	.046	.021	−.057	.016	.051	.008	−.074	−.085	−.021	−.000				
OC	−.006	.002	−.011	.005	.000	−.021	−.030	.003	−.002	−.032	.007	.036	.015	.019	.000	.000			
PR	−.000	−.000	−.000	−.000	−.000	.006	−.014	.041	.000	−.000	−.000	.000	−.004	.052	−.084	.033	.000		
AG	−.000	−.000	.000	−.000	−.000	.018	.003	−.172	.000	−.000	.000	.000	.010	−.240	.249	−.025	−.000	.000	
RI	−.000	−.000	−.000	.000	.000	−.014	.020	−.007	.000	−.000	.000	.000	−.011	−.035	.073	−.038	.000	.000	.000

[a] $\chi^2 = 26{,}218$, with 138 df.

TABLE 4-5

Reestimated Structural Coefficients for Figure 4-1:
White Primary Families

B	T	HS	HQ	BP	V	NES	DN
T	1.000	.0000	.0000	.0000	.0000	.0000	.0000
HS	.1556	1.0000	.0000	.0000	.0000	.0000	.0000
HQ	.2421	.0000	1.0000	.0000	.0000	.0000	.0000
BP	−.1257	.0346	−.0572	1.0000	.0000	.0000	.0000
V	−.0192	−.0405	.2152	.0000	1.0000	.0000	.0000
NES	.0195	.0171	.3334	.0000	.0000	1.0000	.0000
DN	−.1786	.0176	−.0907	.0000	.0000	.0000	1.0000

Γ	S	SES	PR	AG	RI
T	.0833	.1782	.2551	.3229	−.0822
HS	−.0572	.2819	.2368	.1137	−.0646
HQ	.0313	.4455	.1123	$.0025^a$	−.1272
BP	.0851	−.0781	$.0040^a$	.0463	$.0098^a$
V	.2297	$.0051^a$	−.0589	−.0973	.0152
NES	−.2681	.3365	−.0228	.0340	−.0876
DN	−.0990	.0560	$−.0113^a$	.0847	−.0164

Φ	S	SES	PR	AG	RI
S	1.0000				
SES	−.0840	1.0000			
PR	−.0200	−.0120	1.0000		
AG	−.0550	.0330	−.1770	1.0000	
RI	−.0110	.1220	−.0980	.0740	1.0000

Ψ	T	HS	HQ	BP	V	NES	DN
T	.8173						
HS	.0000	.7876					
HQ	.0000	.1121	.6756				
BP	.0000	.0000	.0000	.9615			
V	.0000	.0000	.0000	.1267	.8946		
NES	.0000	.0000	.0000	−.1935	$.0053^a$	.5613	
DN	.0000	.0000	.0000	.1822	.3742	−.1093	.9427

[a] Indicates that a coefficient is less than twice the size of its standard error.

sive model, the χ^2 value and misappropriation matrix reduces to zero. Thus another standard of evaluation must be applied to the estimated model coefficients obtained at this point. The standard used here is whether or not these coefficients are twice the size of their standard error. As with the model in Figure 3-2, significance is attached only to those relationships with coefficients greater than .09.

1. Results

The coefficients in the B matrix of Table 4-5 show the effects of housing attributes on type of neighborhood inhabited by white primary families.

Relationships for the variables considered in Chapter 3 are essentially the same after the addition of the *NES* variable, with one exception. The effect of tenure status (*T*) on housing space (*HS*) is substantially smaller than reported before, although it is still significant. This reduction probably reflects not only the addition of neighborhood variables to the model, but also the change in measurement of *HS*—it will be recalled that *HS* here is measured by a single weighted sum of attributes rather than by alternative measures.

In line with expectation, tenure is observed to be negatively related both to percentage of blacks (*BP*) in the neighborhood and to population density (*DN*). However, *T* is not significantly related to *NES*. On the whole, then, it appears that the primary difference between white renters and white homeowners is not the *SES* of the neighborhood they live in, but the fact that owners are more likely to live in larger, high-quality houses situated in relatively low-density neighborhoods than are renters.

The zero-order correlation between housing space (*HS*) and *NES* is relatively large and positive (see Table 4-3), but contrary to expectation, this relationship vanishes in the estimation presented here. The relationship between *HS* and neighborhood attributes, then, must represent the joint influence on these variables of other factors. Moreover, there is no compelling reason why the relations between housing space and neighborhood *SES* must be direct, particularly considering that a family's space requirement constitutes only one of several attributes it attempts to maximize in selecting a residential site.

However, housing quality (*HQ*) shows a strong positive relationship to *NES*, as one would expect. As noted earlier, this result is assumed to reflect the characteristics of the housing market; dwellings of comparable quality tend to be grouped together. Thus, unlike space attributes, quality attributes are likely to reflect both dwelling characteristics and externalities peculiar to the neighborhood (and urban location, as will be shown later). Also, quality is a primary component of the social use value of a dwelling and is likely to have a greater impact on the market value of a dwelling and thus on *NES* than on any other set of attributes.

Housing quality was also found to be positively related to the proportion of vacant units for rent or sale in the neighborhood (*V*). The basis of this finding is not clear. It may be that at the time of the 1970 Census, much high-quality housing was in new areas that had not yet achieved full occupancy, or perhaps high-quality units were vacant longer because of a relative scarcity of occupants who could afford them at the time the census data were gathered.

The Γ matrix shows the effects of the exogenous variables on observed demand for neighborhood services. Suburbanization (*S*) was found to be positively related to *NES*. The greater the suburbanization, the higher the status of the average neighborhood. This probably reflects differences in urban size, with larger areas being more suburbanized and exhibiting a more pronounced gradient of neighborhood quality and dwelling unit density as one moves from the central city to the suburbs. As will be shown in subsequent analyses, results of the addition of the metropolitan location variable to the model support this interpretation.

Suburbanization was also found to be related to vacancy levels (V), with the highest vacancy rates occurring in urbanized areas of low urbanization. (The positive sign for this coefficient reflects the assignment of low ranks to areas of highest suburbanization.) This finding may reflect the fact that areas undergoing rapid suburbanization have a relatively high proportion of newly developed areas that have not yet achieved maximum occupancy levels, or perhaps that residential expansion tends to exceed demand most in the least suburbanized urban centers, which have a relatively large peripheral area available for expansion.

Family socioeconomic status appears to be the single most important factor influencing consumption of neighborhood services, with a coefficient of .3365 shown in Table 4-5. This is in addition to the strong positive effect it has on tenure, housing space, and quality. As expected, we can conclude that the family with a moderate to high income and at least middle-class status is able to locate in a relatively high-status residential environment. The point to be made here is that high socioeconomic status not only ensures a family that the residential attributes that it has at its disposal are the most prized in the sense of being "bigger and better," but also ensures that the environment in which such attributes are consumed is more or less insulated from the disruptive influences that often emanate from living in large and complex urban environments.

The compositional structure of families (with respect to age of head and number of persons) appears to affect tenure status and the quantity of space consumed by families, not the character of the neighborhood in which they are likely to reside. This conclusion, supported by previous research, is based on the fact that neither number of persons in the household nor age of head appears to have substantial effects on the demand for neighborhood services. This observation should not be interpreted as implying that families with similar housing preferences are not clustered in identifiable residential areas. As I have already noted, the spatial distribution of housing by type practically ensures that some degree of segregation on the basis of household compositional structure will exist in most large urban areas. What should be emphasized is the fact that the demand for a particular kind of housing service bundle, even though it may arise from the compositional structure of a family, may result in families being selectively distributed in different kinds of neighborhoods.

The coefficients reported in the Ψ matrix in Table 4-5 show the extent to which residuals leading to each endogenous variable are correlated with each other. It will be recalled that the model in Figure 4-1 postulates correlated error among the endogenous unobserved variables *HS* and *HQ* and between neighborhood variables. This gave recognition to the assumption that the joint spatial distribution of these variables is mainly a consequence of past behavior of residential decision units active in the residential market. The residuals shown in Table 4-5 are all statistically significant, with the exception of that between vacancy level (*V*) and *NES*. These findings are consistent with the general trend seen in the factorial ecology literature (Timms, 1971). We seem justified in assuming, then, that the joint spatial distribution of these variables is mainly a consequence of past behavior of residential decision units. That is, it is not family SES and family composition that determine the basic character of neighborhoods (although these may have some effect) but rather the structure of the construction industry and the residential market. The residential behavior of individual families provides neighborhoods with continuity in occupancy and land use patterns but does not have a direct effect on the existing structure of the residential market.

C. Summary and Conclusions

In summing up the results of this chapter, we can note that tenure status is not associated with neighborhood status attributes but is negatively associated with the percentage of black people in the neighborhood and dwelling density. Housing space is not associated with characteristics of neighborhoods but with other considerations, and housing quality attributes are positively associated with neighborhood status attributes as well as with vacancy level. Urban areas currently undergoing rapid suburbanization (e.g., in general the small- to moderate-sized urbanized areas) exhibit high vacancy levels, lower dwelling unit density, and lower concentrations of high-quality residential neighborhoods in their peripheral areas. Finally, we note that the socioeconomic attributes of families are the most important factors associated with the socioeconomic status level of residential neighborhoods.

In a later chapter, the discussion will return to the model that this chapter has focused on, after variables representing intrametropolitan locational aspects of demand for residential services have been considered. The questions yet to be explored are whether consideration of intrametropolitan location provides additional insights into family residential behavior and whether the inclusion of residence and workplace location variables alters the pattern of relations observed up to this point. Subsequent chapters will then develop further the issue of how forces external to individual family residential demand determine neighborhood attributes and their persistence over time.

Before going on, however, it should be emphasized that the data presented in this chapter are mainly relevant for understanding what families of different types demand by way of residential services, rather than for understanding the dynamics of neighborhood life. The neighborhood unit defined here, as pointed out before, is not the same as that which is perceived by individual families as their neighborhood, nor is it the same as units that reflect use of local facilities, neighborhood volunteer associations, etc. (Keller, 1968; Hunter, 1975). Another consideration also beyond the scope of this chapter, concerns how forces external to individual residential areas affect neighborhood identity and the delineation and persistence of perceived neighborhood boundaries (see Suttles, 1972).

5

Residential Location:
Central City versus Suburbia

In this and the next chapter attention is focused on factors of location in the demand for residential services. Among the external factors that influence families' residential demand are the location of family residence relative to workplace and the public services structure of municipalities located within metropolitan areas. Municipal attributes relevant for residential decision making include the availability and quality of public services provided and the tax structure. These attributes tend to vary by intrametropolitan location. The location of the family head's workplace is unlikely to be close to the most desirable residential neighborhoods, and there may be no desirable neighborhoods in the municipality in which the workplace is located. Thus the influence of workplace location on residential decision making involves not only journey-to-work considerations, but also the negative externalities associated with living adjacent to major employment centers. Metropolitan residents who want to maximize consumption of residential services and avoid commercial and industrial spillover effects have no real choice of living close to their workplace. However, for other metropolitan residents, particularly those with low incomes, residential choice is dictated by the availability of housing they can afford, and thus they may have little choice of any locational attributes.

In the present chapter I will deal with the sociological significance of suburban versus cental city residence as a reflection of the relatively high-quality housing and low-density environment and the provision of a desirable mix of public services to be found in the suburbs. In Chapter 6, the effects of employment location on residential behavior will be considered, with a focus on journey-to-work factors.

I. SUBURBANIZATION OF THE POPULATION

During the 1960s the United States passed a landmark with respect to the spatial distribution of its population. What had previously been a highly urbanized society now can be described as a highly suburbanized society. The modal form of family living is no longer high-density, big-city living, but low-density, suburban living. Of course American-style suburbanization has always been a part of the pattern of urban expansion outward from special nodal points. However, Guest's (1975) analysis of suburbanization between 1940 and 1970 indicates that the process seen in the United States involved both great movement of the population away from the center of the city and actual decreases in central city density.

Before 1870, cities had the political capacity to expand their boundaries quite freely and so, as their settled periphery expanded, their political boundaries expanded (Greer and Greer, 1976). This growth was facilitated by developments in transportation and communication that helped maintain contact between the central city and the newly developed peripheral settlements and made it possible for those who could afford these services to live in high-quality new housing at the uncongested, quiet periphery while working in the central city. At the same time there was a trend toward local municipal autonomy which, by the end of the nineteenth century, began to severely restrict the ability of central cities to annex peripheral settlements.

Suburbanization was briefly halted during World War II when the major part of national production was diverted from residential needs to the war economy. But the end of the war was followed by a boom in all sectors of the national economy, including a tremendous increase in manufacturing and commerce as well as residential construction outside of the political boundaries of central cities. Thus the process of suburbanization, which had begun about three-quarters of a century earlier, picked up momentum after World War II, resulting in a significant alteration of the structure of the greater urban landscapes in this country. The explosive quality of this development caught the attention of both the public and the scholarly community, and we now have several decades of research into the implications of all this for individual metropolitan areas and the nation as a whole.

In 1974, 38.6% of the United States population lived in metropolitan suburbs, an increase of 1.5 percentage points over 1970 figures (see Table 5-1). The average annual rate of suburban growth was 2.4% in the 1960s and 2.0% between 1970 and 1974. In contrast, central city growth was only .6% in the 1960s and declined at an annual rate of .4% during 1970–1974. Thus

TABLE 5-1

Distribution of the Total U.S. Population by Metropolitan Status, 1970 and 1974

Type of residence	Number (in 1000s)		Percentage		Average annual percentage change	
	1974	1970	1974	1970	1970–1974	1960–1970
Total	208,105	199,819	100.0	100.0	1.0	1.3
Metropolitan	142,223	137,058	68.34	68.59	.9	1.5
Central cities	61,836	62,876	29.71	31.47	−.4	.6
Suburbs	80,386	74,182	38.63	37.12	2.0	2.4
Nonmetropolitan	65,882	62,761	31.66	31.41	1.2	.7

Source: U.S. Bureau of the Census, Current Population Reports, Series P-20, no. 279, Table 15.

the suburbs are still expanding, although perhaps at a negatively accelerated rate, while the central city's population density is slowly decreasing.

There are a number of sources of suburban growth. Both population and industry have shown patterns of redistribution from the city to the suburbs. Population growth may stem from natural increases (when the birth rate exceeds the death rate), from migration from rural areas, and from expansion of the boundaries of metropolitan areas engulfing outlying settlements that sit astride the path of movement (Glenn, 1973). The following are among the most significant factors encouraging this pattern of growth and redistribution: (a) the continuing demand for single-family dwellings located in low-density, uncongested, and unpolluted environments; (b) the acquisition by suburbs of such urban services as utility and sanitation plants; (c) the attractive mix of residential amenities and tax rate structures found in the suburbs; (d) improvements in public transportation and the increase in the use of private vehicles for daily transportation, made possible by the development of intraurban freeways; (e) the development of federal housing programs by the Federal Housing Authority (FHA) and the Veterans Administration (VA) which, by means of low down-payment provisions and easy financing, have enabled some families to purchase new housing in outlying suburban areas; and (f) the changing racial composition and increased racial polarization in central city politics.

As the last point suggests, the majority of those involved in the movement to suburbia have been white primary families. Part of the reason for this is economic: There are proportionately more white families who can afford to purchase housing in the suburbs. In addition, white families have found it easier to get financing and have been the primary beneficiaries of FHA and VA programs. There are other reasons too, of course; the racial factor so prominent in this redistribution pattern will be discussed more fully in Chapter 7.

Although the population moving to the suburbs has been quite homogeneous with respect to race, there has been a shift over the years to a more heterogeneous mix of families with respect to SES and family status in the suburbs. One reason for this is the increase in differentiation in suburban housing, due in part to natural aging processes and in part to increased variety in newly constructed housing. By the 1970s it was no longer necessary for the aged and single populations to restrict their housing search to the central city, since suitable units (such as apartments) became more available in the suburbs. But in spite of the overall increase in heterogeneity of class and family type in the suburbs as a whole, residential segregation by SES is as prevalent among suburban neighborhoods as it is in central city neighborhoods (Farley, 1976, 1977; Logan, 1976). The forces that shape the cyclical growth, maturation, and deterioration of neighborhoods are at work in the suburbs as well as in the central city.

Probably the most important factor contributing to suburbanization is the first one listed previously, the continuing demand for single-family dwellings in desirable environments, a demand that increased as the proportion of primary families who could afford such housing increased in the population as a whole. This demand has been met largely by developers who are best able to practice economies of scale by building large tracts of dwellings, with the latest technological gadgets and currently popular design features, at the periphery or sometimes even beyond the settled areas of urban centers. A number of factors have encouraged this pattern. Land is cheaper and tracts large enough for volume housing production are more plentiful at the periphery. The tax structure makes it more profitable to continue to use old and deteriorating buildings in the central city than to raze them and make the sites available for developments that meet current demand. And finally, land use regulations and tax laws are such that development in suburban municipalities is usually less restricted than in the central city.

The fragmentation of governmental units in metropolitan areas—a result of the historical trends described earlier—has resulted in a wide variety of tax and public service structures that directly affect residential decision making. Many families have specific demands for residential services, and favorable tax structures are undoubtedly a factor in the residential decision making of many families as well as developers of rental properties. Tiebout (1956) developed a theory of local expenditures that suggests that the residential services offered by most municipalities outside the central city are in part determined by consumer preferences. For example, demand for public goods such as high-quality police and fire protection or education can best be met by choosing housing in areas populated by others with similar tastes.

Tiebout's hypothesis concerning the manner in which residential mobility provides an equilibrating mechanism leading to an efficient supply of local government services has been supported by empirical studies (Oates, 1969; Premus, 1976). His position has been criticized, however, on the grounds that the ability to "vote with one's feet" is an option usually available only to those at middle- and upper-income levels. Furthermore, people at these income levels often want to avoid municipalities that have heavy concentrations of low-income populations because the latter have a greater demand for some fairly costly public services but not the income necessary to pay taxes to support them. Thus, for a variety of reasons, Tiebout's hypothesis about the influence of consumer preference on the residential services offered by individual suburbs probably applies only to middle- and upper-class residential suburbs.

II. ANALYSES OF CITY–SUBURB LOCATION DIFFERENTIALS

The empirical analysis presented in this chapter is an extension of that reported in Chapter 4. Essentially, an effort is made to determine whether the decision to reside in the suburbs reflects the demand for various housing and neighborhood services, including tenure. Previous research has established that the residential populations of suburbs tend to be of higher socioeconomic background than central city populations. In the sections that follow an effort is made to refine this specification by determining whether city–suburb socioeconomic status disparities are a function of differential demands for residential packages of varying quantity and quality.

A. Perception of the Residential Environment: HUD Data

In addition to relevant data on the 1970 Census tape, the *Annual Metropolitan Housing Survey,* sponsored by the U.S. Department of Housing and Urban Development (HUD), furnishes data appropriate for the analysis of city–suburb location differentials. Before continuing the analyses begun in preceding chapters, I will report the results of two supplemental analyses using these HUD data to explore city–suburb differences. The first analysis, which concerns residents' perceptions of the quality of their housing and neighborhoods, provides data on some of the qualitative differences between the suburbs and the central city.

1. Sample and Methodology

This analysis uses data from the HUD file for the period between April 1974 and March 1975. In the present analysis only data from white respondents are used, and analysis is limited to the 12 SMSAs (Standard Metropolitan Statistical Areas) that allow analysis of central city–suburb differences.

Respondents were asked a number of questions about their experiences with and perception of their residential environment. They were asked, specifically, to indicate the following:

1. Whether they had experienced a complete breakdown in any of the following dwelling unit facilities: running water, sewage, heating equipment, and electrical circuits. Persons saying that their dwellings were infested with rats or mice, had leaks in basements or roofs, or cracks or holes in walls or ceilings were also included in this category.
2. Whether the following conditions characterized their neighborhood and were objectionable to them: noise from street; highway or airplane traffic; heavy vehicle traffic; streets needing repair; poor street lighting; trash, litter, or junk in streets or other parts of the neighborhood; boarded-up, abandoned, or rundown structures; commercial, industrial, or other nonresidential activities; air pollution from odors, smoke, or gas.
3. Whether the level of crime in their neighborhood was objectionably high.
4. Whether police and fire protection and schools were inadequate or unsatisfactory.

2. Results

Table 5-2 gives the percentage of white respondents indicating at least one problem in each of the categories of residential inadequacy. These data show a smaller percentage of suburban than urban residents reporting problems across all categories. The most consistent difference is seen for complaints about the level of crime, which are less frequent among white suburban residents in all comparisons. Another major difference in volume of complaints concerns the physical condition of the neighborhood; this difference is about the same size as that seen for crime complaints, but it is not found quite as consistently across urban areas. Complaints about inadequate neighborhood services also differentiate suburban and urban residents, although to a lesser extent. Complaints about breakdowns in dwelling facilities are not consistently more frequent among central city residents across SMSAs, although the average difference is in the expected direction.

Note that the data reported here concern residents' *perceptions* of their environment and are not direct measures of actual conditions. Thus some caution should be exercised in interpreting these results. However, the literature on differentials in residential quality suggests that these perceptions are correct. That is, suburban areas generally provide better quality residential packages.

B. Property Tax Rate Differences: HUD Data

Other data available from the HUD *Annual Housing Survey* that are useful here concern residential property values and tax rates. The sample and period covered in the present analysis are the same as in the preceding section (1974–1975) except that only data from white owners of single-family dwelling units are used.

The central city–suburban disparity literature suggests that not only do suburban areas provide bigger and better quality residential packages, but also that the per unit cost of these packages is lower. The explanation given is that the level of residential property taxation in central cities is higher due to a greater mix of public services provided, and central cities have to spend more (because of their size and the condition of their physical plants) to produce the same output of services (see Katzman, 1977).

Table 5-3 gives the city–suburb differences across 12 SMSAs in value of dwelling units and annual real estate taxes expressed as percentage of property values. As expected, the average value of single-family dwelling units is higher in the suburbs in all but three cases, whereas the tax rate is lower in all SMSAs but one. In general, suburbanites' taxes might be as high as that of central city residents in absolute terms, but the former have a real estate tax advantage when the value of their property is taken into account.

C. Determinants of Suburban versus Urban Location: Census Data

The results reported in the preceding sections show that suburban residence, in comparison with central city residence, is associated with the consumption of relatively high-quality residential packages and relatively low tax rates. A further analysis was made of data from the 1970 Census tape, employed in Chapters 3 and 4, to determine whether white families of differing composition and SES show different propensities to select suburban locations for their homes.

One common observation in the literature is that middle- and upper-class families with school-age children make the greatest demand for suburban location. This may be so simply because these families generally demand high-quality residential packages, which are more easily obtained in the suburbs than in the central city. If so, then one would not expect family SES to have a direct effect on suburban location. Rather, the status factor in location patterns would reflect the correlation of suburban location with high-quality generally in a family's residence. Furthermore, while middle- and upper-class families are better able than lower-class families to afford high-quality suburban residences, they are probably more sensitive to city–suburb disparities in fiscal structure, since higher levels of residential con-

TABLE 5-2

Percentage White Central City and Suburban Residents Reporting at Least One Problem in Dwelling or Neighborhood: Selected SMSAs, 1974–1975

SMSA	Percentage indicating at least one problem				Total observations
	Breakdown in dwelling unit facility	Poor physical condition of neighborhood	Crime	Inadequacy of neighborhood services	
Phoenix					
Central city	27.7	39.1	23.3	11.2	2243
Suburbs	24.9	33.8	13.3	14.8	1725
Pittsburgh					
Central city	43.8	54.2	18.6	17.9	742
Suburbs	47.1	45.6	10.4	15.2	3448
Boston					
Central city	41.8	53.0	24.9	20.0	4605
Suburbs	44.9	42.0	13.8	8.2	6745
Detroit					
Central city	40.1	50.0	28.8	13.5	3148
Suburbs	40.3	43.9	11.8	9.4	6531
Minneapolis–St. Paul					
Central cities					
Minneapolis	50.3	50.5	24.9	10.7	1038
St. Paul	45.7	51.4	18.1	9.9	728
Suburbs	45.1	40.4	11.6	6.6	2512

Newark					
Central city	41.9	47.1	24.4	25.0	344
Suburbs	44.6	38.1	9.9	5.4	3205
Los Angeles					
Central cities					
Los Angeles	38.9	50.1	22.4	14.9	4540
Long Beach	31.9	46.5	25.9	12.5	721
Suburbs	29.1	43.7	16.1	12.2	5862
Washington, D.C.					
Central city	48.7	45.9	24.2	10.5	1956
Suburbs	40.9	37.9	16.6	10.8	5596
Anaheim–Santa Ana					
Central cities	27.6	45.2	25.3	11.8	1200
Suburbs	24.7	39.5	14.9	10.8	3169
Albany–Schenectady–Troy					
Central cities	43.5	47.3	16.8	13.3	1373
Suburbs	41.6	43.9	7.9	11.5	2828
Dallas					
Central city	35.0	39.4	i6.3	10.5	1690
Suburbs	41.6	44.4	9.8	11.4	1808
Fort Worth					
Central city	39.4	42.9	13.7	11.8	1740
Suburbs	41.6	47.9	8.9	12.7	2136

Source: HUD, Annual Housing Survey File for SMSAs, 1974–1975.

TABLE 5-3

Mean Value of White Owner-Occupied Housing and Annual Real Estate Taxes as Percentage of Property Value: Selected SMSAs, 1974–1975

SMSA	Property value (mean)	Real estate tax as percentage of property value	Total observations
Los Angeles			
Central cities			
Los Angeles	$42,515	2.0	1524
Long Beach	36,606	1.7	235
Suburbs	36,210	1.8	2442
Washington, D.C.			
Central city	58,403	1.3	414
Suburbs	54,759	1.4	2529
Anaheim–Santa Ana			
Central cities	35,264	1.6	458
Suburbs	47,178	1.5	1371
Albany–Schenectady–Troy			
Central cities	27,802	2.9	331
Suburbs	32,460	2.2	1410
Dallas			
Central city	33,019	1.4	538
Suburbs	28,916	1.3	670
Fort Worth			
Central city	21,362	1.7	781
Suburbs	25,056	1.3	880
Minneapolis–St. Paul			
Central cities			
Minneapolis	27,246	2.1	395
St. Paul	28,455	1.7	301
Suburbs	35,973	1.8	1466
Newark			
Central city	26,093	4.0	24
Suburbs	49,575	2.7	1653
Phoenix			
Central city	29,879	1.4	974
Suburbs	32,298	1.1	690
Pittsburgh			
Central city	20,092	2.3	283
Suburbs	25,663	2.2	1855
Boston			
Central city	27,968	3.6	574
Suburbs	40,285	3.1	2895
Detroit			
Central city	19,434	2.7	1485
Suburbs	34,521	2.0	3865

Source: HUD, Annual Housing Survey File for SMSAs, 1974–1975.

sumption could translate into higher property taxes. Thus the status factor in location patterns may also reflect a greater avoidance of the relatively high central city property tax rates by middle- and upper-income groups in comparison with less well-off groups. To test this hypothesis, a dummy variable for suburban location (*SL*) was added to the model in Figure 4-1, and the final analysis reported in Chapter 4 was repeated with this addition.

1. Results

The resulting structural coefficients are presented in Table 5-4. Relationships for the variables considered previously are essentially unchanged. As the B matrix shows, suburban location is related to tenure (*T*) among white primary families; there are more owners in the suburbs than in the central city. Suburban neighborhoods also tend to have lower population density (*DN*) and higher socioeconomic status (*NES*) than urban locations. Hence, families who choose to own their unit and choose high-status neighborhoods and low-density environments are also more likely to choose to live in the suburbs.

Suburban residence appears not to be affected directly by dwelling size and quality, as indicated by the relative sizes of the coefficients for these variables exhibited in the B matrix. This appears to be inconsistent with the results obtained from the 1974–1975 HUD data. This apparent contradiction can readily be explained by assuming that suburban neighborhoods tend to be more homogeneous with respect to dwelling attributes, for example, suburban neighborhoods tend to have a much higher contiguous concentration of new and better quality housing. Thus, while *average* dwelling size and quality is not higher in the suburbs than in the central city net of other considerations, these two attributes are more similar within individual neighborhoods, yielding a positive correlation coefficient between *NES* and *SL*.

White family residential decision making, then, apparently reflects choice of homogeneous and relatively high-quality, low-density neighborhoods. As noted previously, this end result is in part due to the structure of post-World War II residential construction, as well as to white family residential preferences.

As the Γ matrix in Table 5-4 shows, the only significant effect involving exogenous variables is that for the relationship between *SL* and suburbanization of population and employment (*S*). Naturally, the more suburbanized the area, the higher the proportion of white primary families residing in the suburbs. More importantly, consistent with the rationale presented earlier, family *SES* and family composition (*PR* and *AG*) have no directly significant effect on suburban location. The zero-order relationship between *SES* and suburban location apparently reflects the effect of *SES* on residential choice concerning tenure status and neighborhood quality. In other words, the

TABLE 5-4

Structural Coefficients for Figure 4-1 with Additional Variable of Suburban Location: White Primary Families

B	T	HS	HQ	BP	V	NES	DN	SL
T	1.0000	.0000	.0000	.0000	.0000	.0000	.0000	.0000
HS	.1513	1.0000	.0000	.0000	.0000	.0000	.0000	.0000
HQ	.2458	.0000	1.0000	.0000	.0000	.0000	.0000	.0000
BP	−.1217	.0426	−.0481	1.0000	.0000	.0000	.0000	.0000
V	−.0080	−.0202	.2391	.0000	1.0000	.0000	.0000	.0000
NES	.0090	−.0125	.3061	.0000	.0000	1.0000	.0000	.0000
DN	−.1833	−.0085	−.1010	.0000	.0000	.0000	1.0000	.0000
SL	.1117	−.0297	.0216	−.0579	.0293	.1962	−.1272	1.0000

Γ	S	SES	PR	AG	RI
T	.0097	.1705	.2522	.3246	−.0822
HS	−.1270	.2978	.2436	.1257	−.0650
HQ	−.0457	.4461	.1118	.0022	−.1269
BP	.0960	−.1007	−.0064	.0324	.0122
V	.2512	−.0545	−.0866	−.1341	.0214
NES	−.3368	.4107	.0117	.0796	−.0950
DN	−.1107	.0819	.0007	.1007	−.0191
SL	−.2572	.0018	.0569	−.0433	.0486

Φ					
S	1.0000				
SES	.0840	1.0000			
PR	.0200	−.0120	1.0000		
AG	.0550	.0330	−.1770	1.0000	
RI	.0110	.1220	−.0980	.0740	1.0000

Ψ	T	HS	HQ	BP	V	NES	DN	SL
T	.8241							
HS	.0000	.7749						
HQ	.0000	.1046	.6745					
BP	.0000	.0000	.0000	.9552				
V	.0000	.0000	.0000	.1041	.9033			
NES	.0000	.0000	.0000	−.1794	.0850	.5310		
DN	.0000	.0000	.0000	.1750	.3714	−.1046	.9311	
SL	.0000	.0000	.0000	.0000	.0000	.0000	.0000	.8062

primary families in this sample were attracted to suburban areas because of a preference for home ownership and relatively high-quality neighborhoods, a preference most easily satisfied in the suburbs.

2. Conclusions

One interpretation of these findings is that the greater number of attractive single-family dwellings in the suburbs, as compared with the central city, reflects not a suburban–urban dichotomy, but rather a continuous variable of availability for which distance from the central city stands as a proxy

(Farley, 1976; Redding, 1977). However, it should also be noted that the suburbs are by and large divided into municipalities that have distinct characteristics and tend on the whole to be distinctly different from the central municipality in terms of services offered and property tax levels. Both interpretations of the findings probably have some validity. That is, families choose locations relatively far from the central city because that is where they are able to find the type of housing they want, and they choose locations in the suburbs because they are attracted by the suburban mix of municipal services and by the lower suburban property tax rates that allow them to consume more housing in the suburbs than they could in the central city.

6

Journey to Work

The dwelling unit is the point from which family members pursue activities in various sectors of urban areas. Physical structures that are used for residential purposes stand in fixed relation to each other and other forms of land use activities to be found in urban areas. People place a premium on accessibility to these activities and those with whom they frequently interact. Accessibility is defined here as physical proximity of households to other residential and nonresidential units (Hoover, 1968). The importance of accessibility stems from the costs of intraurban travel. Those who have to travel to locations away from their residence incur monetary costs in proportion to the distance traveled, mode of travel, and frequency of trips. There are also opportunity costs in intraurban travel. These costs are defined as the amount of time individuals consume in travel that could have been used for other purposes had the individual's residence been situated close to the unit with which he or she wished to interact.

The location of employment centers is a major factor relevant to residential decision making. As noted in Chapter 5, the influence of workplace location on residential decision making involves not only journey-to-work considerations, but also the negative externalities associated with living adjacent to major employment centers and the relative advantage of living in suburban communities rather than central cities. The preceding chapter considered the latter factor, among others. The present chapter concerns the journey to work.

Of course location of the household head's workplace is not the only accessibility factor that is important in residential decision making. The location of the workplace of other adults in the household may also be important, and there are other dwelling-originated trips besides journey to work. Members of the household must make trips to purchase goods and services for which there is frequent demand (such as food and household supplies), they must make trips to purchase goods and services for which there is occasional demand (such as clothing, repair services, and durable goods), and they make trips for social and recreational purposes. Kain's (1968) analysis shows that travel expenditures for the journey to work account for the greatest portion of costs in time and money incurred in dwelling-originated trips (see also, Berry and Horton, 1970; Yeates and Garner, 1972). Most residential areas are within easy reach of the various commercial areas to which frequent trips are made for purchase of goods and services, and the longer trips that take household members far from their residence are relatively infrequent. Thus, limiting consideration of location factors mainly to those related to journey to work (this limitation is also necessary partly because of the unavailability of other data) should not result in serious distortion of the test of residential decision making presented here.

Results of previous investigations suggest that mode of travel and distance traveled in the journey to work are determined in part by demographic and socioeconomic characteristics of households, as well as by cost considerations related to the actual trip. To briefly summarize these results, it has been found that employed household heads with high incomes, white-collar jobs, and medium-sized families are likely to travel greater distances to work than heads of other types of households. (For these results and extensive reviews of the literature on this topic see Duncan, 1956; Meyer *et al.*, 1965; Schnore, 1965; Lansing and Hendricks, 1967; Wheeler, 1967; Hoover, 1968; Kain, 1968, 1970; Duncan and Duncan, 1970; Poston, 1972; Whitbread and Bird, 1973; Clemente and Summers, 1975.)

I. MODELS OF THE RELATIONSHIP BETWEEN RESIDENCE AND WORKPLACE LOCATION

A. Early Models

Several models have been developed to explain the observed relationship between workplace accessibility and residential location. The first models were based on the principle of least effort, which states that industrial workers seek to minimize the distance from home to work, locating as close to their workplace as possible (Carroll, 1949; Schnore, 1965; Wheeler, 1967). This hypothesis is consistent with what is known about the relationship between residence and workplace before the advent of efficient, low-cost, intraurban transportation systems and the rise of the factory system as a major form of productive organization (Sjoberg, 1960; Pirenne, 1962; Hawley, 1971). But it has little predictive value for residents of the modern metropolis. As Schnore (1965:333) suggests, "The hypothesis offers a plausible explanation of the concentration of residences near work sites but fails to account for the equally obvious scatter away from those sites."

Duncan (1956) reformulated the least effort hypothesis to state that urban workers will reside in areas nearest their workplace that are compatible with their socioeconomic status. I know of no study that has tested this reformulation directly, although Wheeler (1967) observed that individuals in different occupational statuses do appear to try to minimize workplace–residence separation, in accord with Duncan's reformulated hypothesis.

B. Structural Model

Another type of model developed to explain the relationship between residence and workplace location is the structural model (Wingo, 1961; Alonso, 1964a,b; Mills, 1967; Muth, 1969, 1970; Kain, 1970; Richardson, 1971). This approach uses the consumption of residential space (land) as the basic independent variable. The objective of the model is to show how households' preferences for ample living space and convenient access to employment and residential consumption goods are converted into the observed demand for urban real estate. The key assumptions of the model, as stated by Kain (1970:211) are:

> (1) the assumption that the household's transportation cost function increases with distance from its workplace, (2) the existence of a market for residential space in which the price per unit a household must pay for residential space of a given quality decreases with distance from its workplace, (3) a fixed workplace, (4) utility maximization on the part of the households, and (5) the assumption that residential space is not an inferior good.

If it is also assumed that households have a strong taste for land and that the quantity of land possessed by any single household varies with income and unit value of the land possessed, then higher income households will be relatively less affected by the costs of commuting to work because land consumed at some distance from their workplace may cost less than the same quantity of land consumed close to their workplace. In other words, the cost of commuting to work can be offset by the relatively low price of land for distance residential locations. Therefore the ideal location for a household with a given income is that point in urban space beyond which further savings in land costs will fail to cover added commuting costs. Thus the model argues that whereas the poor are location oriented, the rich are price oriented, and as households acquire more income, accessibility comes to be regarded as an inferior good.

A number of theoretical works have attempted to clarify or modify the structural model, but little empirical work has been done thus far that either clearly supports or refutes it (see Harris, 1968; Hoover, 1968; Kain, 1968, 1970; Muth, 1969; Goldberg, 1970; Richardson, 1971; Nelson, 1973). Kain (1970) did attempt to evaluate the plausibility of the trade-off hypothesis with data on the travel behavior of Detroit residents. He found that high-income occupational workers whose workplaces were in the inner rings of Detroit had the longest journey to work, whereas those whose workplaces and residences were both in the outer rings had the shortest journey to work. Middle-sized families had the longest journey to work, whereas the smallest and largest families had the shortest—the small families because of low space preferences and the largest families because of income constraints. Finally, families living in single-family dwellings had the longest journey to work.

Examination of the variables Kain (1970) used shows that his results partially confirm not only the structural model, but also the ecological model, which I will discuss next. Thus Kain's results cannot help us determine which of the models has the most predictive power to explain the relationship of residence location to workplace location.

C. Ecological Model

Another model developed to explain the relationship between residence and workplace location has been termed the *historical model* (Alonso, 1964b). I prefer to call it the *ecological model* since it involves, most importantly, attention to the existing spatial structure of the housing markets rather than attention to the historical origins of this structure. In this model, the rental value of housing is the focus, rather than the consumption of land, as in the structural model. The basic assumption here is that accessibility to workplace is more strongly determined by characteristics of available housing than by individual attributes. Low-cost rental units are often closer to the urban workplace than high-cost rental units, and single-family detached dwellings available for ownership are most often found at some distance from employment centers. The ability of a worker to pay for residential services imposes a definite restriction on residential choice. This market differentiation serves as a centripetal force for low SES workers when they seek housing, tending to draw them to residential sites close to their workplaces. Conversely, the market differentiation factor serves as a centrifugal force for high SES workers, tending to draw them to residences some distance away from their places of employment because the latter are highly unlikely to be located near the kind of residential neighborhood they prefer and can afford.

Hawley (1950) presents a statement of the ecological model that suggests that households are distributed with reference to land value, the location of other activities, and the cost and time spent in commuting to centers of activity, such as the central business district and other concentrations. These factors in combination influence the rental value of housing, which in turn distributes and segregates households on the basis of their location requirements and income class.

A model that reflects the basic elements of Hawley's theory is presented in Figure 6-1. Housing quality is entered into this model as a determinant of rental value, as Hawley's discussion implies should be the case. In addition I have split the original "location of other activities" variable into two. This term actually refers to two different kinds of activities: (*a*) those that tend to have a centrifugal influence on residential choice because of their negative effects (e.g., industrial and commercial activities that generate noise, pollution, and traffic congestion; and (*b*) those that tend to have a centripetal influence on residential choice because they are central to day-to-day functioning of the family (e.g., commercial, educational, religious, and recreational activities). I have relabeled the second set of activities, in terms of its essential element of effect on neighborhood quality; as "residential amenities." The first set is labeled, in terms of its essential effect on residential decision making, as "accessibility to centers of activity."

It can be observed in Figure 6-1 that land value exerts a negative influence on the rental value of housing. The value of land is determined mainly by its location with respect to the point of maximum accessibility. Competition is keenest for accessible sites. Residential usage is relegated to less accessible sites since it cannot compete for choice locations with consumption- and production-oriented land usages. Hawley's explanation of why residential

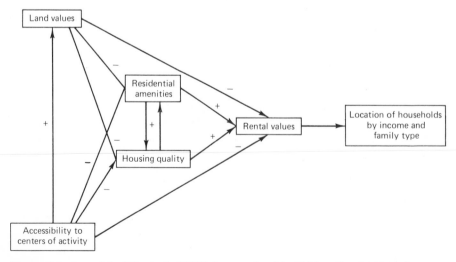

Figure 6-1. A model of Hawley's (1950) theory of residential location and housing consumption.

property on high-priced land commands the lowest rental price involves two points. First, residential property on high-priced land is usually in poor condition as a result of owners' reluctance to maintain it in anticipation of its being razed for replacement by structures making more intensive and remunerative use of the land. Second, residential property on high-priced land is usually close to industrial and commercial activity that generates conditions unfavorable for the optimum performance of family functions. Thus families who can afford to live in other areas tend to shun this housing, which drives its price down.

Figure 6-1 also shows accessibility to centers of activity exerting a negative influence on the rental value of housing. At the same time this accessibility variable is shown as having a negative influence on residential amenities and housing quality, both of which have a *positive* influence on the rental value of housing. Hawley (1950:281) explains these contrasting relationships as follows:

> New residential structures appear on low value lands, lands that have few if any alternative uses. Since buildings are newer and presumably better equipped for family use than those found on high-priced land, they can command a higher rent. Their protection by distance from objectionable land uses and their access to many of the services and utilities family life requires also favor a high rental charge. But again, the tendency of high rental valuation is minimized somewhat by the lowered general accessibility to places of employment and specialized services that greater distances involve.

The final variable included in Figure 6-1, location of households by income and family type, reflects Hawley's observation that rental values selectively distribute and segregate households by income and family type. (Hawley did not discuss exactly what he meant by family type, nor did he offer any explanation as to why the latter would tend to have to share location requirements. However, it can be assumed that family types represent different stages in the family life-cycle.) On the one hand, families in the same income class tend to have similar tastes for transportation services, educational facilities, residential quality, etc. On the other hand, households with similar characteristics tend to have similar location requirements. Generally this means that medium- to high-income families are likely to locate at some distance from their workplaces because of their desire for residential amenities and high-quality housing, whereas low-income families locate closer to their workplace because they cannot afford to purchase housing elsewhere.

In addition, the existing pattern of residential distribution tends to be perpetuated because the location of given family types in an area tends to attract other families of the same type to that area. Once similar families are congregated within an area, they can demand the creation of the various services that they particularly require, services that might not be inherent in the location itself.

Results obtained from studies of intraurban residential mobility are consistent with Hawley's discussion of how the structure of the housing market,
income or SES in general, and family composition influence the residential
distribution of households in urban areas. Analyses of the spatial distribution
of the metropolitan population by Guest (1970, 1971) suggested that a major
reason why families with children are found in peripheral areas of the city or
in suburbia is because in these areas home ownership, detached and roomy
housing, and low population density are easily obtained. In an analysis of the
location of different types of families in Cleveland, Guest (1972) showed how
the location of residential neighborhoods with respect to the central business
district is affected by such factors as: (a) the age of the area or period in
which it was developed; (b) the average internal and external housing space
in the neighborhood dwellings; and (c) site features such as the presence of
nearby industrial or recreational activities. He suggests that these ecological
variables in turn determine the location of families in relation to the center of
Cleveland, with space found to be the most important and site the least
important factor.

D. Deficiencies in Existing Models

There are a number of weaknesses in both the ecological and structural
models. The Hawley (1950) model does not provide an operationalization of
housing quality or space that allows one to see clearly how these variables fit
into the household residence utility function. The Hawley model makes no
distinction between owner and renter households and does not deal with the
probability that owners and renters will differ in their response to accessibility to the centers of activity, land values, and residential amenities.

The structural model has similar weaknesses that stem from some un-
realistic assumptions. This model is most applicable to the residential behavior of owners because renter households do not actually purchase land
but rather pay rent, the level of which is determined by more than the cost of
land. In addition, the structural model assumes that households are
homogeneous with respect to composition; it treats young and mature
families, male- and female-headed families, and single individuals all alike,
without recognition of the probability that these characteristics will affect
the spatial distribution of their households. Finally, the structural model
assumes that residential sites and dwellings are homogeneous goods, which
implies that households are indifferent to any attributes of their residential
package beyond quantity of land or space.

Another question that can be raised about the value of existing models of
residential and employment location relates to the decentralization of employment observed since World War II (Bohl, 1972; Leven, 1972; Berry and
Cohen, 1973; Wilson, 1976). Existing ecological and structural models assume that employment is concentrated near the point of maximum accessi-

bility, for example, the central business district. A variety of studies show that this assumption seriously limits these models' predictive power. Journey to work is very much affected by variation in the concentration of employment about a central point (Duncan, 1956; Duncan and Duncan, 1970; Bohl, 1972; Darrock and Winsborough, 1972; Winsborough, 1972). Furthermore, the existence of housing discrimination based on race and suburban zoning restrictions on type of housing that can be constructed, in combination with the employment decentralization trend, have produced a situation in which many low-income and minority workers cannot locate in the suburbs when employed there and so are forced to commute longer distances to work than middle- and upper-income white workers (Bohl, 1972; Harrison, 1974b; Christian, 1975). The net result of these factors is that there may be two major commuting streams in any large urban area—one of low-income and minority workers going to manufacturing and domestic service jobs in the suburbs, and the other of white-collar workers going to jobs in the central business district.

Both the ecological and structural models imply that accessibility is an inferior good, at least for those households whose income level and race permit them to make a choice between living close to work and consuming relatively large quantities of residential services (Hoover, 1968:271, note). The difficulty in empirically evaluating the services–accessibility trade-off hypothesis becomes obvious when it is considered that white middle- and upper-income groups have options available to them that make such trade-offs unnecessary. These groups can have their cake and eat it too. With the shift of some white-collar employment to the suburbs, many suburbanites do not have to commute to the central city to work. For those who work in the central city and have no desire to own single-family dwellings, there now are renovated areas in most central cities with high-quality apartment complexes tailored for upper- and middle-class occupancy. Thus, having a certain minimum income permits white households to make choices not available to lower-income families (Gans, 1962); and because of the persistence of housing discrimination based on race, these choices are not available to many minority households either. In other words, the residence-accessibility trade-off hypothesis is possibly necessary only when models are applied to low-income and minority households. However Ray (1973) found that journey to work was the least important reason people gave for moving within the metropolitan area.

In general, none of the existing models, considered alone, are able to explain the relationship between workplace location and residential consumption patterns. The ecological model is the most promising in that it has the most general initial statement of the problem. As I will report later, my results tend to support the ecological model, without incorporation of a trade-off hypothesis. However, as Harris (1968) noted, there are other equally plausible models that might be devised and, anyway, given the high correlations between population density, housing quality, residential blight and obsolescence, and socioeconomic status, it would be difficult to distinguish by critical test which of the models is most plausible. My analyses, then, are not designed to test the relative merits of these models so much as to broaden the base of knowledge used to evaluate any of them.

In the following section I will present an empirical analysis of the determinants of journey to work that reflects the points already discussed in this chapter. In Part II of this monograph the effect of suburbanization of employment on commuting patterns and the structure of economic opportunities will be taken up for further consideration.

II. RECENT EVIDENCE ON JOURNEY-TO-WORK PATTERNS

A. Determinants of Journey to Work

The data from the *Panel Study of Income Dynamics* (Morgan, 1974) provide a unique opportunity to analyze the determinants of metropolitan journey-to-work patterns. The uniqueness of this data set lies in several features. First, it represents a national sample of households (with oversampling of the low-income population) interviewed annually since 1968. Second, it permits measurement of two aspects of journey to work: distance and time consumed. Third, the array of independent variables for which data are available is extensive and, since these variables have been measured annually, it provides previously unavailable information on mobility.

1. Methodology

The data used in the present analysis were gathered over a 3-year period, 1972–1974. All white households with heads who worked in 1972 are included. The oversampling of the low-income population is controlled by use of weights developed by Morgan *et al.* (1974).[1]

The two dependent variables are distance from residence to workplace, in miles, and per mile travel time to work (e.g., the ratio of total time consumed to total distance). The latter variable, with the influence of total distance removed, indicates ease of the journey to work as defined by speed of travel (time per mile). An analysis of this variable will aid in determining whether individuals are sensitive to the amount of time consumed in traveling to work, or whether such conditions are dictated by urban scale and choice of location.

The independent variables are organized into sets on the basis of previous

---

[1] The 1972 sample weights are applied (see Morgan *et al.*, 1974).

studies of distance to work. *Geographic location* measures include distance of residence from center of largest city in the primary sampling unit (usually a central city), a dummy variable indicating whether the household lives in the eastern United States, and size of the metropolitan area where the residence is located. *Socioeconomic status* is measured by three variables: (*a*) the occupational status of major occupational group to which respondent belongs (Duncan's SES measure); (*b*) education in terms of years of schooling completed; and (*c*) hourly wage rate. *Stability of employment* (job tenure) is defined as the number of years at current job. *Family status* measures used are age, number of children under 18 years of age in the household, and sex (1 if male) and marital status (1 if married) of head of household.[2] *Geographic mobility* is indicated by dummy variables for whether the household moved for employment- or housing-related reasons between 1972 and 1973. *Housing consumption* measures include number of rooms in the dwelling, tenure status (1 if ownership), and housing quality. The latter was measured by a scale constructed by the *Panel Study* research team (Morgan, 1974). For owners, quality is defined as the market value of the dwelling divided by the number of rooms. For renters, *value* is defined as 10 times annual rent divided by number of rooms. For those who neither owned nor rented their dwelling, an estimate of the value of rent received free or in return for services was used and the measure calculated as for renters. *Transportation to work* is indicated by dummy variables for use of an automobile and use of public transportation. (Walk to work, use of bikes, or other forms of transportation are the omitted categories.)

The two dependent variables and the variables of age, hourly wage rate, and distance of residence from city center are expressed in natural logarithms.

2. Results

Table 6-1 presents the unstandardized and standardized regression coefficients from two equations predicting the determinants of miles and time consumed by household heads traveling to work. The most striking feature of Table 6-1 is that the standardized coefficients show that fewer of the variables are related to distance and time than expected.

Distance traveled to work is positively related to the size of the metropolitan area where the workers are located and to the distance between worker residence and city center. As urban communities increase in size (both with respect to population and territory) and population density, specialization in

[2] An analysis reported by Clemente and Summers (1975) indicates that models of commuting that employ SES, age, and length of employment as predictor variables are not applicable to explaining the commuting patterns of *non*metropolitan residents. Elsewhere (Wilson, 1976) I report the results of a study based on a national sample, which contradicts Clemente and Summers' findings.

TABLE 6-1
Determinants of Journey to Work for White Metropolitan Residents: Panel Study of Income Dynamics, 1972–1974 (Weighted Sample, N = 1450)

Variables	Miles from residence to workplace		Time per mile	
	Unstandardized	Standardized	Unstandardized	Standardized
I. Geographic location				
Size of metropolitan area	.1489	.1114	.0062	.0147
Distance to city center from residence	.4210	.1238	-.1312	-.1212
Eastern United States	.0448	.0204	.0109	.0155
II. Socioeconomic characteristics				
Occupational status	.0041	.0933	.0014	.1010
Hourly wage rate	.2886	.1442	-.0237	-.0377
Education	-.0256	-.0459	-.0180	-.1013
III. Job tenure	.0232	.0401	.0282	.1525
IV. Family status				
Age	-.1916[a]	-.0580	-.0243	-.0232
Sex	-.0137	-.0051	.0973	.1143
Married	.1048	.0446	-.0045[a]	-.0061
Number of children	-.0062	-.0094	-.0090	-.0426
V. Geographic mobility				
Move for job reasons	-.1589	-.0331	.0029[a]	.0019
Move for housing reasons	.0294	.0089	-.0370	-.0352
VI. Housing consumption				
Tenure	.0408	.0193	-.0542	-.0804
Number of rooms	.0031[a]	.0054	-.0008[a]	-.0043
Housing quality	.0613	.0682	-.0052	-.0182
VII. Transportation to work				
Automobile	.9702	.3987	-.2566	-.3312
Public	-.1352	-.0513	-.3646	-.4344
VIII. Constant	.3933		.8245	
Means (log)	1.8853		.3853	
R^2	.3439		.1340	

[a] Regression coefficient is less than twice the size of its standard error.

activities and land use differentiation increase, leading to relatively great geographic separation of residential areas and employment centers. Thus the net effect of increase in urban size is to increase the average distance that workers have to travel to their workplaces. Distance traveled to work also is strongly related to use of automobiles to get there. This suggests that workers who live far from their places of employment find private transportation to work more convenient and efficient than public transportation. Only 2 of the other 13 worker characteristics are related to distance to work. The positive effect of occupational status probably reflects the residential distribution of occupational groups in metropolitan areas. The positive effect of hourly wage rate suggests that the higher paying the job, the greater the distance one is willing to travel to work—and able to afford.

The last column of Table 6-1 reports the standardized regression coefficients for the determinants of time spent traveling to work per mile. In contrast to distance traveled to workplace, time of travel is likely to be affected by the scale of urban spatial systems, the mode of transportation, and the efficiency of existing transportation networks—that is, the extent to which existing transportation networks facilitate the movement of people to various destinations during times when the volume of traffic is heavy.

Time per mile spent traveling to work is negatively related to the distance of a worker's residence from the center of the city. This finding probably reflects the fact that traffic flows faster in areas further from densely populated city centers than it does close in, and it flows faster in residential areas than around centers of employment. Thus the average travel time per mile will be less for those who live at the largely residential periphery of the city than for those who live at the center, because a greater proportion of their journey will be spent in relatively fast traffic flows. Also, travel time per mile is negatively related to both the use of automobile or public transportation to get to work. This probably reflects the time advantage that comes from using an automobile on the one hand and from living near enough one's workplace to make efficient use of public transportation on the other hand. More generally, these results support the proposition that commuters are more interested in minimizing time of travel to work when they make residential decisions than in minimizing distance to work (Ray, 1973). Beesley's (1965) study of London commuters indicates that mode of travel is related to the total time it takes workers to travel to their workplace, and thus affects choice of travel mode but not necessarily residential location.

Two of three indicators of SES have significant but opposite effects on time per mile. The positive effect of occupational status probably reflects the fact that white-collar employment is likely to be concentrated in central business districts where traffic is relatively heavy. The negative effects of education on time per mile and distance traveled to workplace defies conventional wisdom. Moreover, clearly these effects imply that highly educated persons, *ceteris paribus*, appear inclined to live closer to their work-place and are more sensitive to commuting time.

The positive relationship between job tenure (number of years at current job) and travel time per mile is contrary to expectation. It is commonly believed that workers will, at least over time, shift their residence so as to be reasonably close to their workplace. The result here, instead, supports Ray's (1973) view that people are likely to place relatively little importance on location relative to workplace. It may be that, for workers who shift jobs more than residences, the distance of a new job from one's current residence is of little importance in employment-related decisions. Furthermore, the failure to find journey-to-work variables to be related to either moves for job- or housing-related reasons or to housing consumption variables suggests that the hypothesis concerning trade-offs between accessibility and housing vari-ables in residential decision making (as described earlier in this chapter) has little explanatory power.

One final result can be noted here: Sex of head of household is related to time per mile in the journey to work, with male heads experiencing relatively slower trips than female heads. This presumably represents both sex vari-ables in the labor market and the fact that female heads are more likely than male heads to be single parents, a factor that might limit their freedom to choose employment far from their residence.

B. Residential Mobility

The findings reported for the effects of job tenure and whether a household moved for employment-related reasons on the journey-to-work variables have implications for the manner in which the model of the demand for residential services is estimated in the next section. It is assumed that employment location, in contrast to housing and neighborhood attributes, has the least effect on decisions regarding residential consumption. This assumption provides justification for treating accessibility to workplace as endogenous to both housing and neighborhood attributes.

This view contrasts sharply with that presented by Kain and Quigley (1975:37–43) in their attempt to develop an alternative theory of urban housing markets and spatial structure. Their approach assumes that work-places are predetermined, and that households decide their place of work before choosing the type and location of their housing (Kain and Quigley, 1975:38). These authors cite results from a study of residential mobility among persons living in the San Francisco metropolitan area in support of the workplace-dominance assumption. The results they report do indeed indicate that residential mobility is related to changes in workplace loca-tions. However, the small to moderate size of the relationships observed between employment changes and residential mobility, and the fact that no effort was made to control for other factors that affect residential mobility, undermine the plausibility of the workplace-dominance assumption and call into question the predictive value of Kain and Quigley's model.

With respect to the assumption employed here, the issue is not whether location of workplace has any effect on residential location, but rather whether that effect is greater than those reflecting the demand for housing and neighborhood services. Results from three analyses can be cited in support of my contention that employment is not the major reason given by households for moving. Two of these analyses used data from the 1968–1972 wave of the *Panel Study of Income Dynamics* (Morgan, 1974) discussed earlier.

In the first analysis, Roistacher (1974) found that housing was the single most important reason given by families for moving, with 70% giving this reason versus 25% indicating employment-related reasons. In the second analysis, Goodman (1974) set out to determine where intrametropolitan mobility was related to accessibility to place of work. He found that accessibility to place of work was not a major factor in residential site selection. Goodman (1974:104) further noted that

> Respondents spending long hours or substantial sums of money on commuting do not have a significantly higher propensity to move than those nearer to the place of work. The average move is to a location slightly less accessible to the workplace. There is no evidence that movers adjust to equilibrium commuting performance as estimated by income, occupation, urban density, or tenure status.

Tabulations from the 1974–1975 *Annual Housing Survey File* for metropolitan areas provide some additional information bearing on this issue. Respondents who moved within the previous 12 months were asked to indicate the major reasons for moving. I have grouped the reasons given into five major categories, reflecting employment, change in household composition, housing, neighborhood, and others. The employment category includes persons who indicated that they moved because of job transfers, to take a new job, commuting, and other employment reasons. The first three reasons for moving clearly imply a change in workplace location. The reasons for moving information is tabulated by whether respondents moved within central city or suburban sectors, moved between the central city and suburbs, and moved to the SMSA from another section of the country. If Kain and Quigley's workplace-dominance assumption is plausible, one would expect that: (*a*) a higher percentage of persons should move for employment reasons; and (*b*) the preceding percentage should be linearly related to mobility status, since the latter is coded to reflect distance moved.

Table 6-2 reports percentage distributions for reasons for moving by mobility status and SMSA of residence. With respect to the first two mobility status categories, housing is the major reason given for moving, followed by changes in household composition, employment (in some SMSAs), and neighborhood (in other SMSAs). Clearly these results imply that the

TABLE 6-2
Percentage of Persons Moving for Specific Reasons by Mobility Status and SMSA of Residence[a]

Mobility status by SMSA of residence	Employment	Change in household composition	Housing	Neighborhood	Others	Total	
						N	Percentage
Los Angeles, California						2565	100
Within city or suburbs	8.1	25.2	38.4	9.5	18.8	1477 (100%)	57.6
Between city and suburbs	12.1	24.3	33.0	8.8	21.7	678 (100%)	26.4
From outside SMSA	45.6	18.8	2.2	2.2	31.7	410 (100%)	16.0
Anaheim, California						1139	100
Within city or suburbs	6.9	25.7	37.0	10.0	20.4	579 (100%)	50.8
Between city and suburbs	13.9	23.3	37.6	9.9	15.3	202 (100%)	17.7
From outside SMSA	43.0	14.2	12.6	7.5	22.6	358 (100%)	31.4
Phoenix, Arizona						1043	100
Within city or suburbs	7.8	21.8	43.2	6.9	20.3	606 (100%)	58.1
Between city and suburbs	17.6	18.9	41.2	4.1	18.2	148 (100%)	14.2
From outside SMSA	37.7	11.1	.7	1.4	49.1	289 (100%)	27.7
Minneapolis-St. Paul						985	100
Within city or suburbs	7.2	22.3	39.2	4.2	27.2	600 (100%)	60.9
Between city and suburbs	15.8	27.9	30.1	4.9	21.3	183 (100%)	18.6
From outside SMSA	50.5	15.3	2.0	.5	31.7	202 (100%)	20.5
Detroit, Michigan						1255	100
Within city or suburbs	5.7	29.9	39.1	7.1	18.2	879 (100%)	70.0
Between city and suburbs	10.4	30.2	32.2	14.4	12.9	202 (100%)	16.1
From outside SMSA	58.6	14.9	3.4	.6	22.4	174 (100%)	13.9
Washington, D.C.						1577	100
Within city or suburbs	8.4	22.6	39.2	8.5	21.4	970 (100%)	61.5
Between city and suburbs	27.9	18.0	24.3	16.2	13.5	111 (100%)	7.0
From outside SMSA	69.8	8.9	1.2	1.4	18.8	496 (100%)	31.5

	(1)	(2)	(3)	(4)	(5)	N	%
Dallas, Texas						986	100
Within city or suburbs	9.2	18.6	45.7	8.7	17.7	575 (100%)	58.3
Between city and suburbs	20.4	20.4	38.0	4.9	16.2	142 (100%)	14.4
From outside SMSA	58.2	15.6	1.9	.7	23.0	269 (100%)	27.3
Fort Worth, Texas						924	100
Within city or suburbs	8.2	19.2	46.2	8.2	18.2	511 (100%)	55.3
Between city and suburbs	18.1	20.1	32.6	11.1	18.1	144 (100%)	15.6
From outside SMSA	55.0	13.8	6.3	2.6	22.3	269 (100%)	29.1
Boston, Massachusetts						1930	100
Within city or suburbs	5.0	23.0	41.1	9.6	21.2	1272 (100%)	65.9
Between city and suburbs	16.4	26.0	27.4	12.7	17.5	292 (100%)	15.1
From outside SMSA	38.3	13.9	4.1	1.6	42.1	366 (100%)	19.0
Pittsburgh, Pennsylvania						468	100
Within city or suburbs	6.8	31.3	32.9	12.1	16.9	307 (100%)	65.6
Between city and suburbs	7.2	32.5	32.5	10.8	16.9	83 (100%)	17.7
From outside SMSA	56.4	25.6	6.4	1.3	10.3	78 (100%)	16.7
Albany, New York						601	100
Within city or suburbs	4.6	21.8	46.7	8.3	18.6	349 (100%)	58.1
Between city and suburbs	15.4	21.4	32.5	13.7	17.1	117 (100%)	19.5
From outside SMSA	58.5	12.6	3.0	1.5	24.4	135 (100%)	22.4
Newark, New Jersey						371	100
Within city or suburbs	4.6	31.7	39.7	10.7	13.4	262 (100%)	70.6
Between city and suburbs	4.5	22.7	27.3	27.3	18.2	22 (100%)	5.9
From outside SMSA	42.5	29.9	13.8	2.3	11.5	87 (100%)	23.5

Source: HUD, Annual Housing Survey File for Metropolitan Area, 1974–1975.

a Respondents were asked to indicate the major reason they moved during the previous 12 months. The coded responses are grouped here into five categories: (1) employment—job transfer, new job, commuting, and other employment reasons; (2) changes in household composition—widowed, separated, divorced, moved nearer relatives, newly married, family increased, family decreased, and other family reasons; (3) housing—needed larger house, wanted own household, wanted lower rent, wanted better house, and wanted to rent; (4) neighborhood—neighborhood, schools, and more conveniences; and (5) other reasons—to attend school, urban renewal, etc., displaced private act, natural disaster, change climate, entering/leaving armed forces, retirement, others, and not answered.

workplace-dominance assumption as employed by Kain and Quigley is implausible, since the vast majority of persons who move within metropolitan areas do so for reasons other than employment.

In the case of the third mobility status category, moved from outside the SMSA, employment was the major reason given by most households for moving. It should be noted, however, that the variable is not specific with respect to the location of residence or workplace within a metropolitan area once a household moves there from another area. Finally, it can be noted that the percentage of persons who moved for employment reasons does vary by mobility status, with long-distance movers having the highest percentage and local movers the lowest.

C. Analysis of 1970 Census Data

The results reported thus far are consistent with a model that postulates the major determinants of metropolitan journey-to-work patterns in metropolitan areas to be characteristics of the area rather than worker characteristics, that is, an ecological model. In such a model it is assumed that urban scale has direct effects on the degree of specialization of activities and differentiation in land use found in a metropolitan area. The separation of residential and employment centers is assumed to be a function of the distribution within the area of housing and of other activities. Commercial and industrial activities, the major determinants of both employment patterns and traffic flows in urban areas, generally tend to have centrifugal effects on the location of residential areas of high-quality housing and amenity attributes and single-family homes. The results reported for the effects of geographic location and size of place, distance from the center of the city, occupational status, wage rate, and mode of transportation to work on time and distance traveled to work are consistent with this observation. However, the data in that analysis did not allow a direct test of neighborhood characteristics, and so the results only partially refute the trade-off hypothesis. The 1970 Census data allow a more direct test of the latter issue.

1. Methodology

With this objective in mind, the measure of accessibility to workplace (ACC) was added to the models employed in Chapters 4 and 5 (see Figure 4-1).[3] As described in more detail in Chapter 2, the accessibility scores here are a rather crude measure of the ease with which heads of households get to their workplaces. The scale assumes that use of public transportation implies

---

[3] The relative income measure has been dropped from the model at this point because, as shown in Tables 3-4, 4-4, and 5-4, it had little or no net effect on the endogenous variables considered in preceding models.

TABLE 6-3

Structural Coefficients for Model of the Demand for Residential Services: White Primary Families

B	T	HS	HQ	BP	V	NES	DN	SL	ACC
T	1.0000	.0000	.0000	.0000	.0000	.0000	.0000	.0000	.0000
HS	.1576	1.0000	.0000	.0000	.0000	.0000	.0000	.0000	.0000
HQ	.2580	.0000	1.0000	.0000	.0000	.0000	.0000	.0000	.0000
BP	−.1222	.0419	−.0502	1.0000	.0000	.0000	.0000	.0000	.0000
V	−.0090	−.0214	.2355	.0000	1.0000	.0000	.0000	.0000	.0000
NES	.0132	−.0072	.3221	.0000	.0000	1.0000	.0000	.0000	.0000
DN	−.1825	.0096	−.0978	.0000	.0000	.0000	1.0000	.0000	.0000
SL	.1090	−.0324	.0154	−.0589	.0321	.1867	−.1304	1.0000	.0000
ACC	−.0988	.0260	−.0621	.0499	−.1146	−.0895	.1448	−.1250	1.0000

Γ	S	SES	PR	AG
T	.0097	.1607	.2594	.3201
HS	−.1271	.2890	.2476	.1202
HQ	−.0458	.4290	.1197	−.0087
BP	.0959	−.0980	−.0068	.0335
V	.2509	−.0497	−.0871	−.1322
NES	−.3354	.3896	.0143	.0709
DN	−.1104	.0776	.0013	.0989
SL	−.2621	.0167	.0559	−.0375
ACC	−.0177	.0093	.0203	.1841

Φ	S	SES	PR	AG
S	1.0000			
SES	.0840	1.0000		
PR	.0200	−.0120	1.0000	
AG	.0550	.0330	−.1770	1.0000

Ψ	T	HS	HQ	BP	V	NES	DN	SL	ACC
T	.8306								
HS	.0000	.7789							
HQ	.0000	.1125	.6900						
BP	.0000	.0000	.0000	.9600					
V	.0000	.0000	.0000	.1233	.8852				
NES	.0000	.0000	.0000	−.1855	.0230	.5286			
DN	.0000	.0000	.0000	.1844	.3789	−.1263	.9411		
SL	.0000	.0000	.0000	.0000	.0000	.0000	.0000	.8084	
ACC	.0000	.0000	.0000	.0000	.0000	.0000	.0000	.0000	.9244

relatively easy access to workplace and that a workplace located in a different SMSA sector from the worker's residence is less accessible than a workplace located in the same SMSA sector. Some support for the validity of this scale can be found in the result reported previously showing that distance of residence from workplace is positively related to likelihood that the journey to work will be made by automobile.

2. Results

The final analysis reported in Chapter 4 was again repeated, this time with the further addition of the accessibility variable. Table 6-3 reports the resulting structural coefficients. Relationships for the variables considered previously are essentially unchanged. Results for the accessibility variable are consistent with the results reported from the analysis of Morgan's *Panel Study* data: Housing quality (*HQ*) and space (*HS*), tenure status (*T*), and size of the household (*PR*) do not have strong effects on the variable of accessibility. The weak negative effects of both tenure and housing quality do, however, indicate that homeowners and persons who consume high-quality housing are least likely to be accessible to their workplaces. Age of head of household is strongly related to accessibility, a result that is difficult to interpret. This may represent a historical factor in that older heads were more able to settle near their workplace in past decades, before great expansion of some metropolitan areas.

The most important conclusion to be drawn from this analysis is the fact that accessibility to workplace appears to be primarily a function of intrametropolitan location and neighborhood characteristics. Suburban location (*SL*) and neighborhood socioeconomic status (*NES*) are negatively related to accessibility, as was expected from the view of the structure of the housing market presented here. Neighborhood vacancy rate (*V*) is negatively related to accessibility, which also was expected on the assumption that relatively new and so not fully occupied housing developments are likely to be located at the metropolitan periphery.

In short, the results support the prediction that accessibility to workplace is most importantly a function of the structure and scale of urban areas, reflecting the effect of urban scale on degree of specialization of activities and differentiation in land use. On the whole, the results of these analyses of determinants of journey-to-work patterns are consistent with the ecological model discussed earlier. I am reluctant, however, to suggest that the validity of this model is thereby firmly established. The ecological model is essentially a macrostructural one, whereas the results reported here are microanalytic.

7

Race and Residential Behavior

In preceding chapters the emphasis was on estimating the parameters of a model of the demand for residential services, using the behavior of white primary families as the model group. In that discussion, it was assumed that families participate in residential markets for the purpose of acquiring varying quantities of residential services, with the quantity finally acquired being determined largely by economic wealth and household preferences. In this chapter the model is applied to the residential behavior of black families. The primary objective is to determine the extent to which black–white differentials in residential consumption reflect racial discrimination as against differences in income and preferences. The empirical evidence accumulated over the years tends to support a view of black demand not so much responsive to family composition and SES attributes as constrained by the economic position of blacks in the United States and by limitations on their residential choices.

Racial discrimination is postulated as affecting black residential behavior in two ways. First, the differential treatment of blacks in labor markets translates into a reduction of their purchasing ability, which has direct implications for residential consumption. This issue will be discussed in this chapter only in reference to black–white differentials in the relationship of family income to residential consumption. More extensive discussion of this issue will be found in Part II of this monograph. The second way in which discrimination affects black residential behavior is through restrictions on

homeownership and residential location, which has direct effects on the
nature and character of the residential packages blacks consume.

I. HOUSING MARKET DISCRIMINATION

Few empirical studies report direct observations of the effects of racial
discrimination in housing markets (Foley, 1973), although two recent studies
do provide some insight as to its magnitude. Pearce (1976), in a study of the
practices of 97 real estate brokers, found a consistent pattern of racially
differentiated treatment of home buying, both with regard to the showing or
not showing of homes, and in the characteristics and location of the homes
shown. A study by the U.S. Department of Housing and Urban Development (HUD) provides some indication of the extent to which blacks en-
counter discrimination in housing markets (HUD, 1978). This study represents the first serious attempt to study housing discrimination in more than
one community.

In the 1978 HUD study, a pair of governmental auditors were sent to 3264
real estate and rental agencies in 40 SMSAs with black populations of 11% or
more. In each city, a black and a white auditor visited an agency to ascertain
the availability of a dwelling for occupancy that had been advertised in local
newspapers. The preliminary results of this survey were as follows:

1. Of the rental agents, 29.1% discriminated against the black auditor; the
   figure was 21.5% for the sales agents.
2. Discrimination in the rental market was lowest in the Northeast (21%
   versus 33% for the other three regions).
3. Discrimination in the sales market was lowest in the Northeast (12%)
   and highest in the North Central region (40%).
4. Nationally, the odds of a black encountering discrimination when housing search includes visits to four agents is 75% in the rental market and
   62% in the sales market.

HUD officials indicate that these results are conservative and may be revised upward once more detailed analyses are performed. In addition, the
survey made no effort to evaluate the extent of racial steering in these local
housing markets, nor did it discuss the possible role played by financial
institutions in restricting residential choices among blacks.

This study does not make use of information based on direct observations
in assessing the effect of racial discrimination. Instead, an effort is made to
infer the existence of racial discrimination from observations of relationships
among variables such as income, preference, residential location, and consumption. Hence, what is observed are the outcomes of housing market
transactions, some portion of which may reflect the influence of racial
discrimination. The application of this indirect approach renders the results

pertinent to the "effects" of discrimination problematic, and they should therefore be interpreted with caution.

It is taken as axiomatic that the flow of residential services consumed by any given household per unit time is a function of the household's purchasing ability and tastes. If blacks and whites differ with respect to residential consumption after tastes and purchasing ability have been controlled, it is assumed that these remaining differences imply that the two groups are not treated equally by other decision units in housing markets. In addition, it is assumed that differential treatment of blacks is not a phenomenon that is peculiar to housing markets, but rather one that permeates the entire opportunity and reward structure of American society. As suggested before, the appropriate starting point for assessing the effects that differential treatment has on black participation in housing markets should be an analysis of those factors that determine the amount of resources blacks and whites bring to housing markets. As will be reported in Part II of this monograph, labor market discrimination has a substantial effect on the wages earned by black heads of households. Labor market discrimination reduces the potential purchasing ability of black households, which in turn restricts consumption of location, homeownership, and housing services.

Much of the literature on housing market discrimination focuses on what are usually termed *price effects*. These fall into two broad categories (see discussions in von Furstenberg *et al.*, 1974; Yinger, 1974, 1975; Kain and Quigley, 1975). The first kind of racial price differential is caused by landlords who make minority households pay a premium to rent a house at the boundary between black and white areas. It is argued that white landlords and realtors who control boundary property will rent to blacks only at a markup from the price that would be charged a white. This practice is assumed to represent an attempt to compensate for an expected long-run decline in income as whites refuse to rent or buy housing near black–white boundaries. White owners and their agents seem to perceive the movement of blacks into an area as prima facie evidence that the area will eventually become all black, which they believe will cause a drop in returns on their investments. King and Mieszkowski's (1973) analysis of the New Haven housing market and Yinger's (1975) analysis of the St. Louis housing market yield results consistent with these assumptions.

The second kind of racial price differential is partly the result of the funneling effect of residential discrimination against blacks. Blacks, it is argued, incur higher prices for equivalent residential packages because housing discrimination limits their residential choices to the central city where available housing is not, on the average, of very high quality and often not plentiful. Residential segregation, in effect, keeps the supply of housing inelastic with respect to black demand. The result is that blacks pay higher prices for residential packages than whites pay for equivalent packages available to them. Studies by Duncan and Hauser (1960), King and

Mieszkowski (1973), Quigley, (1974), Straszheim (1974), and Wilson (1974) report results consistent with these assumptions.

The inelasticity of the supply of housing available for black occupancy can raise the cost of housing to blacks in several ways. First, it is much more expensive to build new housing on central city land because of the costs associated with razing old buildings and with neighborhood externalities. Thus new housing in the central city, usually of better quality than that which it replaces, is more expensive than housing of similar quality at the metropolitan periphery. These factors also tend to discourage builders from undertaking construction of new housing in the central city; they can more easily make a profit from construction at the periphery. Thus without continuing and relatively rapid conversion of areas from white to black occupancy (or the elimination of housing discrimination), the supply of housing available to blacks fails to keep up with black demand, and the price of renting or buying in black areas is pushed to artificially high levels.

Another way in which the inelasticity of the supply of housing in black neighborhoods affects the prices paid by blacks is through restrictions on the range of quality in residential packages available (Quigley, 1974). If the demand for better quality housing, neighborhood services, and locational amenities rises among blacks as a result of increased income, but these components remain in limited supply, the prices of residential packages not only rise, but also desirable packages become very hard to find. Thus, as Quigley (1974) notes, not only do blacks have to pay higher prices than whites for residential packages of equivalent quality, but certain kinds of desired residential goods may simply not be available in black neighborhoods at any price.

Results from an analysis of mine (Wilson, 1974) confirm Quigley's observation. Indeed, it has become clear to me that the main effect of discrimination on the residential behavior of blacks is a restriction on the range of residential packages that blacks may choose from. However, it is clear that *low*-income black households are most affected by the economic costs of living in segregated neighborhoods. These households are placed at a serious disadvantage when the supply of housing in black neighborhoods is limited because they cannot outbid higher-income households for available decent housing. The economic costs borne by middle- and upper-income black households consist mainly of artificially high prices for what they get and restriction of their ability to consume the full range of desirable attributes rather than inability to obtain any acceptable housing at all.

There are, of course, other interpretations that can be advanced to explain black–white price and consumption differentials. It may be argued, for example, that both of these differentials simply reflect differences in ability to pay for housing at different locations. In other words, blacks consume less space and poorer quality housing mainly because of the limitations of low income. If there is a price differential resulting from the inelasticity of housing supply with respect to demand, it is a phenomenon that can be observed among all low-income households, regardless of race. This situation stems from the fact that, with the exception of publicly subsidized housing, housing for low-income households is obtained through a filtering process. That is, the rate of conversion from high- to low-income occupancy is slow relative to demand for low-income housing, and so low-income groups pay inflated prices for housing (see Muth, 1974).

In line with this interpretation, an analysis of the determinants of rent differentials reported elsewhere (Wilson, 1974) indicated that income differences account for a significant portion of the black–white housing consumption difference. However, I also found that the average income level of blacks living in black neighborhoods and that of blacks living in mixed or white neighborhoods were nearly identical, but the latter consumed substantially more space and better quality residential packages. Thus the findings from the earlier study are consistent with the supply restriction hypothesis presented previously and suggest that black residential consumption is strongly affected by restriction on residential movement stemming from discrimination.

II. EMPIRICAL EVIDENCE FOR DISCRIMINATION

A. Analysis of Race and Perception of Residential Environment

The 1974–1975 HUD *Annual Housing Survey* described in Chapter 5 included a sample of black as well as white households, which provides an opportunity to determine whether blacks and whites differ with respect to their perception of the condition of their dwellings and neighborhoods. Existing evidence indicates that blacks are significantly more likely to live in poor-quality housing and in relatively old and deteriorating central city neighborhoods, even with income or SES controlled. If so one would expect, *ceteris paribus*, that proportionally more black households would indicate the presence of objectionable conditions or serious problems in their dwellings and neighborhoods when asked about these, as they were in the HUD study described in Chapter 5. Again, it should be emphasized that these are data on perceptions of and experience with the physical condition of the residential environment rather than direct assessment of it, and so the data may be somewhat unreliable.

1. Methodology

The sample universe and methodology of the HUD study are described in Chapter 5. In the present analysis the black portion of the sample has been included, and the central city and suburban data have been combined (since location differences are not at issue here). Only the 16 SMSAs with substantial black populations are included here.

2. Results

Table 7–1 shows the proportion of whites and blacks who indicated the presence of at least one problem in their dwelling and neighborhood. In 54 out of 64 comparisons, a higher percentage of blacks than whites reported a problem. For some SMSAs the black–white differences are substantial, reaching more than 20 percentage points. The differences are generally higher for dwelling problems and neighborhood physical condition. The larger and older SMSAs, such as Washington, D.C., Boston, Detroit, Newark, and Pittsburgh have significantly greater racial differences. Furthermore, looking only at those persons who mentioned one or more problems in a category, the mean number mentioned in each category is greater for blacks than whites in 59 out of 64 comparisons (see Table 7–2). In short, more black than white households had serious problems in their dwellings during the sample year and lived in neighborhoods characterized by high levels of noise, traffic, litter, rundown and abandoned structures, pollution and crime, mixtures of commercial and industrial land uses with residential land use, inadequate police and fire protection, and unsatisfactory schools. Among those who had problems, the average exposure to problems was greater for blacks than whites.

B. Analysis of the Effects of Housing Market Discrimination

The preceding analysis illustrates some of the black–white differences in residential consumption experiences. In this section the concern is to determine whether these differences reflect differences in income, preferences, or racial discrimination.

1. Model

Figure 7–1 presents a hypothetical model of the effects of race, income, and preferences for residential consumption. In a competitive housing market—one that responds mainly to people's preferences and ability to pay—the extent of participation of households for the purpose of acquiring residential services should be determined by preferences and the ability to pay. In such a rational market, race (R) would exert only an indirect effect on the demand for and delivery of residential services. This indirect effect would reflect the following: (a) the direct effects of ability to pay, measured here by expected or permanent family income (I), relative income (RI) and wife's proportional contribution to total family income (W); (b) the direct

TABLE 7-1

Percentage of Residents Reporting at Least One Problem in Dwelling or Neighborhood, by Race: Selected SMSAs, 1974–1975

Percentage indicating at least one condition objectionable

SMSA	Housing		Physical condition of neighborhood		Adequacy of neighborhood services		Crime		Total observations	
	Blacks	Whites	Blacks	Whites	Blacks	Whites	Blacks	Whites	Blacks	Whites
Spokane	50.0	37.3	50.0	47.0	12.0	9.9	10.0	13.0	50	4,251
Tacoma	34.3	39.3	50.0	52.1	12.4	18.7	10.1	16.1	178	4,165
Wichita	51.4	39.9	53.8	44.7	22.5	11.8	15.4	11.4	253	4,205
Los Angeles	44.3	33.3	53.2	46.5	25.5	13.4	29.9	19.3	1,448	11,123
Washington, D.C.	56.8	42.9	46.3	40.0	16.3	10.8	18.1	18.6	4,776	7,552
Minneapolis–St. Paul	44.9	46.5	51.3	44.7	19.2	8.1	23.1	16.0	78	4,278
Newark	61.5	44.3	52.2	39.0	25.4	7.3	26.5	11.3	826	3,549
Orlando	48.6	25.3	53.0	43.4	17.3	17.6	12.1	14.9	481	3,354
Phoenix	44.2	26.5	42.0	36.8	18.8	12.8	26.1	18.9	138	3,968
Pittsburgh	58.1	46.5	57.8	47.2	36.1	15.7	18.0	11.9	327	4,190
Boston	60.7	43.6	61.0	46.4	39.9	13.0	32.6	18.3	1,035	11,350
Detroit	55.7	40.3	57.6	45.9	22.6	10.7	30.9	17.3	3,157	9,679
Albany–Schenectady–Troy	63.7	42.2	56.3	45.1	20.0	12.1	14.8	10.8	135	4,201
Dallas	53.6	38.5	46.9	42.0	13.1	11.0	13.6	13.0	612	3,498
Fort Worth	56.6	40.6	51.7	45.7	19.0	12.3	12.3	11.1	447	3,876
Memphis	62.7	38.1	47.0	42.0	12.4	21.4	14.4	14.1	1,385	2,696

TABLE 7-2
Mean Number of Problems Reported in Dwelling and Neighborhoods,
by Race: Selected SMSAs, 1974–1975[a]

SMSA	Housing		Physical condition of neighborhood		Adequacy of neighborhood services	
	Blacks	Whites	Blacks	Whites	Blacks	Whites
Spokane	2.080	1.524	1.920	1.869	1.000	1.119
Tacoma	1.738	1.501	1.831	1.878	1.045	1.161
Wichita	1.785	1.510	2.287	1.805	1.281	1.145
Los Angeles	1.815	1.530	2.184	1.914	1.255	1.162
Washington, D.C.	2.239	1.562	2.031	1.720	1.187	1.140
Minneapolis	1.857	1.528	2.000	1.788	1.333	1.152
Newark	2.352	1.624	2.561	1.829	1.267	1.167
Orlando	1.910	1.462	1.914	1.777	1.193	1.209
Phoenix	2.016	1.476	2.310	1.842	1.308	1.205
Pittsburgh	1.837	1.568	2.291	1.806	1.186	1.180
Boston	2.403	1.663	2.816	2.035	1.315	1.173
Detroit	2.009	1.493	2.350	1.887	1.220	1.183
Albany	2.209	1.532	2.592	1.758	1.259	1.108
Dallas	1.857	1.491	2.185	1.702	1.212	1.232
Fort Worth	2.004	1.541	2.017	1.776	1.271	1.216
Memphis	1.948	1.499	1.955	1.731	1.227	1.131

[a] Only those persons who indicated at least one problem within a category are represented here.

effects of preferences that reflect family life styles or status, measured here by years of schooling (*ED*) and occupational status (*OC*); and (*c*) the direct effects of preferences reflecting household composition or stages in the family life-cycle as measured by size of household (*PR*) and age of household head (*AG*). If, however, it can be shown empirically that race exerts *direct* influence on tenure (*T*) and residential consumption (in dollars, *RC*), net of the intermediate factors, then the alternative hypothesis that discrimination directly affects black residential behavior can be accepted as plausible.

2. Methodology

The variables *PR, AG, ED, T, I, RI,* and *OC* are defined as in preceding analyses. For the dummy variable of race (*R*), black is scored 1. Two other variables that are particularly relevant for the analysis of race differentials are introduced here. First is residential consumption (*RC*), measured in dollars. The methodology generating this measure is described in Chapter 2 and Table 2–A2. This, along with tenure status, constitutes the major de-

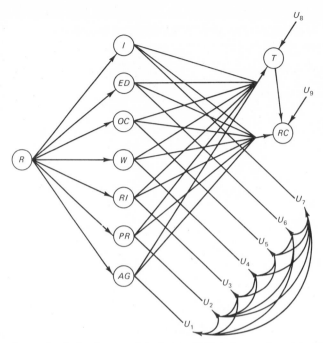

Figure 7–1. A nondiscrimination model of the effects of race, income, and tastes on the demand for residential services.

Variable definitions

R	Race (black = 1)	PR	Number of persons in household
I	Permanent family income	AG	Age of household heads
ED	Years of schooling	T	Tenure status (owner = 1)
OC	Occupational status	RC	Residential consumption (in dollars)
W	Wife's share of total family income	U_{1-9}	Residual
RI	Relative family income		

pendent variable focused on in the present analysis. An additional independent variable introduced here is wife's proportional contribution to expected family income, derived as described in Chapter 2. This was thought to be a necessary control factor, since it has been frequently found to show a marked race differential.

3. Results

Table 7–3 reports the zero-order correlation coefficients, means, and standard deviations for the variables included in Figure 7–1. Table 7–4 reports the results from the regression analysis of effects of income and preference variables on the probability of homeownership by race. The hypothesis that race has no direct effect on tenure status cannot be accepted. The negative unstandardized coefficient for the race variable (Table 7–4) shows the probability of homeownership among black families to be 16

TABLE 7-3

Zero-Order Correlation Coefficients,[a] Means, and Standard Deviations for Measured Variables, by Race: Primary Households (N = 8578 Blacks and 23,612 Whites)

Variables	PR	AG	ED	T	RC	I	RI	OC	W	Blacks Means	Blacks Standard deviations
Number of persons	—	-.059	-.082	.089	.107	-.115	-.045	-.054	-.125	4.253	2.027
Age of head	-.177	—	-.347	.323	.005	.034	-.007	-.007	-.010	40.78	12.53
Years of schooling	.044	.216	—	.024	.274	.470	-.014	.469	.133	10.45	3.36
Tenure	.201	.280	.042	—	.324	.230	-.089	.102	.074	.496	.500
Residential consumption	.189	-.006	.428	.261	—	.408	-.112	.247	.137	$1,438	$427.00
Expected income	-.093	.274	.518	.207	.404	—	-.060	.489	.556	9,013	3,267
Relative income	-.098	.075	.054	-.062	-.103	.163	—	-.037	-.004	1.19	.784
Occupational status	.023	.000	.569	.122	.396	.563	.055	—	.082	26.84	19.57
Wife's contribution	-.130	.055	.036	-.022	.006	.287	.050	.026	—	.204	.223
Correlation between race and other variables[b]	.0885	-.0385	-.1758	-.1326	-.2251	-.1819	.0510	-.2159	.1551		
Whites											
Means	3.73	42.56	12.47	.716	$2039.55	12,191	1.061	45.96	.0198		
Standard deviations	1.57	12.68	3.11	.451	$ 739.20	4,860	.680	24.25	.332		

[a] The figures above the diagonal in the top part of the table are correlation coefficients for black households; those below are for white households.
[b] The coefficients in this row were calculated from the total sample of black and white families weighted by their respective sampling fractions.

TABLE 7-4
Determinants of Homeownership by Race: Primary Families

Dependent variables	Independent variables										
	R	PR	AG	ED	I	OC	W	RI	T	Intercept	R^2
	Unstandardized coefficients										
Total[a]	−.1562	.0665	.0104	.0009[b]	.0015	.0006	−.0635	−.0566	—	−.1403	.1844
Whites	—	.0722	.0102	−.0005[b]	.0015	.0006	−.0660	−.0560	—	−.1336	.1748
Blacks	—	.0136	.0136	.0074	.0035	.0000*	−.0876	−.0419	—	−.5204	.1781
	Standardized coefficients										
Total[a]	−.0939	.2348	.2882	.0068[b]	.1614	.0296	−.0453	−.0851	—	—	—
Whites	—	.2516	.2876	−.0035[b]	.1639	.0311	−.0485	−.0846	—	—	—
Blacks	—	.1320	.3399	.0499	.2271	.0016[b]	−.0389	−.0658	—	—	—

[a] The coefficients reported for the total sample were obtained from a weighted least squares analysis.

[b] Indicates that the regression coefficient is not twice the size of its standard error.

percentage points lower than that of whites, net of income and preference factors. The level of homeownership among blacks, when evaluated at the means for the total sample (e.g., .6975) indicates that the actual level of homeownership among black families is 23 percentage points lower than that of whites.

A number of other findings support the assumption that this difference reflects the influence of housing market discrimination. The probability of homeownership is far more responsive to the income levels of black households than to income levels of white households. As Table 7–4 shows, *ceteris paribus*, black homeowners tend to be older and to have higher incomes and more education than white homeowners. Table 7–5 shows that whites are able to achieve homeownership at a much lower income level than blacks. Over 50% of white households own homes even when they have incomes of less than $2500, whereas blacks do not achieve a 50% homeownership rate until their income exceeds $10,000. More generally, Table 7–5 shows that the point of entry of white households into housing markets for owner-occupied dwellings has a lower threshold than blacks' point of entry. This finding is consistent with the race difference in homeownership shown by the great difference in intercept values reported in Table 7–4.

Table 7–6 reports the results from a regression analysis of the effects of income and preference variables on the dollar level of residential consumption. As was the case with tenure status results, the results here do not support the hypothesis that race has no direct effect on residential consumption. The negative unstandardized coefficient for the race variable, when evaluated at the mean for the total sample ($1989), shows that, *ceteris paribus*, black families in this sample consumed approximately 13% less

TABLE 7-5

Ownership Rates, by Race and Level of Expected Family Income: Primary Families

Income[a] level ($)	Blacks (1)	Whites (2)	Percentage differences[b]
Under 2500	39.24	50.08	−27.62
2500–4,999	36.83	52.48	−42.49
5,000–7,499	38.71	59.65	−54.09
7,500–9,999	46.15	66.70	−44.53
10,000–12,499	52.15	71.70	−37.49
12,500–14,999	66.18	76.33	−15.34
15,000 plus	76.59	80.33	− 4.88
Total	46.47	69.85	−50.31

Source: One Percent Public Use Sample File of Neighborhood Characteristics (1970 Census).

[a] The income categories were derived from the measure of expected family income (I).

[b] Percentage differences were computed as follows:

$$[(1) - (2)/(1)]100$$

TABLE 7-6
Determinants of Residential Consumption by Race: Primary Families

| Sample | Independent variables | | | | | | | | | Intercept | R^2 |
	R	PR	AG	ED	I	OC	W	RI	T		
	Unstandardized coefficients										
Total[a]	-257.718	63.307	-1.9347	48.299	3.869	3.434	-132.227	-110.872	253.527	614.518	.3504
Whites	—	67.510	1.870	52.890	3.795	3.514	-104.119	-144.850	257.500	554.530	.3237
Blacks	—	25.308	-1.510	12.875	4.649	.176[b]	-150.196	-34.013	208.015	802.260	.2623
	Standardized coefficients										
Total[a]	-.0966	.1392	-.0333	.2082	.2554	.1140	-.0493	-.1238	.1579	—	—
Whites	—	.1436	-.0321	.2230	.2496	.1153	-.0470	-.1333	.1571	—	—
Blacks	—	.1199	-.0443	.1012	.3552	.0081[b]	-.0781	.0624	.2432	—	—

Source: One Percent Public Use Sample File of Neighborhood Characteristics (1970 Census).
[a] The coefficients for the total sample were obtained from a weighted least squares analysis.
[b] Indicates that the regression coefficient is not twice the size of its standard error.

than white families in 1970, even after factors of income and preference and tenure status are taken into account.

The intercept value for black families ($802), when evaluated at the mean for the total black sample, indicates that 56% of their total consumption level cannot be explained by income and preference factors. For whites, that portion of total consumption which cannot be explained by income and preferences is only 27%. As the standardized coefficients in Table 7–6 show, consumption is more responsive to differences in education and occupational status among whites than among blacks. In other words, observed white residential consumption is substantially more expressive of demand characteristics for whites than for blacks. In contrast, income and tenure status have more effect on black residential consumption than on white residential consumption. Thus whites are not only able to consume more at lower income levels, but also their level of consumption is affected less by tenure status than is that of black families.

The dependent variable in the analysis reported in Table 7–6 is actually an estimate of annual housing expenditures, the level of which is determined both by housing prices and the kinds (and quantity) of residential attributes consumed. This raises the possibility that the observed racial differences may reflect housing price variations rather than actual consumption. The race and tenure differentials in annual housing expenditures reported in Table 7–7 should dispel any notion that these differentials reflect price variations. There it can be observed that over 88% of the differences in annual expenditures among these groups reflect differences in the kinds and quantity of residential services consumed. Moreover, as was indicated previously, even if price had been shown to have a substantial impact on racial differences in housing expenditures, this does not mean that price does not

TABLE 7-7
Race and Tenure Differentials in Annual Housing Expenditures

Comparison group	Standard group	Annual housing expenditures (in dollars)		Total differences		Percentage of total difference due to consumption of residential attributes
		Comparison group	Standard group	Dollars	Percentage[a]	
White renters	Black renters	$1689	$1300	$389	30.0	91.4
Black owners	Same	1692	1300	392	30.2	92.0
White owners	White renters	2304	1689	615	36.44	98.8
Same	Black owners	2304	1692	612	36.2	87.7

[a] The annual housing expenditure of the standard group is used to compute these percentages.

impact on consumption. Indeed, the net effect of paying higher prices is to reduce the kind and quantity of residential services that can be purchased given a fixed level of income.

An interesting difference in the effect of race on residential consumption versus tenure status emerges when the total effects of race are subjected to decomposition through path analysis (Duncan, 1966; Alwin and Hauser, 1975). The results of this analysis are presented in Table 7–8. The indirect effect of race on residential consumption is greater than its direct effect, whereas the reverse is true for tenure status. The direct effect of race accounts for about 72% of the total correlation between race and tenure status, but it only accounts for 43% of that between race and residential consumption. The indirect effect of race on tenure status is consistent with the assumption that the effect of discrimination on the demand for residential consumption is transmitted primarily through the effect of discrimination on income and ability to pay. Restrictions on the supply of housing available to blacks increase housing costs which, in turn, result in a rise in the level of income required to achieve homeownership status. A similar effect stems from the high level of risk that lenders assign to housing located in areas undergoing racial transition, making it more difficult for households to buy houses in such areas. More generally, discrimination in other spheres (e.g., labor markets) keeps black income and thus demand for residential services generally low. In contrast, the direct effects of race on both tenure and residential consumption are indicative of the restrictive effects discrimination has on black housing supply. Discrimination channels black demand for homeownership and high-quality housing to the oldest and least desirable areas of central cities where the supply of high-quality housing available for owner occupation is quite low.

TABLE 7-8
Decomposition of the Effects of Race on Tenure Status and Residential Consumption

Source of effect	Tenure	Residential consumption
Direct	−.0939	−.0966
Indirect (total)	−.0387	−.1289
Persons	.0208	.0123
Age	−.0111	.0013
Education	−.0012	−.0366
Income	−.0294	−.0461
Occupation status	−.0064	−.0246
Wife's contribution	−.0070	−.0077
Relative income	−.0043	−.0063
Tenure status	—	−.0209
Total	−.1326	−.2251

TABLE 7-9
Structural Coefficients for the Model of Demand for Residential Services, by Race

	T		HS		HQ		BP	
	Whites	Blacks	Whites	Blacks	Whites	Blacks	Whites	Blacks
B								
T	1.0000		—		—		—	
HS	.1576	.2390	1.0000		—		—	
HQ	.2580	.6904	.0000		1.0000		—	
BP	−.1222	.0628	.0419	.0327	−.0502	−.1207	1.0000	
V	−.009	−.5153	−.0214	−.0386	.2355	.1416	.0000	
NES	.0132	.0858	−.0072	.0717	.3221	.1994	.0000	
DN	−.1825	−.3470	.0096	−.0510	−.0978	−.2362	.0000	
SL	.1090	.0515	−.0324	−.0897	.0154	.0979	−.0589	−.1581
ACC	−.0988	−.1087	.0260	.0300	−.0621	−.0698	.0499	.0098

	S		SES		PR		AG	
	Whites	Blacks	Whites	Blacks	Whites	Blacks	Whites	Blacks
Γ								
T	.0097	.1598	.1607	.3090	.2594	.1447	.3201	.3747
HS	−.1271	−.2112	.2890	.2210	.2476	.2680	.1202	.1681
HQ	−.0458	.0706	.4290	.1621	.1197	.0707	−.0087	.0164
BP	.0959	−.0514	−.0980	−.0512	−.0068	−.0127	.0335	.0115
V	.2509	−.0872	−.0497	.0446	−.0871	−.0111	−.1322	−.1479
NES	−.3354	−.2342	.3896	.2623	.0143	−.0303	.0709	−.0427
DN	−.1104	−.0705	.0776	−.0230	.0013	.0530	.0989	.0371
SL	−.2621	−.1138	.0167	.0416	.0559	.0560	−.0375	−.0092
ACC	−.0177	.0023	.0093	−.0791	.0203	.0469	.1841	.0626

C. Analysis of Black Demand for Residential Services

The preceding analyses support a conclusion that the observed effect of race on residential behavior is, to a significant degree, the consequence of discrimination operating to restrict choice of residential location and thus of residential quality and home ownership. In order to determine what specific components of residential packages are affected by these supply restrictions, I will present estimates derived from a structural model of black demand for residential services. The model I use here is the same as the final model used for the analysis of white demand in Chapter 6 (Figure 4–1 with additions). The estimation procedure used previously is repeated here. The information used to generate the structural coefficients for blacks is reported in Tables 7–A1, 7–A2, and 7–A3 in the appendix.

V		NES		DN		SL		ACC	
Whites	Blacks	Whites	Blacks	Whites	Blacks	Whites	Blacks	Whites	Blacks
—	—	—	—	—	—	—	—	—	—
—	—	—	—	—	—	—	—	—	—
—	—	—	—	—	—	—	—	—	—
—	—	—	—	—	—	—	—	—	—
	1.0000		—		—		—		—
	.0000	1.0000		—		—		—	
	.0000	.0000		1.0000		—		—	
.0321	.0093	.1867	.2082	−.1304	−.0443	1.000		—	
−.1146	−.0555	−.0895	.0294	.1448	.1558	−.1250	−.0908	1.000	

1. Results

Table 7–9 reports the structural coefficients for the model of demand for residential services by race of head of household. Those presented in the B matrix show several important black–white differences. First, access to high-quality housing (HQ) is far more dependent on tenure status (T) among black households than among white. This implies that blacks can expect to achieve little improvement in housing without buying a home. But given the restricted housing supply and low income of the average black family, black households find (and will probably continue to find) it very difficult to upgrade their housing through ownership.

A second difference, which is related to the first, is seen in the effect of tenure on housing vacancy level (V) of black and white neighborhoods. As expected, black demand for housing finds its fulfillment primarily in those sections of metropolitan areas in which the housing supply is limited, a limitation reflected in low vacancy rates in black neighborhoods.

Another set of differences indicates that the quality of an individual family's dwelling (HQ) is much less strongly related to general neighborhood quality (NES) in black areas than in white areas. In other words, neighborhoods inhabited predominantly by black families show more intraneighborhood variation in housing characteristics. This could result in an unstable housing price structure over time, which in turn could add another impediment to black residential consumption by causing large swings in housing costs.

Turning to the Γ matrix, the coefficients that show the largest differences between blacks and whites are those for the effects of SES on tenure, housing quality, and neighborhood socioeconomic status. The effect of SES on black ownership is almost twice as great as that for whites. The great majority of white primary families can expect to achieve home ownership status at some point in their lives, as data presented in Table 7–5 suggest, but among black families, achievement of home ownership is tied to their achievement of higher SES. Of equal importance is the finding that housing quality (HQ) and neighborhood quality (NES) are not as responsive to black SES as they are to white SES. In other words, the residential consumption patterns of black households have less to do with social status, income, life style, etc., than the consumption patterns of white households. I have argued in this chapter that this result stems not from differences in black demand patterns but from discrimination in the housing market and in society generally. In the next chapter, these results are summarized and their implications are discussed.

TABLE 7-A1

Zero-Order Correlations among Measured Variables Used to Estimate a Model of the Demand for Residential Services: Black Primary Families ($N = 8578$)

	T	HS	HQ	BP	V	MI	PV	NW	DN	SL	ACC	SE	SP	ED	I	OC	PR	AG	RI
T	1.0000																		
HS	.3366	1.0000																	
HQ	.7405	.3407	1.0000																
BP	-.0279	.0100	-.0806	1.0000															
V	-.4727	-.1633	-.2826	-.0597	1.0000														
MI	.2664	.2730	.3185	-.2345	.0846	1.0000													
PV	.0193	.0982	.1028	-.2016	.1184	.5616	1.0000												
NW	.1240	-.0650	.2296	-.2240	.2034	.2261	.1911	1.0000											
DN	-.5336	-.2191	-.5103	.0816	.2366	-.4592	-.1189	.0041	1.0000										
SL	.1549	-.0506	.1857	-.2141	.0034	.3012	.2687	.2649	-.1890	1.0000									
ACC	-.2038	-.0502	-.2138	.0521	.0259	-.1484	-.0251	-.1141	.2372	-.1475	1.0000								
SE	-.1055	-.2229	-.1059	-.0522	-.1357	-.2889	-.1955	.1704	-.1106	-.1144	-.0139	1.0000							
SP	.0845	-.1788	.0735	-.0693	-.1539	-.2384	-.1364	.1261	-.0923	-.0982	.0210	.9049	1.0000						
ED	.0245	.1051	.1043	-.0573	-.1045	.2356	.1587	.0779	-.0614	.0301	-.0611	-.1162	-.0979	1.0000					
I	.2298	.2578	.2597	-.0229	-.0322	.3702	.1963	.0446	-.1767	.1217	-.1681	-.2621	-.2172	.4704	1.0000				
OC	.1015	.1405	.1530	-.0286	-.0119	.2332	.1639	.0592	-.0641	.0249	-.0185	-.1057	-.0969	.4689	.4890	1.0000			
PR	.0893	.2420	.1132	-.0086	-.0515	-.0244	-.0276	-.0420	-.0189	.0482	-.0239	.0402	.0313	-.0817	-.1152	-.0543	1.0000		
AG	.3231	.1839	.2121	.0194	-.3023	-.0114	-.0058	-.0569	-.1367	.0077	-.0233	.0452	.0403	-.3470	.0337	-.0775	-.0593	1.0000	
RI	-.0885	-.0820	-.1040	-.0127	.0343	-.0940	-.0302	-.0316	.0337	-.0024	.0378	.0213	.0155	-.0141	-.0602	-.0337	-.0449	-.0075	1.0000

TABLE 7-A2

A Confirmatory Factor Analytic Model of the Demand for Residential Services: Black Primary Families

β

	T	HS	HQ	BP	V	NES	DN	SL	ACC	S	SES	PR	AG	RI
T	1.000	.000	.000	.000	.000	.000	.000	.000	.000	.000	.000	.000	.000	.000
HS	.000	1.000	.000	.000	.000	.000	.000	.000	.000	.000	.000	.000	.000	.000
HQ	.000	.000	1.000	.000	.000	.000	.000	.000	.000	.000	.000	.000	.000	.000
BR	.000	.000	.000	1.000	.000	.000	.000	.000	.000	.000	.000	.000	.000	.000
V	.000	.000	.000	.000	1.000	.000	.000	.000	.000	.000	.000	.000	.000	.000
MI	.000	.000	.000	.000	.000	1.000	.000	.000	.000	.000	.000	.000	.000	.000
PV	.000	.000	.000	.000	.000	.562	.000	.000	.000	.000	.000	.000	.000	.000
NW	.000	.000	.000	.000	.000	.226	.000	.000	.000	.000	.000	.000	.000	.000
DN	.000	.000	.000	.000	.000	.000	1.000	.000	.000	.000	.000	.000	.000	.000
SL	.000	.000	.000	.000	.000	.000	.000	1.000	.000	.000	.000	.000	.000	.000
ACC	.000	.000	.000	.000	.000	.000	.000	.000	1.000	.000	.000	.000	.000	.000
SE	.000	.000	.000	.000	.000	.000	.000	.000	.000	1.000	.000	.000	.000	.000
SP	.000	.000	.000	.000	.000	.000	.000	.000	.000	.905	.000	.000	.000	.000
ED	.000	.000	.000	.000	.000	.000	.000	.000	.000	.000	.672	.000	.000	.000
I	.000	.000	.000	.000	.000	.000	.000	.000	.000	.000	.746	.000	.000	.000
OC	.000	.000	.000	.000	.000	.000	.000	.000	.000	.000	.647	.000	.000	.000
PR	.000	.000	.000	.000	.000	.000	.000	.000	.000	.000	.000	1.000	.000	.000
AG	.000	.000	.000	.000	.000	.000	.000	.000	.000	.000	.000	.000	1.000	.000
RI	.000	.000	.000	.000	.000	.000	.000	.000	.000	.000	.000	.000	.000	1.000

Φ

	T	HS	HQ	BP	V	NES	DN	SL	ACC	S	SES	PR	AG	RI
T	1.000													
HS	.337	1.000												
HQ	.740	.341	1.000											
BP	-.028	.010	-.081	1.000										
V	-.473	-.163	-.283	-.060	1.000									
NES	.266	.273	-.319	-.234	.085	1.000								
DN	-.534	-.219	-.510	.082	.237	-.459	1.000							
SL	-.155	.051	.186	-.214	.003	.301	-.189	1.000						
ACC	-.204	-.050	-.214	-.052	.026	-.155	.237	-.147	1.000					
S	.105	-.223	.106	-.052	-.136	-.289	-.111	-.114	-.007	1.000				
SES	.189	.257	.263	-.050	.022	.419	-.159	.096	-.150	-.251	1.000			
PR	.089	.242	.113	-.009	-.051	-.024	-.019	.048	-.038	.041	-.130	1.000		
AG	.323	.184	.212	-.019	-.302	-.011	-.137	.008	.023	.045	-.163	-.059	1.000	
RI	-.088	-.082	-.104	-.013	.034	-.094	.034	-.002	.038	.021	-.056	-.045	-.007	1.000

θ

T	HS	HQ	BP	V	MI	DN	NW	SL
.000	.000	.000	.000	.000	.000	.000	.000	.000

PV	PR	AG	OC	RI	I	SP	ED	SL	RI
.000	.000	.000	.763	.000	.667	.426	.741	.000	.000

V	MI	OC	PV	PR	AG	DN	NW	RI
.667	.763					.000	.000	.000

BP	ED	SP	I	SL	RI			
.741	.426							

T	HS	SE	ACC					
.000	.000	.000	.000					

TABLE 7-A3

Differences between the Information Matrix (Σ) and the Sample Variance–Covariance Matrix (S), Confirmatory Factor Analytic Model of the Demand for Residential Services: Black Primary Families

	T	HS	HQ	BP	V	MI	PV	NW	DN	SL	ACC	SE	SP	ED	IC	OC	PR	AG	RI
T	.000																		
HS	-.000	.000																	
HQ	-.000	-.000	.000																
BP	.000	-.000	.000	.000															
V	.000	-.000	-.000	-.000	.000														
MI	-.000	-.000	-.000	-.000	-.000	.000													
PV	-.130	-.055	-.076	-.070	.071	.000	.000												
NW	.064	-.127	.158	-.171	.184	.000	.064	.000											
DN	.000	-.000	-.000	.000	.000	-.000	.139	.108	.000										
SL	-.000	-.000	-.000	-.000	-.000	-.000	-.100	-.197	.000	.000									
ACC	-.000	-.000	-.000	-.000	-.000	-.006	.062	-.079	-.000	.000	.000								
SE	.000	-.000	-.000	-.000	-.000	.000	-.033	.236	-.000	.000	-.007	-.000							
SP	-.011	.023	-.022	-.022	-.031	.023	.010	.185	.008	-.005	.028	-.000	-.000						
ED	-.103	-.068	-.072	-.024	.090	-.046	.001	.014	.045	.035	.040	.053	.055	-.001					
IC	.089	.066	.064	.015	-.048	.058	.021	-.026	-.059	-.050	-.056	-.075	-.048	-.031	-.001				
OC	-.021	-.026	-.017	.004	-.026	-.038	.012	-.002	-.038	.037	.078	.057	.050	.034	.007	-.001			
PR	.000	-.000	-.000	.000	.000	-.000	-.014	.047	-.000	.000	-.062	-.001	-.006	-.006	-.018	.030	.000		
AG	.000	-.000	.000	.000	.000	.000	.001	-.054	-.000	.000	.000	.000	-.001	-.237	.155	.028	-.000	.000	
RI	-.000	.000	.000	-.000	.000	.000	.023	-.010	.000	.000	.000	-.000	-.004	.023	-.019	.002	-.000	.000	.000

8

Implications of Findings
for Determinants of the Demand
for Residential Services

In this chapter I will summarize and integrate the findings reported for Chapters 3 to 7. The original model of determinants of white primary families' demand for residential services has undergone several revisions in light of the empirical results presented. In view of this, a brief restatement of the major assumptions implicit in my initial approach are in order.

It is taken as axiomatic that families are faced with a fundamental decision in regard to residence—that of how to relate to the existing structure of urban areas. I have argued that this decision is determined in large part by each family's activity pattern. I viewed families as units of production and consumption, units requiring various kinds of input goods and services which, when combined with time, are used by the family to produce goods and services that maximize the welfare of family members. Residential goods can be thought of as input goods that have value according to the services they provide and the activities they support.

The dynamic relation between a family's production and general consumption activities and its consumption of residential services over time cannot be observed directly by means of survey data. What we observe are the relations between attributes of families and characteristics of their residential environments, from which we make inferences about production and consumption activities. It is assumed in this process that: (*a*) social and structural attributes of families are important indicators of the types and quality of goods and services they produce; and (*b*) variations in the social and structural attributes of families can be used to explain variations in residential behavior.

In addition, I stated a number of assumptions dealing with the kinds of residential goods families are likely to consume, the relative importance attached to different kinds of goods, and the external and internal constraints on residential consumption. Specifically, the following were postulated:

1. Families participate in housing markets in order to acquire varying quantities of residential services and so must allocate financial resources to ensure a constant flow of residential services of a specific quality and quantity per unit time.
2. Families with similar production- and consumption-related activity patterns make similar compromises or trade-offs between various types and quantities of residential goods and between residential and other goods.
3. The higher the flow of residential services consumed and the more permanent income left over for consuming other kinds of goods, the more satisfaction families derive from residential consumption.

In addition to confirming some of the results of previous investigations and supporting the general validity of the model, the results reported in preceding chapters provide the basis for increasing our understanding of the determinants of white primary families' residential consumption. This success stems in part from the contribution made by the United States Census Bureau in creating a single data tape incorporating family characteristics, tenure status, and housing, neighborhood, and location attributes. This is the first time it has been possible to enter all these variables into a single analytic framework.

In the following section I will briefly summarize the results presented so far and then comment on their implications.

I. SUMMARY OF FINDINGS, CHAPTERS 3–7

A. White Primary Families

Homeownership was found to have a significant effect on the nature and quality of housing and neighborhood services consumed by white families (and, as later results showed, by black families). To a lesser extent, home ownership also affects where families live in metropolitan areas. Families who choose to own their homes also appear to choose simultaneously bigger and higher quality dwelling units. Thus, increases in internal space, privacy from outside disturbance, and quality housing are important benefits derived from owning one's home, in addition to whatever investment potential is associated with homeownership. However, although homeownership is negatively related to the racial composition and population density of a neighborhood, it does not appear to be directly related to neighborhood socioeconomic status when other residential attributes are taken into account. In spite of this lack of relationship, a higher concentration of owner-occupied housing of high quality is found in the suburbs. Thus the finding of little direct relationship between neighborhood socioeconomic status and tenure status may say more about our inability to estimate functions that take into account the joint distribution of residential attributes than about the true relationship between these two variables.

Dwelling size and structural type (single-family, detached units versus others) do not appear to vary significantly between neighborhoods once the effects of other residential attributes are taken into account. However, dwelling quality is directly related to neighborhood quality. This was expected, since it is known that housing tends to be provided in tracts that are homogeneous with respect to price and quality, and housing of high quality is unlikely to be built in areas where existing housing is of low quality. Unlike space attributes, quality attributes are much more strongly related to externalities peculiar to neighborhoods and general metropolitan locations (suburb versus central city). This is assumed to reflect the fact that quality is a major component of the social use value of a dwelling (in contrast to its technical use) and thus is more likely to have a major impact on the market exchange value of a dwelling than any other set of attributes.

Where families choose to live in metropolitan areas is affected by their demand for various kinds of housing and neighborhood services. Suburban neighborhoods tend to be characterized by much higher concentrations of owner-occupied housing located in low-density environments of higher socioeconomic status attributes than central city neighborhoods. It should be emphasized that there are probably two important factors responsible for the observed central city–suburb differential. One is distance from the center of the city, with progressive changes in quality and space attributes in housing along this gradient (Farley, 1976; Redding, 1977). New housing available for owner occupancy tends to be constructed at the periphery of urban areas. Thus dwelling age decreases as one goes from the center of the city to the constantly expanding periphery. However, the city–suburb variable as a dichotomy also reflects the effects that municipal differences in tax and fiscal structure have on the demand for residential services. Suburbs, for example, often provide fewer public services than central cities, but they may provide specific services of higher quality and at lower unit cost. The suburbs also tend to have lower tax rates than the core municipality. Generally, as the data on perceptions of dwelling and neighborhood problems indicate, suburban residents purchase relatively problem-free residential packages, but they pay less for what they get than they would pay in the central city.

Within metropolitan areas, accessibility to workplace does not appear to be as important to families as housing and neighborhood environment. The oft-stated hypothesis that families make a trade-off between accessibility to workplace and consumption of housing and neighborhood services was not supported by results from the analyses reported here. This finding is supported by previous research that indicates that commuting is the least important reason people give for moving within metropolitan areas. For the majority of metropolitan residents, particularly those in middle- and upper-income categories, the choice of living close to their workplace is not a practical one, since they cannot do this and still avoid the noxious effects of concentrated commercial and industrial land uses. Thus these major generators of employment in urban areas tend to have centrifugal effects on the location of high-quality housing, single-family homes, and residential amenities; households who want these usually have to go toward the periphery of the city to find them. Furthermore, the larger the general metropolitan area, the further workers generally have to travel to work. It is assumed that this reflects the increase in specialization of land uses as urban size increases. The net effect of all these factors is that accessibility to workplace is largely a function of the spatial structure of the housing market and of urban scale. This does not mean that workers are completely insensitive to considerations of their journey to work when making residential decisions. There are many people, for example, who probably cherish the ability to walk or bicycle to work—college professors being one such group. However, it should be understood that cheap, efficient, and individualized forms of transportation have allowed many people so much geographic mobility that the importance of residential location relative to their workplace is very low, and many of those who would like to live close to work have no real choice of doing so.

A second set of findings concerns the effects of family composition (life-cycle stage, as indicated by age of head and number of persons in the household) and family SES on the demand for residential services. Family composition primarily affects families' demand for housing space and the choice of owning versus renting. It appears to have no direct relationship to the character of the neighborhood they live in once other considerations are taken into account. Family SES, in contrast, appears to most strongly influence the quality of the dwelling and neighborhood they choose to live in. All things considered, SES is the single most important factor influencing residential demand, having an effect on both demand for goods that yield technical services and demand for intangible social goods relevant to status maintenance. For white families with at least moderate incomes, this demand is met in the suburban portions of the metropolitan area; these families are able to and do consume relatively high-quality residential goods, plentiful space, and desirable environments, and they escape from some of the negative attributes of American urban areas.

B. Race and the Demand for Residential Services

In a competitive market, the consumption patterns of black and white families would be similarly determined by ability to pay, by needs according to life-cycle stage, and by preferences according to life style. In such a perfect market, racial differences would stem from differences in these income and preference factors. The proportion of black primary families owning their homes is, however, 22 percentage points lower than the white proportion in the sample of primary families analyzed here. White primary families were seen to consume approximately 13% more residential services in 1970 than black families with similar incomes and preferences. It was found that approximately 72% of the total effect of race on homeownership levels can be attributed to the direct effect of race and 42% of the effect of race on residential consumption in dollars.

The results from the annual housing survey involving households' perceptions of their dwelling units and neighborhood, and those obtained from the analysis of black demand for residential services, indicate that blacks are significantly more likely to live in poor-quality housing and in relatively old and deteriorating central city neighborhoods. It was also noted that black demand for housing finds its fulfillment primarily in those sections of metropolitan areas in which the housing supply is limited both with respect to the number of units and their physical conditions. Finally, it was noted that the neighborhoods inhabited by black families exhibited more variation in housing attributes than is true of those inhabited by whites, which indicates that the supply of housing to black households is not as responsive to socioeconomic status attributes as is true of whites. Intraneighborhood variations in housing characteristics contribute to unstable housing price structures over time, which in turn adds another impediment to black residential consumption by causing large swings in housing costs.

These results very strongly support the conclusion that housing market discrimination is a major determinant of black families' residential consumption patterns. They also suggest that the effects of discrimination are transmitted through two major channels. The effect on tenure status is probably transmitted directly through such factors as the application of more stringent requirements for blacks than for whites who want mortgages and insurance, and indirectly through restrictions on residential location by black families. The effect of discrimination on black residential consumption patterns is probably transmitted mainly through indirect channels, via such factors as restrictions on residential location and the attainment of homeownership status.

II. IMPLICATIONS

The most important implication of the results reported for white primary families is that they relate to their urban environment in a manner consistent with expectations based on knowledge of their life styles and family composition. This does not mean that we can predict with any great accuracy when families will make housing adjustments in line with changes in socio-economic status and family composition, although some of the information necessary to such predictions may be provided in the results reported here. These results stem from analysis of cross-sectional data that do not capture the dynamics of change over time in local housing markets. We can do no more here than observe the association between current attributes of families and their present consumption patterns, which reflect past decision making.

The structure and operation of local housing markets are constantly in a state of change, of course. Changes in social norms governing attitudes and behaviors toward residential consumption—ownership, space needs, desirable structural and design features, quality, and neighborhood and metropolitan location—affect residential decision making and thus leave their imprint on the physical structure of local housing markets. These changes do not occur in a vacuum but are shaped significantly by changes in the demographic structure of families, in construction and design technologies, and in economic conditions. The factors of per capita income, capital formation, and investment activities are particularly important. The improvement in the housing environment of the average urban white American family over the past century would not have been possible without changes in residential production and delivery systems.

One very important change has taken place within relatively recent history. De Leeuw, Schnare, and Struyk (1976) report that the cost of the average new single-family home increased from $20,000 to $40,000 between 1964 and 1974. During the last 4 or 5 years the rise in residential costs has exceeded the rise in average family income. This has made necessary certain adjustments both in people's expectations for what they can consume and in the production of housing services. There have been reductions in the amount of services (space and quality alike) built into new dwellings, increases in the production of multifamily units and mobile homes, and increases in efforts to renovate existing housing, particularly in central cities.

However, the desire for a single-family home is probably as strong today as it was a generation ago, and the absolute number of households who want to own their own house has increased with the entrance of the postwar baby boom generation into adulthood and thus into the housing market. Some of this increased demand is absorbed by production of mobile homes and multifamily units, but it also has an effect on the price of single-family homes. It is likely that a smaller proportion of those who want to own single-family homes will be able to do so in this generation—at least in the immediate future. And those who are able to buy homes will not be able to afford as much housing service as previous generations and may have to allocate a greater portion of their resources to satisfy minimum needs. Note also, though, that the rise in housing prices increases the investment potential of homeownership. This may be a positive stimulus to home buying even in the face of rising prices and reduced services afforded by the average home.

What does all of this imply for the consumption of residential services by blacks? It would seem to imply an increase in black residential problems rather than improvement in the next decade, unless certain other changes occur. In an earlier paper (Wilson, 1974) I suggested that the availability of residential services to blacks could be significantly improved if: (a) existing antidiscriminatory laws were more stringently enforced and publicized; (b) blacks were encouraged to seek housing in the outer sections of metropolitan areas; and (c) the economic costs to blacks and to society of maintaining segregation were more widely publicized. In the remainder of this chapter these suggestions are discussed and elaborated upon in light of recent findings on this issue.

The degree of segregation by race in metropolitan areas is very high and has changed very little in the past three decades in spite of some legal sanctions against housing discrimination (Taeuber and Taeuber, 1965; Sørensen et al., 1975; de Leeuw et al., 1976). As noted previously, discrimination is an important explanatory factor here. Black families are channeled away from predominantly white residential areas through a number of discriminatory practices (Foley, 1973; Feagin and Feagin, 1978). This has had the effect of increasing the average costs blacks pay for residential services and has imposed restrictions on blacks' access to several important components of residential packages (such as new housing and better quality neighborhoods).

The policing of subtle forms of discrimination is made difficult by the fact that most housing market decisions are so decentralized that it is difficult to describe, locate, and prove that specific acts are of discriminatory intent. Individuals discriminate for specific reasons, and no amount of moral persuasion is going to alter that fact. Thus it is reasonable to hypothesize that significant reductions in discrimination are not likely to occur in the absence of incentives to individuals not to discriminate.

One of the major benefits whites receive from discriminating is that it reduces the uncertainty associated with fears of what will happen to their neighborhoods if blacks are allowed to move in (see Pettigrew, 1973; Colasanto, 1977). Much white resistance to black neighbors is based on misconceptions about the impact of the presence of blacks on both property values and white life styles. Many whites see blacks as having values and behavior patterns that would lead to conflict and disruption of white neighborhoods if they were allowed to live there. Thus it is necessary not only to change the racial prejudices of whites, but also to convince them that in fact there would not be disadvantages, but rather long-run advantages to opening up residential housing markets to all races. That is, there would be an advantage in meeting black demand for residential services as the white demand is met, thereby reducing rather than increasing racial tension and its sequelae.

Of possibly equal importance with respect to changes in segregation is the continuing black perception that efforts to buy or rent in white neighborhoods will be met with discrimination and abuse. This realistic fear, plus the benefits that blacks have historically derived from their residential concentration, means that some segregation is voluntary on the part of blacks. Thus, some improvement in residential consumption levels among blacks might occur if more blacks were encouraged to seek housing in the outer sections of metropolitan areas. The results of an opinion poll reported by Pettigrew (1973) show that 70% of blacks would prefer to live in mixed residential areas. This would seem to suggest that black opposition to ghetto dispersal may not actually be very strong. However, Pettigrew notes that his respondents may be motivated more by desires for better housing and neighborhood services than by a desire for interracial living.

Pettigrew's results also showed that major black movement out of the central city and into the suburbs might not be welcomed by the white population in those areas. Only 40% of Pettigrew's white respondents were willing to live in close proximity to blacks. A further complication becomes apparent when we look at the meaning of the term *mixed neighborhood*. To whites it seems to mean a neighborhood that is less than 5% black, whereas for blacks it means a neighborhood not dominated by whites.

The net effect of white and black attitudes is that the burden of neighborhood integration may depend more on the residential mobility of blacks than of whites, but because white resistance both directly and indirectly affects the ability of blacks to improve their residential consumption (through maintenance of economic inequality as well as through direct restriction on blacks' ability to purchase residential services), blacks are unlikely to be able to make significant improvement in their residential environment. A substantial change must occur both in the attitudes and behaviors of whites before blacks will feel free to increase their residential mobility.

Few housing analysts would disagree with the generalization that the relative wealth position of black and white households is a contributing factor in racial segregation and race differentials in residential consumption. If housing in urban areas is segregated by price, then households with differing ability to pay for housing will be similarly segregated. Blacks and whites are segregated partly because the average black household cannot afford to purchase the same kind of residential package as the average white household. There is less agreement on the magnitude of the effects of income on racial segregation and residential consumption (Taeuber and Taeuber, 1965; Pascal, 1967; Taeuber, 1970, 1975; Muth, 1974; Marshall and Jiobu, 1975; Roof et al., 1976). The bulk of the evidence indicates that the economic factor is not the only (and perhaps not the most important) causal force underlying racial segregation and black residential consumption patterns. For example, several studies have noted that high levels of residential segregation still obtain between blacks and whites of the same income, occupation, and educational level (Erbe, 1975; Farley, 1977; Schnare, 1977; Wilson and Taeuber, 1978). Nonetheless, there is little doubt that improvement of black economic well-being would raise the level of black residential consumption substantially and that this rise has potential for realization in mixed or previously all-white neighborhoods, thereby reducing segregation by race.

Thus, another alternative that can be pursued to improve the residential environment of black households would be to direct efforts toward programs that show more potential for increasing black income level. The payoff to be gained from pursuing this alternative could have as great an impact on black residential consumption as reducing levels of housing discrimination and racial prejudice. Some of the important issues related to race differentials in income are discussed in Part II. This discussion includes the presentation of some analyses that attempt to identify factors associated with race differentials in income. The results of these analyses will be used to evaluate alternative ways of improving black income levels.

INTRAMETROPOLITAN LOCATION
AND ECONOMIC WELL-BEING

The primary objective of the analysis presented in Part II is to investigate the relationships among racial discrimination, residential location, and economic opportunity. Researchers studying residential behavior usually treat income as one of the primary factors determining residential consumption. In this section I will reverse the issue and ask whether intrametropolitan residential location affects economic well-being.

A basic premise underlying the discussion in this section is the assertion that differential treatment of minorities is a phenomenon that permeates the opportunity and reward structure of American society. The uniqueness of this approach is to be attributed to the fact that a more comprehensive analysis of the presumed effects of discrimination can be pursued, particularly a more systematic treatment of the manner in which institutional discrimination in other areas of American life affect the residential behavior of black households. For example, the more traditional approach to analyzing the effects of discrimination on residential behavior focuses only on isolating those forces operating within housing markets that lead to differential patterns of response to black and white households. Moreover, it can be argued that the appropriate starting point for assessing the effects of discrimination on the extent of blacks' participation in housing markets would be analysis of those forces operating in other institutional spheres (namely, labor markets) that might impact on the amount of resources blacks bring to housing markets as a necessary condition for participation.

In Chapter 9 I will examine whether the incidence of commuting from the central city to the suburbs has increased among black workers between 1960 and 1970. If employment has been increasingly decentralized, as argued earlier, but the black work force remains residentially concentrated in the central city, then one would expect to see a steady rise in black city-to-suburb commuting.

In Chapter 10 I will then examine whether workplace and residence locations affect wages and whether blacks (and whites) who work in the suburbs are paid at a higher wage level than comparable workers in the central city. I will also examine the impact of labor market discrimination on black workers' wages. Here the focus is on the hypothesized link between discrimination and economic well-being, one component of which is residential consumption.

9

The Spatial Structure of Economic Opportunity in Metropolitan Areas

In the past several years, a great deal has been written on the residential distribution of populations in relation to the structure of metropolitan employment opportunity (see Gold, 1972; Masotti and Hadden, 1973; Harrison, 1974a,b; von Furstenberg *et al.*, 1974; Hughes, 1975; Christian, 1975; National Academy of Political and Social Sciences, 1975). The central issue in most of these discussions has been the suburbanization process and the impact it is believed to be having on the economy of central cities and the socioeconomic well-being of their resident populations.

The continuing redistribution of activities within metropolitan areas makes one fact very evident: The spatial structure of metropolitan areas is still evolving. Every new development in the technology of transportation and communication, in building design and operation, in marketing and production techniques, and in organizational forms tends to be reflected in changes in the spatial distribution of activities in metropolitan areas.

Historically, the centralization of employment activities in the core of metropolitan areas was very much influenced by the centralized character of intraurban transportation networks, by the difficulty of moving goods and people efficiently within the urban area, and by the existence of an economic infrastructure that provided cost-reducing externalities for industries located near the core area. But in the last few decades the cost constraints on peripheral location have declined substantially while negative externalities associated with congested central locations have increased. As a result, industrial activity has been decentralizing, at an increasing rate, over the past several decades. Christian (1975:214) describes the underlying process as follows:

> On a different level, industrial land uses have suffered from industrial firm outmigration from the central cities, primarily resulting from the inabilities of central cities to offer adequate space for industrial firm expansion, reasonable land costs, and efficient transportation networks for the necessary flows of goods, services, and employees. The decline of industrial activity within major central cities has resulted from industrial relocation from the central cities to suburban and outlying rural areas; limited and/or declining industrial firm expansion; firm closures and failures; and declining new starts of industrial establishments within central cities.

The decentralization trend was led in the 1940s and 1950s by industries that were expanding or newly developing and by retail trade in convenience goods. During the mid 1960s many central cities experienced a new boom in office construction, and a number of observers thought that headquarters and main office functions, financial and marketing activities, and many professional and specialized services would continue to require central location. Because such industries are the expanding portion of the postindustrial service economy, these observers forecast a new vitality for the central business district (Berry and Cohen, 1973). Evidence culled from the 1970 Census data and the 1973 County Business Patterns indicate that the long-term trends may not follow such a neat division of function favoring the central city and that the optimism engendered in the mid 1960s may have arisen from particular short-term cycles (James, 1976; Wilson, 1978). Gold (1972:464) described the probable reason for the shift in the location of corporate activities as follows:

> For many corporations, the desire of top executives to move closer to their residences in the suburbs appears to be the principal motive for relocating headquarters facilities out of the urban core. The negative factors expelling corporate executives from the central city . . . include racial unrest, decline in the skill level of the central-city labor force, extensive and costly commutation patterns, the proliferation of commuter income taxes, and the general tensions that result from doing business in a crowded and impacted environment.

In addition, as Gold suggests, it is likely that many of the business establishments that provide auxiliary services to corporations will be following them to the suburbs (see also Quante, 1976).

It has been suggested that one result of the decentralization of economic activities (and of the general population) is the loss of the competitive advantage that central cities once held over the suburbs. This advantage originally stemmed from the central city's tax base (which included the area's major thriving industries), the relatively abundant job opportunities and labor pool in the big cities, and the relatively high socioeconomic status of its resident population (Bahl, 1972; Masotti and Hadden, 1973; Harrison, 1974a; von Furstenberg *et al.*, 1974; Christian, 1975). The tax base is eroded, of course, as industry moves away, and we have seen that in 1970 the socioeconomic status of the central cities' resident population was clearly not on the average higher than that in the suburbs. It is beyond the scope of this monograph to consider the full impact of decentralization on the central city's economy, but I will be concerned in the rest of this chapter with one other aspect of this impact—the drop in economic opportunity for central city residents.

I. THE MISMATCH HYPOTHESIS

It has been suggested that a severe imbalance between where people live and work has developed in metropolitan areas. This is thought to be a direct result of the suburbanization of employment opportunities for blue-collar, semiskilled, and low-skilled workers, particularly black workers, who continue to be concentrated mainly in the central city residential areas. Christian (1975:237) outlines several critical features of the relocation of employment activities from central cities that impact adversely on black workers:

> (1) The fact that the great majority of these job relocations are skilled and unskilled blue collar jobs; (2) industrial firms which are relocating are primarily the firms which traditionally have employed the greatest number of black employees; (3) the fact that employment in most suburban areas demands ownership or accessibility to a private automobile readily excludes many blacks from maintaining jobs or, for that matter, even seeking employment in these areas; (4) the low wages often paid to central city residents related to the cost of commuting presents an insurmountable barrier for many; and (5) the perceived level of discrimination practiced in the numerous suburban municipalities has the effect of diminishing the desire to work in alien locations.

There is more to the problem than the suburban relocation of industries that have traditionally provided jobs to low-income and minority populations, and the solution will involve more than simply encouraging low-income and minority populations to move to the suburbs where jobs presumably are available. As Gold (1972) pointed out, the problem also involves constraints on just such moves. Housing in suburban areas is unavailable to minorities and low-income workers because of racial discrimination and because of zoning restrictions that prevent the construction of low-cost housing. In addition, it is difficult for minorities and low-income workers to find out about suitable jobs that might be worth moving for, and low-cost, efficient transportation, which might serve as an alternative to moving, is not available.

A. Previous Evaluations of the
Mismatch Hypothesis

The presumed mismatch between residential and employment locations is believed to have the following adverse effects on the economic well-being of centrally located minority populations: (*a*) higher rates of unemployment; (*b*) longer periods of unemployment while seeking appropriate jobs; (*c*) the necessity of accepting jobs beneath one's capabilities and the low wages that go with such jobs; and (*d*) high transportation-to-work costs (Bahl, 1972; Gold, 1972; Glenn, 1973; Harrison, 1974b; Christian, 1975). A review of the variety of studies that have attempted to evaluate these assertions can be found in Harrison (1974a,b), von Furstenberg *et al.* (1974), and Masters (1975). I will summarize Harrison's important discussion (which is based on a review of previous studies as well as his own results), and in the following section I will present results from my current analysis.

Harrison was concerned with evaluating the assertion that suburbanization of employment opportunity leads to increased unemployment among minority residents of the central cities. Two assumptions underlie this assertion: (*a*) the supply of labor in central cities is relatively fixed while employment opportunity has declined; and (*b*) suburbanization has led to a skill mismatch in metropolitan areas.

With respect to the first assumption, Harrison concluded that while the greatest growth in blue-collar jobs has occurred in suburban areas in the past two decades, there has also been growth of blue-collar employment opportunity in the central city. Most importantly, growth of blue-collar jobs in the central city has been sufficient to accommodate virtually all unemployed central city residents. However, practically all of the net increase in blue-collar jobs in the central city is being absorbed by suburban commuters. Thus the first assumption is not valid; the supply of labor in central cities is *not* relatively fixed. Therefore the second assumption cannot be correct; the problem is not one of skill mismatch but rather that practically all of the net increase in jobs in the central city are being absorbed by suburban commuters, leaving suburban blue-collar jobs (which are increasing more rapidly) for reverse-commuting urbanites. Harrison (1974b:59) concludes that "high unemployment rates and low incomes of central city residents are not simply a matter of the jobs not being there, or of the jobs being of the wrong type. Therefore proposed solutions based on an assumed geographical and skill mismatch will not resolve the employment or income problem."

There is, however, a major problem with Harrison's results. The data he used to analyze job and employment growth were not fine enough to provide a critical test of the mismatch hypothesis. What he was unable to do (but what will be done in analyses reported in the next section of this chapter) was to examine the change over time in employment, taking into account not only suburban–central city and race differences, but also occupation, industry, and other factors that affect employment and commuting patterns.

The analyses to be presented in the rest of this chapter and in the following chapter are extensions of those reported by previous researchers, particularly Gold (1972), Harrison (1974b), Christian (1975), and Kasarda (1976). First I will present some analyses of location differentials in the labor market structure (central city versus the suburbs), with attention to factors of industry type, occupation, region of the country, and size of the greater metropolitan area. Second, the variables of residential location and race will be introduced to assess the effects of the observed employment and residential redistributions on commuting patterns for black and white workers. Finally, the following chapter will assess the relative merits of the mismatch hypothesis in regard to its ability to explain wage differentials by race and residence–workplace combinations.

II. FURTHER ANALYSIS OF THE MISMATCH HYPOTHESIS

A. Methodology

The data used in this chapter (and in Chapter 10) were obtained from the *One Percent State Public Use Samples* drawn from the 1960 and 1970 Census data (U.S. Bureau of the Census, 1972). The samples here are more comprehensive than that from the 1970 *Public Use Sample of Neighborhood Characteristics* employed in the analyses reported in earlier chapters. The present analysis includes all persons who were reported as being at work at the time of the 1960 or 1970 Census and for whom information on workplace location was available, with one major exclusion. Since I wished to control for the effect of regional differences in the analyses with 1960 data, I was able to include only those metropolitan areas identified by state on the data tape, which meant that those living in other than the 24 most populous states were excluded.[1] In addition, those whose workplace or residence was outside an SMSA (but who resided or worked inside an included SMSA) were dropped. The exclusion of those who worked but did not live in the SMSA results in an underestimation of the universe of persons employed in the suburbs of 3–5% for both 1960 and 1970. (See the 1970 Census volume on *Journey to Work* for statistics consistent with this estimate of the present

---

[1] The 24 states represented in the reduced sample are Alabama, California, Connecticut, Florida, Georgia, Illinois, Indiana, Kansas, Kentucky, Louisiana, Massachusetts, Michigan, Minnesota, Missouri, New Jersey, New York, Ohio, Oregon, Pennsylvania, Tennessee, Texas, Virginia, Washington, and Wisconsin.

sample bias.)[2] Another minor source of bias in these data results from the fact that industry and occupation were not reported for some people. The information for the 1970 data set is more complete than for the 1960 set, but some of the 1970 information had to be dropped in order to make the two sets of data comparable in terms of occupation and industry categories.

B. Analyses of Labor Market Structure: Central City versus Suburbs

1. Analyses of Industry and Occupation Employment Differentials: 1960 and 1970

As noted earlier, one of the most important labor market trends, continuing through the 1960s, has been the redistribution of employment from central cities to the suburbs. Tables 9–1 through 9–4 illustrate this trend.

Table 9–1 reports the percentage of persons employed in central city versus suburban locations for 1960 and 1970 and the change between census years. In 1960, only agriculture and mining showed higher percentages of workers employed in the suburbs. By 1970, the number of industry groups with a majority of their labor force employed in the suburbs rather than in central cities increased to seven (including agriculture but not mining). All of the additions to the suburban category were durable goods manufacturing industries, which also showed a smaller central city–suburb differential in 1960.[3] Apparently these industries have been decentralizing over a longer period than the other industry groups. Although at both time periods the majority of the metropolitan labor force was employed in the central city rather than in the suburbs, the percentage had declined in all major industry groups with the exception of agriculture and mining (which are, of course, rather unimportant industries in metropolitan areas). The overall decline in the central city share of employment was approximately 8%.

Another way to observe the changing location of employment opportunities in metropolitan areas is through analysis of differential growth rates in subsectors of the metropolitan economy.[4] Table 9–2 shows the absolute

[2] The exclusion of persons who work outside of the SMSA in which they reside does not bias the estimates of the labor force structure of central cities or suburban areas.

[3] Industry grouping in the durable goods category includes nonmetalic manufacturing, metal industries, electrical equipment, transportation equipment, and professional and photographic equipment.

[4] Some researchers might argue that if the employment growth distribution were adjusted for annexations by central cities during the 1960–1970 period, the rate for central cities would be even less than that presented in Table 9–2. I did not do this for two reasons. First, it is not theoretically necessary. The reason usually given for adjusting for annexation when working with central city population data is that apparent growth may reflect annexation more than any net gain from migration and natural increase (Kaufman and Schnore, 1974). However, it is not theoretically necessary to do this when studying employment because, at least in the present

(continued on page 144)

TABLE 9-1

Intrametropolitan Employment Location by Industry: 1960 and 1970

Industry	1960 Central city (%)	Suburbs (%)	N	1970 Central city (%)	Suburbs (%)	N	Percentage change in central city 1960–1970
Agriculture, forestry, fisheries	16.24	83.76	5,430	21.46	78.54	5,070	5.22
Mining	40.20	59.80	1,306	51.81	48.19	1,465	11.61
Construction	57.73	42.27	17,809	51.10	48.90	18,698	−6.63
Nonmetallic manufacturing	55.85	44.15	5,739	48.93	51.07	5,379	−6.91
Metal industries	55.84	44.16	16,482	50.43	49.57	14,310	−5.41
Electrical equipment	57.83	42.17	19,071	47.60	52.40	22,590	−10.23
Transportation equipment	52.52	47.48	12,599	44.04	55.96	13,360	−8.48
Professional and photographic equipment	65.83	34.17	5,087	46.64	53.36	6,631	−19.19
Food and kindred products	72.36	27.64	9,867	65.15	34.85	7,033	−7.21
Textile mill productions	76.96	23.04	9,129	68.60	31.40	7,653	−8.36
Paper and allied products	72.91	27.09	10,409	62.74	37.26	11,481	−10.17
Chemical and allied products	50.76	49.24	6,479	45.96	54.04	6,327	−4.80
Rubber and misc. plastic products	65.05	34.95	3,951	53.58	46.42	3,796	−11.46
Not specified manufacturing	73.33	26.67	345	57.12	42.88	716	−16.21
Transportation and communication	75.08	24.92	19,607	66.04	33.96	21,555	−9.03
Utilities and sanitary services	68.79	31.21	4,720	63.27	36.73	5,069	−5.53
Wholesale trade	78.22	21.78	13,106	63.87	36.13	17,795	−14.35
Retail trade	65.86	34.14	50,645	53.92	46.08	62,472	−11.95
Finance, insurance, and real estate	77.86	22.14	17,389	71.13	28.87	23,171	−6.73
Business and repair services	70.82	29.18	9,598	61.41	38.59	13,677	−9.41
Personal services	66.81	33.19	19,363	56.99	43.01	16,496	−9.82
Entertainment	61.84	38.16	2,877	54.67	45.33	3,221	−7.16
Professional and related services	63.63	36.37	40,172	58.41	41.59	68,400	−5.22
Public administration	67.03	32.97	17,323	64.12	35.88	21,520	−2.91
Not reported	68.79	31.21	3,076	56.71	43.29	7,522	−12.08
Total	64.95	35.05	321,579	57.06	42.94	385,407	−7.89

Source: One Percent State Public Use Samples (1960 and 1970 Censuses).

143

and relative employment growth rates for separate industry groups and for the sample as a whole. Looking first at the absolute figures, it can be seen that again only agriculture and mining are exceptions to the trend toward greater employment growth (or at least less decline) in the suburbs than in the central city. Overall, industry in the suburbs employed 47% more in 1970 than in 1960, compared with only 5% more for the central city. The proportion of persons employed in eight industrial groups in the metropolitan area as a whole declined in the 10-year period. This may reflect shifts in plant location away from metropolitan areas altogether as well as overall reduction in the labor force because of automation or because of a decline in the demand for the goods and services produced by these industries.

Turning to the relative growth figures we can see that over all industry groups, 83% of total employment growth occurred in the suburbs rather than in the central cities. These relative percentage figures represent the ratio of each sector's absolute change to the total SMSA absolute change. For industry groups showing total growth, positive figures greater than 100 show that a sector captured all of the growth in an industry plus an amount shifted from the other sector. In all such cases except mining, these 100 plus figures are in the suburbs column. For industry groups showing total decline, positive figures greater than 100 show that a sector absorbed all of the decline plus an amount lost to the other sector. In all such cases except agriculture, these negative 100 plus figures are in the central city column. For only 3 of the 25 categories do the figures indicate that the central city experienced more of the total growth than the suburbs and in all three cases the difference is very small; in most other cases the difference is large and favors the suburbs.

The decentralization of employment in metropolitan areas has not only been selective with respect to industry, but also with respect to occupation. Kasarda (1976) found that decentralization resulted mainly in the removal of blue-collar jobs from the central cities. Tables 9–3 and 9–4 illustrate this occupational differential in the suburbanization of employment. Table 9–3 shows that all major occupational categories showed a lower percentage of employment in the central cities in 1960 than in 1970. The decreases are

---

context, I am interested in the social, political, and economic attributes that go with location in the city. The presumed adverse consequences of suburbanization are reduced by annexation— for example, the central city gains in tax base and land use control. These attributes and effects are part of the focus on the analysis here and not effects to be controlled for.

The second reason for not adjusting the employment growth figures is that such adjustments would lead to understatement of the level of employment in central cities (see Harrison, 1974b; Kasarda, 1976). Previously unincorporated areas are likely to have had relatively great population growth in the years preceding annexation—this may be why they were annexed. But they are unlikely to have had growth in employment because industry is unlikely to settle in unincorporated areas that do not have full municipal services and the tax benefits that lure industries in. The population in annexed areas was probably mainly employed in the central city before annexation.

TABLE 9-2

Absolute and Relative Change in the Intrametropolitan Location of Employment, by Industry: 1960–1970

Industry	Absolute change			Change relative to total	
	Central city (%)	Suburbs (%)	Total (%)	Central city (%)	Suburbs (%)
Agriculture, forestry, fisheries	23.36	−12.45	−6.63	−57.22	157.22
Mining	44.57	−9.60	12.17	147.17	−47.17
Construction	−7.06	21.45	4.99	−81.66	181.66
Nonmetallic manufacturing	−17.88	8.41	−6.27	159.17	−59.17
Metal industries	−21.59	−2.54	−13.18	91.48	8.52
Electrical equipment	−2.51	47.20	18.45	−7.87	107.87
Transportation equipment	−11.08	24.97	6.04	−96.32	196.32
Professional and photographic equipment	−7.64	103.57	30.35	−16.58	116.58
Food and kindred products	−35.83	−10.12	−28.72	90.26	9.74
Textile mill productions	−25.28	14.27	−16.17	120.33	−20.33
Paper and allied products	−5.09	51.70	10.30	−36.10	136.01
Chemical and allied products	−11.58	7.18	−2.35	250.66	−150.66
Rubber and misc. plastic products	−20.86	27.59	−3.92	345.81	−245.81
Not specific manufacturing	61.66	233.70	107.54	42.05	57.95
Transportation and communication	−3.29	49.79	9.94	−24.90	124.90
Utilities and sanitary services	−1.23	26.41	7.39	−11.46	111.46
Wholesale trade	10.97	125.26	35.78	23.76	76.24
Retail trade	0.97	66.53	23.35	2.75	97.25
Finance, insurance, and real estate	21.73	73.77	33.25	50.88	49.12
Business and repair services	23.57	88.43	42.50	39.27	60.73
Personal services	−27.33	10.39	−14.81	123.30	−23.30
Entertainment	−1.01	32.97	11.96	−5.23	105.23
Professional and related services	56.29	94.72	70.27	50.97	49.03
Public administration	18.84	35.19	24.23	52.11	47.89
Not reported	101.61	239.17	144.54	48.36	51.64
Total	6.28	46.84	19.85	17.29	82.71

Source: One Percent State Public Use Samples (1960 and 1970 Censuses).

TABLE 9-3

Percentage of the Metropolitan Labor Force Employed in Central Cities, by Occupation: 1960 and 1970[a]

	1960		1970		
Occupation	Central city	Total employed SMSA	Central city	Total employed SMSA	Difference in percentages (1960–1970)
Professional	62.51	40,620	56.81	61,955	−5.70
Manager	67.46	28,592	59.63	30,950	−7.82
Sales-clerical	70.90	83,423	61.17	108,595	−9.73
Services	67.30	29,936	57.29	41,826	−10.02
Craftsmen	60.86	46,501	54.29	49,313	−6.57
Operatives	64.06	59,798	54.63	61,598	−9.43
Private household	61.46	7,860	51.42	4,850	−10.04
Laborers	61.32	14,492	53.57	14,927	−7.75
Not reported	67.77	6,056	56.54	7,946	−11.22

Source: One Percent State Public Use Samples (1960 and 1970 Censuses).

[a] Only SMSAs in the 24 most populous states are included.

greatest for private household and service workers. While in 1970 there is an absolute increase in the number employed in the central cities in all categories except private household workers, the lowest percentage is for the craftsman category. It can be noted also that the percentage employed in central cities is slightly lower for blue-collar occupations at both time periods, except for services.

TABLE 9-4

Absolute and Relative Rate of Growth in Metropolitan Employment, by Occupation: 1960–1970[a]

	Absolute growth			Relative to total	
Occupation	Total (%)	Central city (%)	Suburbs (%)	Central city (%)	Suburbs (%)
Professional	52.52	38.61	75.72	46.00	54.00
Managers	8.25	−4.32	34.30	−35.33	135.33
Sales-clerical	30.17	12.31	73.70	28.92	71.08
Services	39.72	18.94	82.49	32.09	67.91
Craftsmen	6.05	−5.40	23.85	−54.40	154.40
Operatives	3.00	−12.15	30.04	−258.67	358.67
Private household	38.30	−48.38	23.80	77.64	22.36
Laborers	3.00	−10.02	19.12	−204.60	304.60

Source: One Percent State Public Use Sample Tapes (1960 and 1970 Censuses).

[a] Only SMSAs in the 24 most populous states are included.

Table 9–4 shows that during the 1960–1970 decade, central cities experienced growth in professional and sales-clerical (but not managers) categories and substantial declines in all blue-collar occupations except services. In contrast, during this decade the suburbs not only experienced greater absolute increases in all employment categories (except private household workers), but also captured a disproportionately greater share of the total SMSA growth in these occupations.

In summary, the trends reported in Tables 9–1 through 9–4 document the pervasiveness of the decline in central city employment and support the proposition that industries that employ relatively large numbers of blue-collar workers are decentralizing at a greater rate than others. I have so far treated the occupation and industry variables as if they were independent of each other, but of course this is not the case. Also there are other metropolitan attributes that affect the spatial distribution of employment. Kasarda's analysis suggests that such factors as national region and size of the metropolitan area should be controlled. The following analyses will include these two variables and estimate the interactive effects of several variables on labor market structure.

2. Determinants of Workplace Location

a. The odds of working in the central city, 1960 and 1970. Of the several metropolitan attributes that might be considered in analysis of employment location, only regional effects can be assessed for both 1960 and 1970 with the census data (state sample) for those years. A detailed table showing a complete cross-classification of the workplace structure of central cities and suburbs with region, industry, occupation, and time period is not presented here.[5] Goodman's (1972) log-linear model for the analysis of multidimensional contingency tables is employed in order to reduce the greater volume of information contained in the detailed table to a set of meaningful parame-

[5] The detailed table is a complete cross-classification of 14 industry groups, eight major regions, eight occupational categories, two workplace categories, and two time periods. The categorical breakdown of these variables was as follows:

1. *Industry*—agriculture and mining; construction; durable goods manufacturing; nondurable goods manufacturing; not specified manufacturing; transportation, communications, and utilities; wholesale trade; retail trade; finance, insurance, and real estate; business and repairs; personal service and entertainment; professional and related services; public administration; and a not reported category

2. *Region*—West, West North Central, East North Central, Middle Atlantic, New England, South Atlantic, West South Central, and East South Central

3. *Occupation*—professional and technical; managers and officials; sales and clerical; craftsmen and foremen; operatives; services; laborers; and an "others" category that included private households and occupation not reported

4. *Workplace*—central city; suburbs

5. *Year*—1960 and 1970

The detailed table is available from the author upon request.

ters. This model evaluates for each specific attribute or combination of attributes the odds (probability) that a person possessing those attributes works in the central city (rather than in the suburbs).

The general model being evaluated can be estimated with the following equation, in which the dependent variable is the logarithm of the odds of working in the central city:

$$\log_e E = \mu_E + \lambda_A + \lambda_B + \lambda_C + \lambda_D + \lambda_{AB} + \lambda_{AC} + \lambda_{AD}$$
$$+ \lambda_{BC} + \lambda_{BD} + \lambda_{CD} \tag{9.1}$$

$\log_e E$ is the natural log of the odds of working in the central city; μ_E is the grand mean effect—for example, the average cell value of E when variables A through D are zero; the parameters λ_A through λ_D represent the effects of industry, occupation, geographic regions, and time periods (1960 versus 1970) respectively, on the odds of working in the central city; and the parameters λ_{AB} through λ_{CD} represent two-way interaction effects. The general model expressed in Eq. (9.1) is hierarchical; each parameter is added sequentially to a baseline model. (All of the log-linear models evaluated in this chapter are of this form.)

Table 9–5 reports the log-linear estimates of the χ^2 values associated with the hierarchical model defined by Eq. (9.1). The log-linear χ^2 value associated with the "total" row provides a test of the hypothesis that the odds of a metropolitan resident working in the central city do not vary by industry, occupation, geographical region, or year. The very large χ^2 value (51,523) indicates that this hypothesis cannot be accepted. The other χ^2 values in

TABLE 9-5

Log-Linear χ^2 Derived from a Hierarchical Model Predicting Employment in the Central City: 1960 and 1970 (N = 686,528)[a]

Variables	χ^2	df	Percentage reduction in χ^2
Total	51,523	3199	—
Industry	38,230	3175	25.80
Occupation	35,548	3168	5.21
Region	21,021	3161	28.20
Year (1960 versus 1970)	15,265	3160	11.17
Industry × Occupation	11,359	2992	7.58
Industry × Region	7,254	2824	7.97
Industry × Year	6,482	2800	1.50
Occupation × Region	5,814	2751	1.30
Occupation × Year	5,645	2744	.33
Region × Year	4,759	2737	1.72

Source: One Percent State Public Use Samples (1960 and 1970 Censuses).

[a] Only SMSAs in the 24 most populous states are included.

Table 9–5 were generated to evaluate the relative importance of the sequential additional of each variable to the baseline model. The full model (if the three-way and four-way interactions also were shown) will by definition completely explain the observed cell frequencies. Hence the log likelihood χ^2 reduces to zero. The percentage reduction in χ^2 due to the addition of a new parameter to the model indicates the relative ability of the parameter to explain the total variation observed in the dependent variable.[6]

Table 9–5 shows that the workplace distribution in metropolitan areas is heavily influenced by industry and region variables. The 11% reduction associated with time period reflects the substantial shift in distribution between 1960 and 1970 also seen in preceding analyses. Occupation alone accounts for relatively little reduction but the industry by occupation interaction accounts for somewhat more.

The Industry × Region interaction term also results in a fairly large reduction in the χ^2 value. This probably reflects two factors. First the development of the eight regions into which the sample was divided took place at different periods and were shaped by somewhat different forces. Second, as the next analysis will show, the regional variation is correlated with variation in the size of urban areas, which has an independent effect on the spatial distribution of employment. (It was not possible to separate region and urban size effects when using 1960 data.)

b. The odds of working in the central city, 1970, SMSA size controlled.
Table 9–6 shows an analysis of the odds of working in the central city using 1970 Census data (neighborhood characteristics sample), with the variable of size of urban area used as a control—in addition to the regional variable.[7] Since only 1970 data are used it is possible to include all SMSAs (rather than only those in the 24 most populous states, as in the preceding analyses). Another refinement made is the exclusion of nonwhites other than blacks. This exclusion reduces the sample of employed persons by only 3%.

Approximately 41% of the total χ^2 value can be attributed directly to variation in the size of SMSAs, and the addition of this variable to the model reduced the direct effects of both region and occupation to close to zero. Size has further effects in interaction with industry and region. Also note

[6] The χ^2 values for the combined years are presented because the ranking of the variables in regard to the reduction each produced in the total χ^2 value for 1960 and 1970 considered separately are identical to that reported in Table 9–5.

[7] The category breakdown of the region and occupation variable differs from that reported for Table 9–5. The region variable is separated into West, East (New England and Middle Atlantic), North Central (East and West), and South (South Atlantic, and East and West South Central). Occupations are grouped into five categories: skilled white collar (professionals and managers); semiskilled white collar (sales and clerical); skilled blue collar (craftsmen and foremen); semiskilled blue collar (operatives and service workers); and unskilled blue collar (laborers and private household workers). The size variable is separated into urbanized areas of less than 500,000, 500,000–999,999, and 1 million or more population, respectively.

TABLE 9-6

Log-Linear χ^2 Derived from a Hierarchical Model Predicting Employment in the Central City: 1970 (N = 352,333)[a]

Variables	χ^2	df	Percentage reduction in χ^2
Total	22,443	839	—
Industry	15,799	826	29.6
Occupation	15,659	822	.62
Size of urban area	6,424	820	41.15
Region	6,039	817	1.71
Industry × Occupation	5,101	765	4.18
Industry × Size	4,398	739	3.13
Industry × Region	3,585	700	3.62
Occupation × Size	3,497	692	.39
Occupation × Region	3,374	680	.55
Size × Region	1,871	674	6.70

Source: One Percent Public Use Sample of Neighborhood Characteristics (1970 Census).
[a] SMSAs in all states are included. Nonwhites who are not black are omitted.

that the Industry × Occupation and Industry × Region interactions seem substantially less important in Table 9–6 than in Table 9–5. It is clear, then, that the scale of urban areas has a profound effect on the distribution of employment between the central cities and the the suburbs, with industry (but not occupation) having a smaller but still significant independent effect.

These χ^2 values provide some indication of at least the relative magnitude of the effects of the variables considered, but they do not show patterns of variation within levels of these variables. In order to observe these patterns, another set of statistics generated from Goodman's log-linear model were studied. These statistics are the log odds of having a given characteristic and are expressed as deviations from the average cell mean. Table 9–7 reports the log odds of working in the central city for urban area residents of different occupation–industry classifications, and Table 9–8 reports these odds classified by region and size of urban area in which they reside. These figures were generated from the same model used to produce Table 9–6 and represent the net effect of the row and column variables with the other variables controlled.

The odds of working in the central city vary substantially by industry with occupation controlled. For construction, durable manufacturing, and whole-sale trade, the odds are negative while for transportation communications, utilities, and retail trades (and the unspecified occupation category), the odds are positive. Looking at occupational differences within industries shows some occupational differences but not simply by a blue-collar–white-collar division. Although results presented earlier suggest that decen-

TABLE 9-7

Log-Linear Additive Parameters Indicating the Effects of Industry and Occupation on the Odds of Working in the Central City, 1970

| | Occupation | | | | |
Industry	Skilled white collar	Semiskilled white collar	Skilled blue collar	Semiskilled blue collar	Unskilled blue collar
Agriculture-mining	.0541	.1644	-.6387	-.5311	-.4029
Construction	-.1121	-.0667	-.1947	-.2328	-.1487
Durable manufacturing	-.3347	-.2168	-.2249	-.2150	-.2434
Nondurable manufacturing	.0221	.0726	.1009	.0822	-.0158
Not specified manufacturing	.2410	.2701	.0704	.0922	.2259
Transportation, communication utilities	.1046	.1174	.1029	.0705	.0549
Wholesale trade	-.0552	-.0823	-.0853	-.1184	-.1212
Retail trade	.3291	.2727	.3939	.5175	.3460
Finance, insurance, real estate	.0630	.1302	-.0634	.0637	.1025
Business and repairs	-.0219	-.0230	.0926	.2056	-.0942
Personal service, entertainment	.0359	-.0270	-.0217	-.0055	-.2997
Professional and related	-.0194	.0962	.0328	.0772	-.0291
Public administration	.1162	.1671	-.1430	-.1076	.1193
Not reported	-.0765	.1647	-.0942	-.1895	.0840

Source: One Percent Public Use Sample of Neighborhood Characteristics (1970 Census).

TABLE 9-8

Log-Linear Additive Parameters Indicating the Joint Effects of Urban Size and Region on the Odds of Working in the Central City, 1970

Region	Urban size		
	<500,000	500,000–999,999	>1,000,000
East	−.0242	−.0697	−.2066
North Central	.0910	.0821	−.2458
South	.2092	.2868	−.3213
West	.3116	.0725	−.1856

Source: One Percent Public Use Sample of Neighborhood Characteristics (1970 Census).

tralization of blue-collar employment (not including service work) has gone further than that of white-collar employment, the results here suggest that there is not, as yet, any strong trend toward central city–suburban specialization along occupational lines controlling for industry.

As would be expected, the odds of working in the central city are also inversely related to size of the full metropolitan area. However, this is most strikingly so in the West, with only small or reverse differences between the two smallest size categories for the other three major regions. The sharpest distinction across all regions is between SMSAs of more and less than 1 million population. Thus as expected, the odds of working in the central city are lowest in the very largest metropolitan areas and the varying pattern of differences suggests that historical, economic, political, and geographic growth patterns vary across regions.

C. Summary of Analyses of Location Differentials in the Labor Market Structure

In summary, a number of conclusions can be drawn from the results of the analyses of labor market structure in the central cities and suburbs. First, central cities are still the major centers of employment within metropolitan areas. But between 1960 and 1970 a substantial redistribution of employment from the central cities to the suburbs took place, particularly among manufacturing, wholesale, and retail trade industries and in the most developed regions of the country (East and North Central). Furthermore, most of the new employment growth in *all* industries occurred in suburban districts. Finally, the central city–suburban distribution of employment is in large part a function of industry type and of size of the greater metropolitan area, with regional variation and occupation accounting for little variance. Although suburban blue-collar employment is growing faster than suburban white-collar employment, neither central cities nor suburbs appear as yet to be strongly specialized along occupational lines. It is probable that the economic activities concentrated within metropolitan areas are being spread out over a broader territorial area via the decentralization process. I should point out, however, that the recency of this shift prompts caution in making long-range forecasts.

D. Analysis of the Relationships among Employment Redistribution, Residential Redistribution, and Race

I will turn now to assessment of the relationship of the employment distribution changes over the decade to the residential distribution of blacks and whites, particularly with respect to changes in the incidence of central city-to-suburb commuting. Table 9–9 shows the city–suburb residential distribution of the employed white population in 1960 and 1970. The general residential redistribution of the employed white population from city to suburbs has been far greater than that of workplace redistribution. It appears that the modal metropolitan residence of white workers is now suburban. The proportion of whites living in the central cities was 8 percentage points lower in 1970 than in 1960, whereas the difference for blacks was only 2 percentage points. Only in the East South Central and West South Central regions do central cities still house the majority of white workers. However, the vast majority of black workers still live in the central cities, as Table 9–10 shows.

The relative stability of black residence patterns and the great shift in white residence patterns, along with major shifts in economic activities, have had significant effects on commuting patterns. Before the 1960s, most

TABLE 9-9

Percentage of Employed White Metropolitan Population Living in Central Cities, by Region: 1960 and 1970

	1960		1970		
Region	Central city (%)	Total N	Central city (%)	Total N	Percentage difference
Pacific	41.12	39,863	39.23	49,268	−1.89
West North Central	58.64	14,613	43.50	19,008	−15.14
East North Central	51.34	72,276	40.15	87,144	−11.19
Middle Atlantic	51.54	83,892	41.68	86,434	−9.86
New England	40.34	14,156	34.41	18,864	−5.93
South Atlantic	44.64	22,753	37.61	32,419	−7.03
East South Central	54.68	9,811	55.51	12,785	.83
West South Central	72.86	17,452	62.22	23,822	−10.64
Total	50.67	274,816	42.31	325,744	−8.36

Source: One Percent State Public Use Samples (1960 and 1970 Censuses).

TABLE 9-10

Percentage of Employed Black Metropolitan Population Living in Central Cities, by Region: 1960 and 1970

	1960		1970		
Region	Central city (%)	Total N	Central city (%)	Total N	Percentage difference
Pacific	73.55	2,321	70.05	3,493	−3.49
West North Central	87.32	1,033	81.08	1,353	−6.24
East North Central	89.85	7,036	87.44	9,337	−2.42
Middle Atlantic	82.30	8,094	80.33	9,460	−1.97
New England	81.02	332	77.13	376	−3.90
South Atlantic	73.18	4,317	70.88	4,914	−2.30
East South Central	77.43	2,592	77.33	2,634	− .10
West South Central	87.33	3,638	85.76	4,228	−1.57
Total	82.43	29,363	80.30	35,795	−2.13

Source: One Percent State Public Use Samples (1960 and 1970 Censuses).

metropolitan-resident whites both worked and lived in the central cities, as Table 9–11 shows. By 1970 the percentage of whites who lived and worked in the central city declined about 10% across all occupations. This decline results from shifts in both white residence and workplace distributions. Historically, as whites began to settle in the suburbs, the volume of commuting from suburb to city increased, since most jobs were in the central cities. However, as more and more jobs became available in the suburbs, a smaller proportion of whites had to commute to central city workplaces. Furthermore, as the income levels of white blue-collar workers increased, they too were able to find suitable housing in suburban areas where employment opportunities were growing.

Blacks were not part of this residential redistribution because of lower income levels and housing market discrimination. Moreover, as jobs (particularly blue-collar jobs) decentralized, commuting by blacks from city to suburb increased substantially. For the black population, the decline in the percentage who both live and work in the central city, observable in Table 9–12, represents mainly employment redistribution, and not both employment and residential redistribution, as is the case with whites. Furthermore, central city-to-suburb commuting by blacks varies more by occupation than it does for whites. The level of city-to-suburb commuting among black blue-collar workers is twice as high as that for black white-collar workers.

These patterns can be seen more clearly when percentage change in city-to-suburb commuting rates are calculated. As Table 9–13 shows, while city-to-suburb commuting increased for both black and white workers in all occupational groups, the absolute increase is almost twice as high for blacks as for whites. The relative change columns show (as do Tables 9–11 and

TABLE 9-11

Residence—Workplace Distribution of Employed White Metropolitan Residents, by Occupation: 1960 and Percentage Change, 1960–1970

| | Percentage SMSA workers who— | | | | | | | | | |
| | Live and work in the central city | | Live and work in the suburbs | | Live in central city, work in suburbs | | Live in suburbs, work in central city | | Total N | |
Occupation	1960	1960–1970	1960	1960–1970	1960	1960–1970	1960	1960–1970	1960	1970
Skilled white collar	42.96	− 8.63	31.13	5.73	4.97	1.61	20.94	1.29	66,100	86,442
Semiskilled white collar	50.62	−11.32	26.28	8.54	3.71	2.07	19.38	.71	78,867	98,941
Skilled blue collar	39.43	− 9.70	33.71	5.60	6.37	1.51	20.49	2.60	43,378	44,433
Semiskilled blue collar	45.24	−12.14	32.11	7.51	6.22	2.27	16.43	2.35	50,755	50,120
Unskilled blue collar	48.22	−10.25	36.64	6.11	4.22	2.13	10.91	2.01	35,716	45,808
Total	45.71	−10.17	31.04	6.78	4.96	1.81	18.28	1.57	274,816	325,744

Source: One Percent State Public Use Samples (1960 and 1970 Censuses).

TABLE 9-12
Residence–Workplace Distribution of Employed Black Metropolitan Residents, by Occupation: 1960 and Percentage Change, 1960–1970

| | Percentage SMSA workers who— | | | | | | | | Total N | |
| Occupation | Live and work in central city | | Live and work in suburbs | | Live in central city, work in suburbs | | Live in suburbs, work in central city | | | |
	1960	1960–1970	1960	1960–1970	1960	1960–1970	1960	1960–1970	1960	1970
Skilled white collar	78.45	− 9.42	10.26	2.92	5.77	3.55	5.52	2.95	2,046	4,239
Semiskilled white collar	85.05	− 9.47	6.52	2.77	3.92	4.59	4.51	2.11	3,238	6,946
Skilled blue collar	71.66	− 7.66	14.15	−1.00	8.88	6.95	5.31	1.71	2,241	3,248
Semiskilled blue collar	75.46	−12.58	11.00	2.29	8.89	8.67	4.65	1.62	7,156	8,383
Unskilled blue collar	72.78	− 6.25	15.03	0.08	7.31	5.10	4.88	1.07	14,682	12,979
Total	75.10	− 7.60	12.71	0.44	7.33	5.47	4.86	1.69	29,363	35,795

Source: One Percent State Public Use Samples (1960 and 1970 Censuses).

TABLE 9-13

Percentage Change in Central City-to-Suburb Commuting, by Race: 1960–1970

Occupation	Blacks		Whites	
	Absolute	Relative to total change	Absolute	Relative to total change
Skilled white collar	234.75	44.24	73.15	17.56
Skilled blue collar	158.29	74.12	26.71	20.63
Semiskilled white collar	365.35	51.67	95.45	16.91
Semiskilled blue collar	131.45	71.88	34.78	23.57
Unskilled blue collar	49.95	183.6	93.03	17.75
Total	112.92	71.37	61.84	18.20

Source: One Percent State Public Use Samples (1960 and 1970 Censuses).

9–12) that most of the increase in the white suburban work force reflects increases in the number of persons who both live and work in the suburbs. In contrast, the increase in the black suburban work force reflects a shift to working in the suburbs while living in the central city.

If the increased city-to-suburb commuting among blacks were simply a result of the decentralization of employment, one would find the same size increases for whites when occupation was controlled. Tables 9–11 through 9–13 show that this is not the case. The white shift is seen in residence as well as in workplace, unlike black shifts. On the whole, then, these results provide strong support for the proposition that blacks, particularly blue-collar workers, have been more or less forced to commute to suburban workplaces as employment has decentralized because they are not as free as whites to shift their residence to the suburbs.

Of course other factors may affect residence and workplace locations besides race and occupation. Table 9–14 presents log-linear estimates of χ^2 values for the effects of industry, occupation, sex, and region as well as race and time period (1960 versus 1970). The dependent variable here has four categories: live and work in the suburbs, live and work in the city, live in the city and work in the suburbs, and live in the suburbs and work in the city. The addition of race and industry variables produced the largest reduction in the χ^2 values, followed by region, time, and occupation. The results for industry, occupation, and region are consistent with the analyses presented previously (Tables 9–5 and 9–6) and need no further explanation. The results for the time period variable of course reflect the general shift in the residence–workplace distribution observed in other tables presented in this

TABLE 9-14
Log-Linear χ^2 Derived from a Hierarchical Model Predicting the Residence–Workplace Distribution of Metropolitan Residents: 1960 and 1970 (N = 665,718)

Variable	χ^2	df	Percentage reduction in χ^2
Total	98,744	6717	—
Industry	77,855	6678	21.15
Occupation	71,292	6666	6.65
Race	43,717	6663	27.93
Sex	42,457	6660	1.28
Region	29,805	6651	12.81
Year	21,422	6648	8.49
Industry × Year	20,486	6609	.95
Occupation × Year	20,361	6597	.13
Race × Year	20,228	6594	.13
Sex × Year	20,189	6591	.10
Region × Year	19,190	6582	1.01
Industry × Occupation × Year	15,590	6272	3.65
Industry × Race × Year	14,911	6192	.69
Industry × Sex × Year	14,069	6114	.85
Industry × Region × Year	11,418	5880	2.68

chapter. Interactions representing this important shift (e.g., the time period variable) and industry variations, which has been seen to have very strong effects, were chosen for entry into this analysis. None of the interaction additions resulted in substantial reductions in the χ^2 values. Again, these results are consistent with those seen in Tables 9–5 and 9–6.

The strong effect for race observable in Table 9–14 turns out not to be what it appears, once residence is taken into account. In the model represented in Table 9–15, residence is treated as an independent variable predicting the odds of working in the central city rather than as a component of the dependent variable (as in Table 9–14). This change shows that residence has a major effect, with its addition reducing the total χ^2 by nearly 82%. The subsequent addition of the race variable now has almost no effect at all. Furthermore, the interactive effects of residence account for other substantial reductions in χ^2 values, whereas the interactive effects of race are close to nil.

So far, then, it has been established that the incidence of city-to-suburb commuting among blacks varies substantially by occupation and that the apparently strong effects of race are accounted for by the fact that black residence is concentrated in the central city. One final question to ask is whether there are different patterns of results within the occupation, race, and sex categories when residence, industry group, and region are controlled. In this final model the occupation and race categories are nested

TABLE 9-15

Log-Linear χ^2 Derived from a Hierarchical Model Predicting Employment in the Central City, 1960 and 1970 (N = 665,718)

Variable	χ^2	df	Percentage reduction in χ^{2a}
Total	245,295	4479	
Residence	44,560	4478	81.83
Industry	34,911	4465	21.65
Occupation	33,094	4461	4.08
Race	33,037	4460	.13
Sex	32,722	4459	.71
Region	28,138	4456	10.29
Year	25,817	4455	5.21
Residence × Industry	19,846	4442	13.40
Residence × Occupation	18,482	4438	3.06
Residence × Race	18,480	4437	.00
Residence × Sex	17,717	4436	1.71
Residence × Region	13,047	4433	10.48
Residence × Year	11,631	4432	3.18
Industry × Year	11,049	4419	1.31
Occupation × Year	10,974	4415	.17
Race × Year	10,973	4414	.00
Sex × Year	10,967	4413	.01
Region × Year	10,484	4410	1.08

[a] The percentage reduction in χ^2 values reported for all parameters other than residence, were computed using the χ^2 value obtained once the effect of residence is controlled (e.g., χ^2 = 44,560).

TABLE 9-16

Log-Linear Additive Parameters Indicating the Effects of Occupation, Race, and Sex on the Odds of Working in the Central City, 1970[a]

Occupation	Males		Females	
	Blacks	Whites	Blacks	Whites
Skilled white collar	.0814	.1055	.1724	−.0571
Semiskilled white collar	.0809	.0619	.2499	.0361
Skilled blue collar	−.0789	.0333	−.0177	.0145
Semiskilled blue collar	−.1783	−.0223	−.0639	−.0775
Unskilled blue collar	−.0377	−.0723	−.0693	−.1610

[a] These coefficients were generated from a model in which the effects of residence, and 14 industry and four regional categories were controlled.

within sex categories, yielding 20 categories in all. As in similar analyses presented earlier (Tables 9–7 and 9–8), entries in Table 9–16 are the log odds of working in the central city, expressed as additive coefficients. Each represents the net effect of the row and column variables with the other variables controlled.

The odds of working in the central city vary substantially by occupation. White-collar males are more likely to work in the central city, whereas blue-collar males are more likely to work in the suburbs. The largest differences between black and white males is found for the workplace of blue-collar workers, with black blue-collar males more likely to be found in the suburbs than white blue-collar males. These results reflect the higher city-to-suburb commuting by black blue-collar workers. Turning to females, black white-collar females are more likely to work in the city than any other group, male or female. However, the differences between black and white blue-collar females are much smaller than parallel differences for males. The explanation for these sex differences may lie in the greater trend of women to be in part-time work and to be less mobile for employment purposes.

E. Summary

While central cities are still the major centers of employment in metropolitan areas, during the 1960s a substantial redistribution of employment from central city to suburban areas occurred, with industries characterized by blue-collar occupational structures experiencing the greatest shift. White workers appear to have responded to this shift by taking up residence in the suburbs. For blacks, the response has been increased city-to-suburb commuting.

This does not mean that there is more black than white commuting in general. As Tables 9–11 and 9–12 show, there is much more suburb-to-city commuting by whites than by blacks, and thus total commuting by whites in either direction is greater. This suggests that whites are attracted to suburban living perhaps not for employment location reasons but mainly for other reasons—for the consumption of housing and public services. Thus the commuting patterns of black workers can be assumed to mirror constraints on their residential location, whereas those of whites mirror residential choice. It is within the context of these results that one can assume that the financial costs of commuting impose a greater burden on blacks than on whites. In Chapter 10 I will present an analysis of wage rates designed to test this assumption.

10

Wage Differentials: Race, Residence, and Workplace

The results reported in Chapter 9 document some of the changes that have occurred in metropolitan employment patterns and the impact that these changes have had on patterns of commuting with respect to industry, occupation, region, race, and sex variables. The major portion of metropolitan economic growth is occurring in suburban areas. The suburbs have both captured the major share of new growth in many industries and gained from shifts of industry from the central cities. In both cases suburbs gain doubly because these new and transferring industries tend to be technologically progressive and capable of further growth and expansion (Stanback, 1974; Thompson, 1974; Quante, 1976). The issue to be addressed in this chapter is whether such central city–suburban trends in employment growth are associated with similar differentials in wages, and whether the wages of blacks and whites are affected in the same or different ways.

One observation made repeatedly in the literature is that the earning potential of black workers is affected by their residential location within metropolitan areas. It is thought that residence in the central cities restricts the range of jobs available to blacks to industries characterized by low wages and lack of stability in employment—for example, declining or marginally productive industries and service occupations. The effects of this situation on the economic well-being of the black population are assumed to be threefold:

1. Low demand for skilled black labor discourages skill development in the black labor force.

2. Lack of opportunity has a dampening effect on the economic aspirations of black workers.
3. Economic underdevelopment in the black population is self-perpetuating because low wages restrict the residential choices open to blacks, thereby limiting access to better paying jobs.

The remedies most commonly proposed for this situation are the development of more efficient metropolitan transportation, which would enable blacks to get to the better jobs, and increasing blacks' access to suburban housing, one way or another. The assumption behind these recommendations is that the jobs available to blacks in the suburbs are superior to those in the central cities in terms of wages, fringe benefits, and tenure. In line with this assumption, Stanback (1974) in a study of 10 metropolitan areas found that workers in industries that are growing rapidly in suburban areas (namely, manufacturing and construction) are paid a higher average weekly wage than comparable central city workers. However, the results of a study by Masters (1975) cast doubt on the value of residential location in terms of getting better paying jobs. He found that the earnings of blacks and black–white differentials were insensitive to residential location. Unfortunately, the macroanalytic character of Master's analysis weakens the importance of his results in regard to assessing the impact of residential location on the economic status of individuals.

Harrison (1974b) sought to determine whether residential location was related to the economic well-being of metropolitan residents. His review of previous studies indicated that the average wages paid to suburban workers was no greater than that paid to city workers. However, when he compared whites and nonwhites from different metropolitan areas on measures obtained in the 1966 *Survey of Economic Opportunity*, he did find some significant differences. For nonwhites the findings were that: (*a*) earnings were significantly higher among those who reside *outside* the ghetto but not outside the central city as a whole; (*b*) unemployment rates were similar for ghetto and nonghetto residents; (*c*) occupational status was not related to residential location (comparing city poverty and nonpoverty areas and the suburbs); and (*d*) only the relative importance of the household head's wages to total family income and not the total itself diminishes with distance from the ghetto. On the whole these results suggest that nonwhites would not gain much by shifting their residence from the central city to the suburbs. One of the major problems with Harrison's results is that he was unable to compare economic well-being of those who live and work in the same sector with those who live and work in different sectors (e.g., he was unable to cross-tabulate residence with workplace location).

Another analysis relevant to the analysis of the impact of residential location on the economic status of black central city workers and on the general plausibility of the mismatch hypothesis is that reported by Danziger and Weinstein (1975). They tested the hypothesis that suburban jobs held by urban poverty residents were economically superior to jobs held by those who both live and work in this area. Three alternative models of this hypothesis were presented. The first one assumed that metropolitan labor markets are spatially segmented and that high transportation costs and housing segregation prevent poverty-area residents from enjoying the economic advantage of suburban employment. The second model assumed that suburban wages would be higher because employers felt compelled to offer workers incentives to commute from the central city. The third model assumed that workers commuting to the suburbs would receive higher wages because, although urban markets do not provide enough employment opportunities for poverty-area residents, market imperfections prevent the bidding down of suburban wages.

Danziger and Weinstein evaluated their hypotheses by calculating three different estimates of the difference between the imputed hourly wage for poverty-area residents who worked in suburban areas and the wage they would receive if they worked in poverty areas at prevailing wage rates. These three estimates were (a) gross wage differentials; (b) net wage differentials after adjustment for the greater travel costs of those who commute to the suburbs; and (c) net wage differentials after adjustment for the greater travel time of those who commute to the suburbs. Their results did not confirm the hypothesis that suburban jobs available to poverty-area residents are economically superior to those offered in the poverty areas. Danziger and Weinstein (1975:14) concluded:

> The evidence from examination of UBD (gross wage differential) suggests that no systematic wage-rate improvements would accrue to blacks merely from suburban employment. This remains true even if additional commuting burdens were reduced by either residential relocation or transit improvements. Lowered travel costs or residential relocation will, of course, benefit commuters, but will not be sufficient to make suburban employment more remunerative than poverty-area employment.

As to which of the three models of suburban poverty-area wage differentials is the most plausible, Danziger and Weinstein concluded that the supply model is more consistent with the data. This is because their results indicate that poverty-area residents are simply "rationed" out of jobs near their homes and are forced to commute to the suburbs without full compensation for the commuting burden (1975:15). Hence, the conclusion of these authors is similar to that suggested by Harrison (1974b), namely that ghetto dispersal (mainly to the suburbs) will not improve significantly the economic status of black central city residents.

Although Danziger and Weinstein's results rather strongly support the conclusion that suburban jobs are not economically superior to central city jobs for poverty-area residents, Danziger and Weinstein caution that the most rigorous test of the mismatch hypothesis would require data on non-pecuniary characteristics of jobs such as working conditions and fringe benefits, data that were not available to them. Another useful extension of their analysis would have been to include a sample of workers who live and work in suburban districts, which would have allowed examination of the question of whether blacks who both live and work in suburban areas have higher wages than blacks who live and work in central cities or live and work in different sectors. If blacks who live and work in the suburbs were found to receive the highest wages and blacks who live and work in central cities the lowest, then one might suggest that Danziger and Weinstein's results were insensitive to biases produced by labor market imperfections, particularly as they affect the dissemination of information on employment opportunities and shifts in residential location.

In an analysis presented elsewhere (see Taeuber, 1976:74–78), I found results contradictory to those reported by Harrison (1974b) and by Danziger and Weinstein (1975). The sample in this analysis is the same as that used in Part I of this monograph, consisting of male heads of primary families who worked at least 48 weeks in 1969. It was reported that blacks who live and work in central cities are paid a significantly lower hourly wage than blacks who work in the suburbs. Commuters, of course, have higher average journey-to-work costs than those who live and work in the same metropolitan sector. These costs are not compensated for by higher wages; thus commuters would increase their net income if they were able to establish residence in the same areas as their workplace. However, the earnings of black city-to-suburb commuters are probably not high enough for them to afford housing in the suburbs, even if housing discrimination did not by and large prevent them from moving to the suburbs.

Since no substantial hourly wage differentials were found for white workers with different residence and workplace locations, it appeared that the city–suburb differential observed for blacks might be associated with differences in the distribution of different types of industry between the city and the suburbs. If, as noted earlier, suburban industries tend to be high-growth industries, they are least likely to be resistant to change and most likely to adopt various innovations, including personnel as well as product, marketing, or organizational innovations. Such industries might have less rigid occupational structures and might offer employment and advancement opportunities to a greater variety of workers than older industries. In addition, they also might be more susceptible to governmental regulation than the solidly established industries that characterized the central cities in previous decades. In short, suburban industries may be less likely to practice racial discrimination in hiring and may offer relatively greater opportunities for advancement for black workers. This tentative conclusion is supported by the findings for wage differentials between blacks and whites: The gap is smaller for those who work in the suburbs.

In the following section I will present an extension of this analysis, using a more heterogeneous sample of male workers and observations taken at two points in time, a decade apart. It was expected that the residence–workplace differentials for blacks would be sharper in 1969 than in 1959 and that the differential between races would be smaller, both results reflecting ongoing industrial development and at least some small gains for black workers in the decade of the 1960s.

I. ANALYSES OF WAGE DIFFERENTIALS

The census data available on the 1960 and 1970 *One Percent State Public Use Sample* tapes offer the possibility of further tests of the mismatch hypothesis, as it relates to the effect of race, residence, and workplace location on wages (U.S. Bureau of the Census, 1972). The samples used in the analyses to be reported here are described in Chapter 9. Note that the data on wages pertain to the year preceding each census, for example, 1959 and 1969, and are so identified here. The first set of analyses is based on data for women and men who worked at least 48 weeks during 1959 or 1969. In the second set of analyses, which examine the components of residence, workplace, and race differentials, only male data are used.[1]

A. Central City–Suburb Differentials

Table 10–1 presents the 1969 wage differentials between the central city and the suburbs for the combined sample and the change from 1959 to 1969. As expected, the average weekly wages of workers in construction and durable goods manufacturing were substantially higher in the suburbs in 1969. However, the other industry groups that have shown great suburban growth over the decade (all except personal services) pay only slightly greater or even lower average weekly wages in the suburbs than in the central city. The higher suburban wages for construction and durable goods manufacturing, then, may reflect the fact that a relatively great proportion of their labor force works in the suburbs (see Table 9–1).

Table 10–2 shows that the 1969 results for construction and durable goods manufacturing hold for both black and white workers. However, black

---

[1] The exclusion of data for women from the second set of analyses stems from previous findings suggesting that women have somewhat less flexibility in regard to job location than men. While it seems necessary to control for this possibility, it should be noted that the locational factors affecting men's wages probably affect women's wages in the same way, or perhaps have a stronger effect since travel-to-work considerations may be more important to women.

TABLE 10-1

Average Weekly Wages of Metropolitan Workers, by Industry and Workplace: 1969 and Percentage Change: 1959–1969[a]

| | Place of work | | | |
| | Central city | | Suburbs | |
Industry	1969	Change (%)	1969	Change (%)
Construction	$131.30	22.92	$144.28	26.79
Durable goods manufacturing	123.93	12.84	132.12	13.77
Nondurable goods manufacturing	108.94	17.84	110.71	14.82
Transporation, communication, and utilities	121.02	19.55	120.86	11.41
Wholesale and retail trade	95.56	17.66	93.05	17.37
Finance and business	113.40	16.21	116.99	13.13
Personal services	57.99	40.82	52.77	26.15
Professional and related services	111.35	17.28	112.59	14.32
Public administration	123.87	26.11	123.50	21.20
Others[b]	110.05	16.81	108.29	24.16

[a] Wages are expressed in 1959 dollars.
[b] Includes agriculture, mining, entertainment, and unreported categories.

suburban workers, unlike white suburban workers, also have higher wages in nondurable goods manufacturing, in the wholesale and retail trades, and in the "others" category, which includes agriculture, mining, and entertainment. Table 10–3 shows that these race–workplace wage differentials are related to occupational category. The average weekly wage of black white-collar workers does not vary by workplace. Only black skilled and semi-skilled blue-collar workers earn more in the suburbs. For white workers the reverse is true, with all but the skilled and semiskilled blue-collar workers earning more in the central city.

B. Is There a Commuter Differential?

Tables 10–4 and 10–5 add the dimension of residence to these wage differential data for black and white workers. It was predicted that workers who incur the expenses of commuting relatively great distances to work would be rewarded with higher pay than noncommuters. The findings, however, are mixed. For construction, durable goods manufacturing, the wholesale and retail trades, and the "others" category, black city-to-suburb commuters do earn higher weekly wages than workers who live and work in

TABLE 10-2
Average Weekly Wages of Metropolitan Workers, by Industry, Workplace, and Race: 1969 and Percentage Change, 1959–1969[a]

	Black				White			
	Work in central city		Work in suburbs		Work in central city		Work in suburbs	
Industry	1969	Change (%)	1969	Change (%)	1969	Change (%)	1969	Change (%)
Construction	$ 96.48	27.40	$104.25	32.57	$147.76	18.72	$153.26	25.64
Durable goods manufacturing	101.06	16.43	107.92	12.43	134.35	13.62	139.29	16.06
Nondurable goods manufacturing	84.86	25.29	94.37	25.56	120.63	18.01	114.56	15.01
Transportation, communication, and utilities	99.08	24.21	89.42	14.04	133.41	20.91	128.52	12.81
Wholesale and retail trade	74.71	37.77	78.09	50.58	104.19	13.53	95.16	14.98
Finance and business	84.31	34.42	84.42	38.17	124.13	16.28	122.16	13.05
Personal services	47.93	40.89	40.74	27.27	76.46	26.34	63.97	18.55
Professional and related services	89.16	35.98	84.91	27.90	127.09	14.26	119.46	14.06
Public administration	109.18	26.88	100.93	23.42	135.22	27.34	130.00	21.18
Others[b]	66.17	27.77	113.67	85.86	127.87	7.70	107.13	13.77

[a] Wages are expressed in 1959 dollars.
[b] Includes agriculture, mining, entertainment, and unreported categories.

TABLE 10-3

Average Weekly Wages of Metropolitan Workers, by Workplace, Occupation, and Race: 1969 and Percentage Change, 1959–1969

Occupation	Black				White			
	Work in central city		Work in suburbs		Work in central city		Work in suburbs	
	1969	Change (%)	1969	Change (%)	1969	Change (%)	1969	Change (%)
Skilled white collar	$124.80	39.43	$125.61	40.05	$176.38	15.62	$170.99	19.73
Skilled blue collar	103.42	29.97	109.59	23.63	138.71	17.54	140.75	16.37
Semiskilled white collar	83.18	16.60	83.69	21.62	96.91	14.08	92.04	14.88
Semiskilled blue collar	89.10	27.74	98.09	20.96	103.15	16.30	104.58	12.56
Unskilled blue collar	65.60	31.99	63.39	25.92	79.47	16.30	71.40	10.13

TABLE 10-4

Average Weekly Wages of Black Workers, by Industry, Workplace, and Residence: 1969 and Percentage Change, 1959–1969

| | SMSA workers live and work in— | | | | SMSA workers— | | | |
| | Central city | | Suburbs | | Live central city, work suburbs | | Live suburbs, work central city | |
Industry	1969	Change (%)	1969	Change (%)	1969	Change (%)	1969	Change (%)
Construction	$ 96.94	27.23	$100.06	34.22	$108.59	25.61	$ 92.67	30.63
Durable goods manufacturing	100.98	16.42	100.77	9.26	112.09	12.25	101.86	16.28
Nondurable goods manufacturing	84.59	25.19	94.89	29.19	93.85	20.82	87.34	23.97
Transportation, communication, and utilities	99.20	25.41	85.11	15.69	94.63	6.73	97.75	9.39
Wholesale and retail trade	74.81	37.49	76.68	60.55	79.73	34.93	73.61	43.57
Finance and business	83.41	33.48	85.50	47.77	83.35	24.40	95.02	41.65
Personal services	48.28	41.33	39.29	24.26	42.50	28.98	42.68	35.11
Professional and related services	88.40	36.69	83.64	33.14	87.07	18.24	96.56	21.32
Public administration	107.79	25.32	102.29	28.39	99.59	18.21	120.55	39.24
Others	67.20	33.04	89.59	56.38	145.41	109.68	56.00	−17.16

the same sector. Black suburb-to-city commuters have the highest wages
in finance and business, professional and related services, and public administration. Other differences that can be seen in Table 10–4 are either very
small or are the reverse of expectation.

Turning to white workers, Table 10–5 shows more consistent results, with
suburb-to-city commuters earning the highest wages in all industry
categories. Many of these white suburb-to-city commuters are highly skilled
or highly placed employees of business and professional organizations that
have their central offices in or near the central business districts of major
cities. The average white suburb-to-city commuter is relatively well paid, as
Table 10–5 shows, and can well afford the expense of commuting to work. In
contrast, when white city-to-suburb commuters are compared with those
who live and work in the same sector, no consistent differential appears. The
expected commuter advantage here is seen only for workers in the wholesale
and retail trades and public administration. The other differences are either
very small or the reverse of expectation.

C. Components of Residence–Workplace
Wage Differentials

The gross wage differentials reported up to this point conceal the influence
of several factors that are relevant to a determination of whether residential
location per se affects wages. A component difference analysis permits
examination of these factors through decomposition of observed gross differences into additive components. The first stage of the procedure is estimation of a series of hourly wage determination equations of the following
form:

$$\log (HW) = B_o + B_{ij}X_{ij} + B_{ij}W_{ij} + B_{ij}Z_{ij} + e \qquad (10.1)$$

where $\log (HW)$ is the natural logarithm of the hourly wage figure, B_o and B_{ij}
are unstandardized regression coefficients, X_{ij} represents background characteristics, W_{ij} represents labor force characteristics, Z_{ij} represents geographic location characteristics, and e is the residual. Table 10–6 lists and
defines the variables used in estimating Eq. (10.1). This analysis is restricted
to males who worked at least 48 weeks in 1959 or 1969 (see footnote 1 in
this chapter). Equation (10.1) was applied to each of 32 subgroups defined by
race, occupation (blue collar versus white collar), time period, and the four
residence–workplace location combinations. The latter are designated as CC
(live and work in the central city), CS (live in the city, work in the suburbs),
SS (live and work in the suburbs), and SC (live in the suburbs and work in
the city). Variable means and unstandardized regression coefficients are
reported in Table 10–A1 in the appendix for the total sample of black and

TABLE 10-5

Average Weekly Wages of White Workers, by Industry, Workplace, and Residence: 1969 and Percentage Change, 1959–1969

Industry	SMSA workers live and work in—				SMSA workers—			
	Central city		Suburbs		Live central city, work suburbs		Live suburbs, work central city	
	1969	Change (%)	1969	Change (%)	1969	Change (%)	1969	Change (%)
Construction	$137.03	16.46	$153.79	25.50	$150.53	27.67	$161.85	16.84
Durable goods manufacturing	123.76	11.17	140.48	17.05	134.45	12.03	146.96	12.67
Nondurable goods manufacturing	109.08	15.11	113.98	16.25	117.61	8.11	140.33	14.49
Transportation, communication, and utilities	124.60	18.52	128.92	14.57	126.41	3.97	146.60	20.46
Wholesale and retail trade	95.76	12.41	94.04	15.33	101.92	9.80	121.74	10.29
Finance and business	115.47	17.97	122.59	12.50	119.76	19.31	140.70	10.44
Personal services	71.99	21.05	63.98	25.57	63.89	−24.47	92.43	40.13
Professional and related services	119.66	17.42	119.29	14.62	120.73	8.89	144.07	2.50
Public administration	129.01	25.54	129.02	21.00	135.04	22.33	146.98	27.09
Others	123.53	7.14	104.43	15.84	122.34	2.77	137.71	4.50

TABLE 10-6
Definitions of Variables Used in Estimating Equation (10.1)

Variable	Definition
I. Background factors	
A. Years of schooling	Number of years of schooling completed (scaled from 0 to 18 or more years of schooling).
B. Head of household	Dummy variable—value of 1 if person is head of household, 0 otherwise.
C. Married	Dummy variable—value of 1 if person is married, 0 otherwise.
II. Labor force characteristics	
A. Occupational status score	1960 Duncan score.
B. Seniority	Age minus years of schooling completed plus five.
C. Class of worker	Two dummy variables—value of 1 for *private* if work in private industry, value of 1 for *government* if work in public administration. Omitted category is self-employed.
D. Work full-time	Dummy variable—value of 1 if person worked 40 hours or more a week in 1960 and 1970, 0 otherwise.
E. Industry	Nine dummy variables—values of 1 if industry of work was construction, durable manufacturing, nondurable manufacturing, transportation–communication–utilities, retail–wholesale, finance–business, professional services, public administration, and personal services. The omitted category includes persons employed in agriculture, mining, and entertainment.
III. Geographic location	
A. Region	Three dummy variables—value of 1 if region of residence is Pacific, East, or North. The omitted category is South region.
B. Migration status	Seven dummy variables—value of 1 if person lived in different metropolitan area, or moved from nonmetropolitan area between 1955 and 1960, and 1965–1970. The omitted category includes persons who lived in the same metropolitan area.
IV. Dependent variable	
log(*HW*)	Natural logarithm of 1959 or 1969 earnings (from wages and self-employed income) divided by weeks worked in 1959 or 1969, and hours worked in 1960 or 1970, respectively. Wages for 1969 are expressed in 1959 dollars.

white males.[2] In the final analysis step the mean differences between standard and comparison groups were decomposed into: (*a*) a sum representing differences in background and labor force attributes; (*b*) the difference in average wages of equally productive workers in different groups; and (*c*) a sum representing residuals for the interactions between the various attributes and wage rates.

Table 10–7 reports the results for the comparisons relevant to the questions of whether suburban employment is economically superior to that available in the central cities and whether city-to-suburb commuters are paid more than those who live and work within the same metropolitan sector. I am interested in comparing the relative contributions of the components representing background and labor force attributes versus the wage rate differential.[3]

The comparisons of interest are, specifically, *CS* versus *CC, SS* versus *CC,* and *CS* versus *SS*. On the one hand, if city-to-suburb commuters (*CS*) do not receive higher wages than workers who live and work in the city (*CC*), then they are worse off financially by reason of having a suburban job because they must bear commuting costs. On the other hand, if city-to-suburb commuters do receive higher wages than those who live and work in the city, but suburban workers are generally paid at a higher wage rate than central city workers (*SS* versus *CC*), then the higher wages for the city-to-suburb commuters might just reflect generally superior wage rates paid in the suburbs. Only if city-to-suburb workers (*CS*) receive higher wages than those who live and work in the suburbs (*SS*) as well as those who live and work in the city (*CC*), can we conclude that commuters to the suburbs receive a wage differential to offset commuting costs. If we cannot draw this conclusion (e.g., if *CS* = *SS*), then it would appear that suburban workers would stand to gain wage benefits by moving to the suburbs and thus reducing travel-to-work costs.

In 1959 it appears that for black workers, and to a very minor extent for white workers, *CS* commuters were compensated at least in part for the costs of commuting to the suburbs, as shown by the differences attributable to wage rate (Table 10–7). That is, the highest average wages were paid to city-to-suburb commuters and the lowest to those who lived and worked in the suburbs. For whites the major portion (but not all) of the total differential was attributable to productivity, whereas for blacks only the *SS* versus *CC* difference was mainly attributable to productivity, with the *CS* versus *CC* and *CS* versus *SS* differences attributable to wage rates. Thus in 1959, both white and black city-to-suburb commuters would have been better off if they had lived in the suburbs and so avoided some journey-to-work costs. The

---

[2] Comparable tables for white- and blue-collar workers are omitted from the presentation. These tables can be obtained from the author upon request.

[3] Results for the other comparisons and for the interaction component are omitted from the presentation.

TABLE 10-7

Selected Components of Residence and Workplace Wage Differentials, by Race, Occupation, and Time Period[a]

	Log hourly wage			CS versus CC			SS versus CC			CS versus SS		
				Differences attributable to:			Differences attributable to:			Differences attributable to:		
	CS	SS	CC	Worker attributes	Wage rates	Total	Worker attributes	Wage rates	Total	Worker attributes	Wage rates	Total
All males												
1959												
Blacks	.6482	.4650	.5351	3.94	7.78	11.31	−4.34	−.59	−7.01	6.81	5.29	18.31
Whites	.9832	.9159	.9220	4.04	1.12	6.12	1.28	.11	−.61	7.71	1.67	6.74
1969												
Blacks	.8979	.7548	.7908	5.78	2.55	10.71	−2.36	−2.05	−3.60	8.12	7.18	14.32
Whites	1.1402	1.1411	1.0928	1.50	2.99	4.75	2.86	2.73	4.84	−.41	−.07	−.09
Blue-collar males												
1959												
Blacks	.6334	.4472	.5094	5.59	6.98	12.40	−3.53	.02	−6.22	8.09	4.65	18.62
Whites	.9375	.8143	.8375	5.76	4.88	9.99	.61	.80	−2.32	9.33	2.85	12.31
1969												
Blacks	.8811	.7157	.7452	7.64	3.93	13.58	−2.18	−1.63	−2.95	9.82	8.20	16.54
Whites	1.0313	1.0050	.9635	3.87	3.33	6.79	2.74	2.86	4.16	1.47	−.34	2.63

[a] A positive cell entry indicates that the first member of each comparison pair had higher wages. The interaction terms are not entered in this table.

main difference between blacks and whites is that the wage rate disadvantage of black commuters is high enough to be interpreted as commuting compensation.

In 1969 the situation was somewhat but not greatly different. Black city-to-suburb commuters again had the highest average weekly wage, whereas blacks who lived and worked in the suburbs had the lowest. Only the CS versus SS differential (and not the CS versus CC differential) is substantially attributable to the wage rate component rather than to productivity in 1969. For whites, city-to-suburb commuters also received the highest wages, but those who lived and worked in the central city had the lowest wages, and those who lived and worked in the suburbs had nearly as much as the city-to-suburb commuters. Generally the 1969 white differences are very small and neither productivity nor wage rate components are very large. Thus black (but not white) commuters would have been better off if they could have lived in the suburbs and avoided commuter costs.

Since the controversy over whether suburban employment makes a difference with respect to wages was focused primarily on blue-collar workers (because the majority of black workers fall into this category), the component difference analysis was repeated with data for blue-collar workers only. The pattern of results, shown in the bottom half of Table 10–7, is substantially the same, with a few noticeable exceptions. The CS versus CC differentials are sharper, particularly for whites. However, for both groups the CS versus CC wage rate differential declined between 1959 and 1969 (rather than increased, as had been expected). With respect to the CS versus SS comparisons, among whites the wage differentials virtually disappear. Among blacks the total wage differential is smaller but the differential due to the wage rate component almost doubles.

A number of conclusions can be drawn from these results. First, as to the question of whether suburban jobs are superior to those in the central city, the answer is no. The results reported in Table 10–7 do not show that suburban workers consistently received higher wages than central city workers, although CS commuters did receive higher wages than those who both lived and worked in the suburbs. This differential was found to reflect both productivity and wage rate factors. (If suburban jobs generally were better paid, the observed pattern should have been CS greater than or equal to SS, and SS greater than CC.) Second, the results clearly established the existence of a higher wage differential in favor of city-to-suburb commuters among blacks.

On the basis of these results a strong case can be made for the argument that black city-to-suburb commuting workers would reduce their journey-to-work costs by moving to the suburbs. If the total wage differentials in favor of black CS workers merely reflected higher wage rates, these workers would not be better off than their central city counterparts because of higher commuting costs. It is primarily because these workers have productivity skills that match the kinds of jobs available in the suburbs that a suburban residence is made more appealing. The persistence of the locational wage differentials among blacks (but not whites) implies that the residential mobility of black labor is less responsive to employment demands originating from different locations within the metropolitan area.

These results contrast sharply with those reported in my earlier study reported in Taeuber (1976). That earlier analysis yielded results clearly suggesting that suburban employment for blacks was economically superior to that available to them in the central city. A replication of that analysis using the 1960 and 1970 state samples indicates that the earlier observed differences were mainly a function of the composition of the sample. The 1970 neighborhood sample, although a national sample, was restricted to male heads aged between 21 and 60 of primary families only. The sample used in the analysis of this chapter, although restricted to those living in the most urbanized states, included heads over 16 years of age of all types of households.[4]

D. Components of Black–White Wage Differentials

A large black–white wage differential is observable in Table 10–7. In a further analysis the components of this differential were analyzed directly. Table 10–8 shows this analysis for the full male sample, and Table 10–9 shows it for the blue-collar sample. As the "Total" columns show, the black–white difference is smaller in 1969 than in 1959 but still substantial, and it is smaller for central city than for suburban residents in both periods. The differences are greatest for suburb-to-city commuters (SC) and least for reverse commuters (CS).

The component attributable to wage rates is substantial in all comparisons. Labor force characteristics account for more of this difference than wage rates among suburban residents, particularly for the suburb-to-city commuters. Note that the industry and occupation categories employed in this analysis are somewhat crude, and thus some workers may be similarly classified who are actually different in both skills and remuneration. Thus the higher racial differential for suburb-to-city commuters (SC) is probably due to racial differences in labor force characteristics.

Although the total wage differences between races are substantial, the patterns are not consistent with expectations. It had been expected that the

---

[4] The contrasting results from the two analyses raise the possibility of whether employers respond more favorably to married male heads of households than males in other marital status categories. The fact that the coefficient for the effect of being married is significant for virtually all of the race, time period, and residence–workplace regressions reported in Table 10–A1 (in the appendix to this chapter) clearly indicates that such a "favorability" bias may exist among employers. Employers may view married male heads of households as more dependable and as motivated to work more efficiently.

TABLE 10-8

Components of Black–White Wage Differentials, by Residence and Workplace: All Males, 1959 and 1969

Group	Log hourly wages		Differences (white minus black) attributable to:			
	Standard: whites	Comparison: blacks	Mean attributes	Wage rate	Interaction	Total
1959						
Live and work, central city (CC)	.9220	.5351	13.94	15.58	9.18	38.69
Live central city, work suburbs (CS)	.9832	.6482	13.27	15.52	4.71	33.51
Live suburbs, work central city (SC)	1.1150	.5524	30.32	19.78	6.16	56.26
Live and work, suburbs (SS)	.9159	.4650	23.02	14.41	7.65	45.08
1969						
Live and work, central city (CC)	1.0928	.7908	13.99	10.76	5.44	30.20
Live central city, work suburbs (CS)	1.1402	.8979	9.13	9.45	5.65	24.23
Live suburbs, work central city (SC)	1.2828	.8300	23.96	18.44	2.89	45.28
Live and work, suburbs (SS)	1.1411	.7548	17.54	14.51	6.59	38.64

TABLE 10-9

Components of Black–White Wage Differentials, by Residence and Workplace: Blue-Collar Males, 1959 and 1969

Group	Log hourly wages		Component differences (%)	
	Whites	Blacks	Wage rate	Total
1959				
Live and work, central city (CC)	.8375	.5094	15.35	32.81
Live central city, work suburbs (CS)	.9375	.6334	14.09	30.41
Live suburbs, work central city (SC)	.9899	.4991	22.27	49.07
Live and work, suburbs (SS)	.8143	.4472	16.39	36.71
1969				
Live and work, central city (CC)	.9635	.7452	10.74	21.82
Live central city, work suburbs (CS)	1.0313	.8811	8.05	15.02
Live suburbs, work central city (SC)	1.1365	.7421	20.64	39.44
Live and work, suburbs (SS)	1.0050	.7157	14.89	28.94

gap would narrow most in the suburbs because the most rapidly growing industries are in the suburbs. The error in this expectation is in the assumption that higher levels of employment growth would translate into greater opportunity for advancement, even among black workers. Apparently this is not the case. The general observed narrowing in 1969 of the black–white gap in hourly wage rates is due to increases in the wages of black workers who live and work in the central city. For black workers who live in the suburbs the narrowing appears to stem from an upgrading of productivity characteristics rather than from less wage rate discrimination. For black city-to-suburb commuters, both improvement in wage rates and productivity upgrading contributed to narrowing the black–white gap. These general observations do not change when only blue-collar workers are included in the analysis, as comparison of Tables 10–8 and 10–9 shows.

E. Summary

In summary, then, black workers can expect to earn substantially less than white workers, both for reasons of productivity characteristics and wage rates, regardless of where they live and work in the metropolitan area. While present data do not offer obvious explanations for these findings, there is strong evidence that a substantial portion of these differentials stem from labor market discrimination (Masters, 1975). This discrimination is reflected both in the level of achievement among black workers of highly paid productivity attributes and in wage rates (Cain, 1976). In the debate over whether working in the suburbs or both living and working in the suburbs offer advantages to black workers, the pervasiveness of labor market discrimination has usually been ignored. While black workers may improve their lot somewhat by commuting to the suburbs, they clearly will not do much to reduce the effects of discrimination by leaving the central city for either work or residence. Thus, eliminating barriers to black residence or workplace location, or both, is unlikely to effect a major reduction in the general black–white wage differential.

TABLE 10-A1

Determinants of Hourly Wages of Males Who Worked at Least Forty-Eight Weeks in 1959 and 1969, by Race, Time Period, Residence, and Workplace

| | Live central city, work— | | | | Live suburbs, work— | | | |
| | Central city | | Suburbs | | Central city | | Suburbs | |
Variable	Mean	Coefficient	Mean	Coefficient	Mean	Coefficient	Mean	Coefficient
				Total white sample, 1960				
Years of schooling	10.937	.0368	11.142	.0260	11.762	.0427	11.064	.0345
Class of worker								
Private	.752	.0696	.814	.3966	.809	.0017[a]	.720	.1779
Government	.126	.0687	.127	.3440	.092	-.1549	.118	.1069
Occupational status	42.965	.0056	41.401	.0053	48.400	.0047	40.695	.0057
Seniority	26.858	.0044	24.845	.0048	24.418	.0064	25.266	.0033
Work full-time	.881	-.2442	.936	-.1112	.899	-.2737	.909	-.2426
Head of household	.879	.2380	.887	.0783[a]	.931	.2250	.891	.2620
Married	.821	.1659	.841	.1233	.911	.1381	.867	.2592
Industry								
Construction	.054	.2354	.053	.3655	.061	.1298	.081	.6703
Durable manufacturing	.184	.1933	.365	.3446	.243	.0678[a]	.258	.6149
Nondurable manufacturing	.145	.1143	.152	.2679	.133	.0256[a]	.132	.5371
Transportation	.113	.1262	.080	.3215	.119	.0086[a]	.073	.5776
Retail-wholesale	.209	-.0526[a]	.126	.1487	.191	-.1102[a]	.165	.3431
Finance-business	.095	-.0298[a]	.050	.1789	.102	-.0986[a]	.063	.3993
Professional	.081	-.1105	.045	.2306	.069	-.0393[a]	.076	.3927
Public administration	.074	.0429[a]	.077	.2808	.057	.0631[a]	.062	.5110
Personal services	.029	-.2349	.022	.1242[a]	.013	-.3712	.023	.0757[a]
Region								
Pacific	.131	.1762	.260	.1188	.189	.1515	.208	.1609
East	.359	.0892	.245	-.0277[a]	.292	.1271	.400	.0850
North	.316	.1384	.324	.0819	.359	.1555	.268	.1414

Migration status								
Move same state								
Metropolitan	.026	−.0405ᵃ	.038	−.1008ᵃ	.108	.0608	.070	−.0239ᵃ
Nonmetropolitan	.020	−.1487	.021	−.0714ᵃ	.020	−.0511ᵃ	.022	−.1028
Move different state								
Metropolitan	.042	−.0572	.060	−.0536ᵃ	.070	.0166ᵃ	.052	−.0319ᵃ
Nonmetropolitan	.021	−.1195	.032	−.1730	.027	−.1224	.029	−.0763
Not applicable	.025	−.1648	.021	−.2420	.017	−.0705ᵃ	.019	−.0788ᵃ
Log hourly wages	.922		.983		1.115		.916	
Intercept		−.1682		−.3879		.0372		−.7275
R^2		.2232		.1830		.2144		.2815
Number of observations		15,867		2,070		7,780		11,656

Total white sample, 1970

Years of schooling	11.800	.0438	11.704	.0491	12.406	.0510	11.883	.0437
Class of worker								
Private	.726	.0101ᵃ	.811	−.0260ᵃ	.791	−.0345ᵃ	.729	.0646
Government	.159	.0049ᵃ	.116	−.1048ᵃ	.123	−.1401	.130	.0304ᵃ
Occupational status	44.393	.0059	42.075	.0044	48.704	.0049	42.684	.0061
Seniority	25.680	.0047	24.682	.0058	24.031	.0075	24.375	.0053
Work full-time	.845	−.2135	.872	−.2374	.860	−.2743	.867	−.2770
Head of household	.899	.2483	.902	.1868	.939	.3910	.908	.3755
Married	.806	.1566	.823	.1666	.900	.1474	.860	.1568
Industry								
Construction	.056	.1844	.072	.3556	.067	.2357	.076	.4986
Durable manufacturing	.164	.1107	.332	.2241	.227	.1284	.265	.4154
Nondurable manufacturing	.106	.0183ᵃ	.097	.1809	.115	.0942	.096	.2967
Transportation	.101	.0805	.074	.1736	.110	.1031	.075	.3528
Retail-wholesale	.211	−.1062	.180	.0398ᵃ	.183	−.0249ᵃ	.189	.1945
Finance-business	.117	−.0642ᵃ	.072	.0598ᵃ	.104	−.0160ᵃ	.071	.2212
Professional	.115	−.0797	.069	.1111ᵃ	.096	.0090ᵃ	.101	.2065
Public administration	.085	.0410ᵃ	.064	.2525	.068	.1365	.064	.3383
Personal services	.026	−.2385	.018	−.2342	.014	−.1107ᵃ	.015	.0121ᵃ
Region								
Pacific	.152	.1352	.233	.1141	.175	.0752	.193	.1271

TABLE 10-A1, continued

| | Live central city, work— | | | | Live suburbs, work— | | | |
| | Central city | | Suburbs | | Central city | | Suburbs | |
Variable	Mean	Coefficient	Mean	Coefficient	Mean	Coefficient	Mean	Coefficient
East	.304	.1156	.221	.0342[a]	.263	.0868	.341	.1014
North	.288	.1191	.356	.1098	.365	.1106	.324	.1443
Migration status								
Move same state								
Metropolitan	.056	−.0249[a]	.047	−.1059	.089	.0189[a]	.074	−.0070[a]
Nonmetropolitan	.020	−.1039	.022	−.1265	.018	−.1103	.018	−.0972
Move different state								
Metropolitan	.048	−.0526	.058	−.0039[a]	.067	.0184[a]	.056	−.0422
Nonmetropolitan	.021	−.0438[a]	.026	−.1012[a]	.020	−.0774	.023	−.0645
Not applicable	.053	−.0865	.046	−.0689[a]	.042	−.0579	.042	−.0485
Log hourly wages	1.093		1.140		1.283		1.141	
Intercept		−.0602		−.0493		−.1302		−.4511
R^2		.2283		.2684		.2867		.2848
Number of observations		14,012		3,089		9,800		15,459
Total black sample, 1960								
Years of schooling	8.992	.0219	8.774	.0043[a]	8.619	.0170	7.878	.0240
Class of worker								
Private	.775	.2820	.801	.4034	.748	−.0595[a]	.746	.3715
Government	.185	.4108	.185	.3375	.210	.0023[a]	.198	.4456
Occupational status	22.556	.0030	20.032	.0042	22.215	.0033	18.939	.0027
Seniority	26.536	.0021	25.583	.0039	26.162	.0012[a]	28.270	−.0001[a]
Work full-time	.900	−.3191	.923	−.3516	.918	−.3918	.870	−.3578
Head of household	.827	.1313	.858	.0903[a]	.846	.0894[a]	.816	.2003
Married	.771	.1081	.818	.1050	.843	.1386	.814	.1962
Industry								
Construction	.060	.2924	.068	.2198	.079	.2018[a]	.082	.5740

Nondurable manufacturing	.124	.2755	.132	.2780	.124	.3901	.113	.6467
Transportation	.123	.3161	.060	.3021	.126	.3299	.086	.6023
Retail-wholesale	.193	.0905	.122	.1485[a]	.205	.0961[a]	.114	.3330
Finance-business	.073	.0828	.040	.0440[a]	.052	.1093[a]	.042	.2937
Professional	.078	.0550[a]	.069	.2943	.086	.1788[a]	.092	.3879
Public administration	.101	.2457	.110	.4655	.115	.3259	.084	.5645
Personal services	.064	−.0850	.044	−.0343[a]	.039	−.2127[a]	.068	.2208
Region								
Pacific	.069	.3201	.146	.2858	.178	.3043	.119	.3994
East	.292	.2357	.239	.2351	.119	.3774	.318	.3079
North	.298	.2783	.294	.2890	.142	.2787	.174	.3631
Migration status								
Move same state								
Metropolitan	.009	−.0583[a]	.022	−.0067[a]	.061	.0574[a]	.039	.0350[a]
Nonmetropolitan	.013	−.1116	.009	.0240[a]	.014	−.2111[a]	.023	−.0318[a]
Move different state								
Metropolitan	.026	−.0503[a]	.039	−.0660[a]	.034	−.1377[a]	.037	−.0293[a]
Nonmetropolitan	.026	−.1388	.038	−.3686	.016	−.1906[a]	.031	.0973[a]
Not applicable	.015	−.0835[a]	.020	−.1571[a]	.006	−.1150[a]	.016	−.1834[a]
Log hourly wages	.535		.648		.552		.465	
Intercept		−.3495		−.2500		.1537		−.8241
R^2	.2570		.3195		.3531		.3965	
Number of observations	8,869		947		619		1,439	
Total black sample, 1970								
Years of schooling	10.186	.0299	10.194	.0238	10.381	.0266	9.761	.0334
Class of worker								
Private	.733	.1119	.842	.0124[a]	.690	−.3194	.756	.1310
Government	.224	.1601	.146	.1007[a]	.265	−.3254	.190	.1560
Occupational status	27.152	.0047	25.094	.0040	28.548	.0043	25.169	.0037
Seniority	25.182	.0039	24.952	.0028	25.027	.0008[a]	26.469	.0018[a]
Work full-time	.868	−.3369	.869	−.3989	.882	−.4249	.877	−.3115
Head of household	.865	.2139	.884	.1712	.872	.2654	.867	.3202

TABLE 10-A1, continued

Variable	Live central city, work—				Live suburbs, work—			
	Central city		Suburbs		Central city		Suburbs	
	Mean	Coefficient	Mean	Coefficient	Mean	Coefficient	Mean	Coefficient
Married	.758	.0757	.780	.0815	.845	.1103[a]	.793	.1164
Industry								
Construction	.055	.2830	.064	.2505	.067	.4239	.079	.2966
Durable manufacturing	.185	.3570	.423	.3022	.193	.3875	.252	.3266
Nondurable manufacturing	.108	.2608	.107	.1835	.106	.3976	.106	.2735
Transportation	.126	.2805	.071	.1507[a]	.121	.3335	.092	.1946
Retail-wholesale	.171	.1196	.116	.0598[a]	.159	.1886[a]	.147	.1031[a]
Finance-business	.083	.1476	.045	−.0223[a]	.068	.3562	.053	.1006[a]
Professional	.107	.1388	.054	−.0227[a]	.107	.3747	.099	.1073[a]
Public administratiin	.105	.2903	.071	−.0325[a]	.139	.4572	.077	.2690
Personal services	.044	−.0456[a]	.028	−.1878[a]	.021	−.0890[a]	.035	.0845[a]
Region								
Pacific	.079	.2057	.124	.2298	.192	.2567	.138	.1761
East	.294	.2425	.188	.1701	.161	.1707	.327	.2274
North	.312	.2577	.452	.2478	.213	.3014	.205	.2065
Migration status								
Move same state								
Metropolitan	.032	−.0310[a]	.018	.1538[a]	.087	−.0315[a]	.050	.1229
Nonmetropolitan	.009	−.0314[a]	.011	−.2862	.010	.1960[a]	.007	−.5574
Move different state								
Metropolitan	.034	−.0559[a]	.035	−.0652[a]	.044	−.0344[a]	.043	−.1430
Nonmetropolitan	.019	−.0592[a]	.030	−.0988[a]	.017	.0108[a]	.019	−.0348[a]
Not applicable	.063	−.0503	.055	−.0806[a]	.040	−.2479	.049	.0014[a]
Log hourly wages	.791		.898		.830		.755	
Intercept		−.1912		.2567		.2964		−.2825
R^2		.2074		.2042		.3032		.2212
Number of observations		9,637		2,154		998		1,927

[a] Indicates that regression coefficient is not twice the size of its standard error.

184

11

Alternatives for the Improvement of Black Residential Consumption and Employment

In this chapter I will discuss the relevance of the various results reported in this monograph for policy on the residential environment and employment situation of black metropolitan families. The complexity of the issues involved and the dynamic nature of residential markets make the formulation of policies designed to improve the socioeconomic well-being of blacks a rather risky venture. Proposals that are designed to provide input into the formulation of public policies should be based on empirically demonstrated generalizations that specify: (*a*) the factors thought to be responsible for the genesis and continued existence of a given condition; (*b*) the particular manner in which such factors operate individually or jointly to produce the condition; and (*c*) the costs and benefits associated with manipulating one or all of the factors in order to produce the desired improvement. Results of the enormous amount of research that has been directed toward sorting out the factors influencing residential consumption in metropolitan areas provide the point of departure for examining those aspects of employment and residential consumption that would require change in order to improve the socioeconomic well-being of the black population.

The initial discussion in this monograph of factors that influence the demand for residential services was based on the proposition that in a competitive housing market the quantity of residential services consumed by the average family is determined by their ability to pay and by their preferences. However, when the attempt was made to account for race differentials in residential consumption, the choice model developed for white residential consumption (which was based on income and preference factors) was found to be inadequate. The results reported in Chapter 7 indicate that a significant portion of the large differential between blacks and whites in tenure status and quantity of residential services consumed cannot be accounted for by differences in income and preference indicators. More specifically, a very substantial portion of the effects captured by the coefficient for race reflects the influence of housing market discrimination. Thus the conditions under which black families acquire residential services tend to be shaped by forces over which they have no direct control.

These kinds of results naturally lead to suggestions that the residential environment of black families could be significantly improved if: (a) current antidiscrimination statutes were more stringently enforced, thereby opening up a broader range of housing to blacks, particularly in the newer areas of central cities and in the suburbs; (b) white prejudices and fears were reduced by educational programs designed to alleviate anxieties that whites tend to associate with having a black neighbor; and (c) blacks were encouraged to seek housing outside of the ghetto, particularly in the outlying sections of metropolitan areas. These recommendations are consistent with proposals to increase the representation of blacks in the suburbs (see Downs, 1973; Hermalin and Farley, 1973; Glazer, 1974; Harrison, 1974a; Sternlieb and Lake, 1975). The presumption is that increased suburban residence by blacks would have the effect of simultaneously reducing existing levels of residential segregation, upgrading the residential environment inhabited by black households, and affording blacks greater access to employment opportunities and higher quality public schools for their children.

Previous chapters that included discussions of blacks focused primarily on their housing and employment experiences as reflected in the 1970 Census data. In this chapter an effort is made to integrate previous discussions with an analysis of post-1960 trends to determine whether significant changes have occurred in the residential concentration of blacks in metropolitan areas. A focus on the experience of blacks during the 1970s will provide a better indication of the extent of progress blacks have made in upgrading their housing environment. During the 1960s, blacks made significant progress in upgrading their socioeconomic standing, particularly among the young and college graduates (see Featherman and Hauser, 1978). In addition, the Civil Rights Act of 1968 explicitly prohibits racial discrimination in the sale and rental of housing. The impact of these events on the housing environment of blacks would not have been visible to any significant extent in the 1970 Census.

Unfortunately, very little information is available regarding locational shifts in the black population since 1970, except for the few central cities that have conducted special censuses. The annual *Current Population Report* series and the 1974–1975 *Annual Housing Survey* for metropolitan areas provide relevant information on trends in the concentration of blacks between central cities and suburbs. I make use of this information to evaluate trends in the redistribution of the black population within metropolitan areas. While an exclusive focus on the city–suburb differential can provide only a crude estimate of the concentration or decentralization of blacks, it does have the advantage of highlighting changes in the size of the black population in a geographical area (e.g., the suburbs) in which their representation has been extraordinarily low—so low, in fact, that significant increases in the representation of blacks would certainly signal a reversal in a long-established trend.

The discussion that follows seeks to answer two questions. First, what has been the extent of suburbanization among the black population? Second, do post-1960 trends in the suburbanization of the black population provide any indication of a substantial change in the residential concentration of blacks within metropolitan areas? One useful way to address these questions would be to focus on trends in residential mobility. It can be suggested that improved economic standing and efforts to reduce racial discrimination in housing should lead to reduced levels of black concentration in central city ghetto areas, as well as an increasing movement of blacks to the suburbs.

I. BLACK SUBURBANIZATION

A. Post-1960 Trends in Black Suburbanization

In 1977 approximately 4.6 million blacks lived in the suburbs, which represents a 35% increase since 1970 (see Table 11–1). In addition, the average annual rate of growth of the black suburban population almost doubled during the 1970–1977 period, up 1.9% from the 2.3% rate that prevailed during the 1960s. The 4.2% annual rate of growth is substantially higher than the .9% rate observed for blacks in central cities and the 1.3% rate of the white suburban population.

The substantial increase in the black suburban population is due primarily to increased net in-migration. Table 11–2 provides estimates of the black suburban population by migration status for two recent periods. There, it can be noted that the number of in-migrants 2 years of age and over during the 1975–1977 period is greater than the number 4 years of age and over who migrated during the 1970–1974 period. It can also be noted that 56% of the in-migrants were former residents of central cities during both time periods. Thus these trends document a substantial increase in the suburban population due primary to an increase in the volume of movement of blacks from central cities to suburbs.

TABLE 11-1

Black Population of the United States by Place of Residence: 1960–1977

Residence	Total black population 1977 (1,000s)	Percentage of total U.S. population			Average annual percentage change	
		1960	1970	1977	1960–1970	1970–1977
Total U.S.	24,472	10.6	11.1	11.6	1.8	1.5
Metropolitan	18,354	10.7	11.9	12.8	2.7	1.7
Central cities	13,737	16.4	20.5	22.8	2.9	.9
Suburbs	4,617	4.8	4.6	5.6	2.3	4.2
Nonmetropolitan	6,118	10.3	9.1	8.9	− .5	1.0

Source: Current Population Reports, Series P-20, No. 324, April 1978, Table 18.

Information available from the 1974–1975 *Annual Housing Survey* for selected metropolitan areas provides some indication as to the characteristics of blacks moving to the suburbs and the major reasons they give for so moving. Movement to the suburbs among blacks appears to be dominated by young heads of households with higher income levels. Table 11–3 presents the distribution of black heads of households by age, household income, residence, and mobility status. Black residents of suburbs and in-migrants to suburbs are younger than residents of central cities. In addition, city-to-suburb movers have higher levels of income than all central city and suburban residents. For example, among city-to-suburb movers, 32% have incomes of $15,000 or more, in contrast to 20% of central city residents and 28% of all suburban residents. It appears that the status selectivity of

TABLE 11-2

Black Suburban Population by Migration Status: 1970–1974 and 1975–1977

Residence	Population 4 years of age and over		Population 2 years of age and over	
	1974	1970–1974	1977	1975–1977
SMSA				
Total (1,000s)	15,373		17,373	
Percentage in suburbs	22.6		25.4	
In-migrants to suburbs				
Total (1,000s)		834		861[a]
Percentage from central city		56.7		55.9
Percentage in-migrants to SMSA living in suburbs		33.2		39.3

Source: Current Population Reports, Series P-23, No. 55, 1975, Tables G. and H. *Current Population Reports*, Series P-20, No. 320, 1978, Table 39.

[a] This estimate does not include migrants from abroad.

TABLE 11-3

Distribution of Black Heads of Households by Age, Total Household Income, and Mobility Status: 1974–1975

	Central city		Suburbs			
					Migrant	
Variables	Total (%)	Moved from outside SMSA (%)	Total (%)	Moved from central city (%)	Moved from outside SMSA (%)	Migrants from central city (%)
Age						
Under 30 years	22.8	68.6	24.3	49.3	62.1	65.2
30–44 years	30.5	20.0	33.4	36.9	23.3	78.9
45–64 years	32.9	10.4	31.4	12.9	12.0	71.7
65 years +	13.8	1.1	10.9	0.9	2.7	43.4
Income						
Under $6,000	42.8	55.7	31.2	21.8	32.2	61.4
$ 6,000– 9,999	20.1	18.0	20.6	20.6	27.0	64.1
$10,000–14,999	17.7	9.9	20.6	25.9	17.4	77.8
$15,000–19,999	9.2	8.5	12.0	11.7	9.9	73.5
$20,000–29,999	7.8	5.5	11.5	16.4	9.3	80.6
$30,000 +	2.5	2.4	4.2	3.6	4.2	67.2
Percentage of total population	78.6	1.0	21.4	1.4	.6	NA

city-to-suburban movers among blacks is increasing at a time when it is decreasing among whites (see Farley, 1976). An important question raised by these data is whether the income selectivity of suburban in-migrants will eventually lead to a widening of the socioeconomic status difference between blacks in central cities and suburban areas.

Table 11–4 reports the percentage of blacks giving main reasons for moving from the central city to the suburbs between 1974 and 1975 by age of head, number of children, and household income. Excluding the "others" category, the main reasons given for moving are ranked housing, family, neighborhood, and employment, in that order. While housing clearly stands out as the major reason given for moving, the percentage so indicating varies positively with age, the presence of children, and level of household income. Not surprisingly, the ranking of main reasons for moving among city-to-suburb black movers is essentially no different from that reported for whites in Chapter 6 (and, I might add, no different from those reported by blacks moving within central cities).

An important question raised by the data presented in Tables 11–1 through 11–4 is whether or not blacks are moving into the suburbs in a segregated pattern or are dispersing among the white population. The latter pattern would suggest reduced discrimination and a widening of the opportunities available to blacks in housing. The suburbanization of blacks in individual metropolitan areas during the 1960s varied substantially (see Farley, 1976) and probably represented different kinds of residence patterns. Connolly (1973) and Rose (1976) report that a significant amount of the suburbanization of blacks in such areas as Los Angeles, Cleveland, St. Louis, Chicago, and Philadelphia represented either the expansion of central city areas or increases in the black population of suburban areas that already had black residents. A definitive answer to this question must await the publication of the 1980 Census. However, this author would be surprised if the current rate of suburbanization among blacks does not lead to greater interracial mixing in neighborhoods.

Regardless of the locational character of black suburbanization, it would be of interest to know whether moving to the suburbs represents an upgrading of housing standards. Table 11–5 presents data that relate directly to this question. The data pertain to the characteristics of housing occupied by black households with respect to residence and mobility status. First, it is quite evident that black suburbanites fare better in terms of acquiring home ownership status and in terms of living in newer and better quality housing than black residents of central cities. Second, black in-migrants to and within suburban areas (particularly those from the central city) are substantially more likely to upgrade their housing situation than movers within and to central cities. The observed differences between residents of central cities and suburbs, with respect to age and value of dwelling and gross rent, are

TABLE 11-4

Percentage of Black Households Giving Main Reasons for Moving from the Central City to the Suburbs: 1974–1975[a]

Variables	Employment	Family	Housing	Neighborhood	Schools	Others	Not answered	Percentage of total
Age of head								
Under 30 years	3.89	36.1	35.1	5.7	.0	15.8	3.4	46.9
30–44 years	8.6	9.1	47.1	15.2	4.3	14.5	1.1	39.5
45 years +	10.5	3.4	44.3	14.1	.0	21.9	5.9	13.6
Number of children								
No children	9.6	28.5	31.0	8.8	2.1	16.8	3.2	39.0
One or more children under 18 years	4.7	16.2	47.5	11.8	1.5	15.7	2.6	61.0
Household income								
Under $6,000	5.7	25.8	23.5	13.0	3.3	22.6	6.3	25.1
$ 6,000– 9,999	4.1	22.2	41.4	14.9	.0	13.5	3.9	20.4
$10,000–14,999	9.2	12.7	43.7	11.1	2.1	21.3	.0	19.4
$15,000–19,999	6.3	26.4	52.8	2.5	.0	12.0	.0	17.9
$20,000 +	8.7	16.2	51.5	10.1	2.8	8.3	2.5	17.1

[a] The SMSAs included in the tabulations are Minneapolis-St. Paul, Newark, Phoenix, Pittsburgh, Boston, Detroit, Anaheim, Albany, Dallas, Fort Worth, Los Angeles, Washington, D.C. See footnote to Table 6-2 for definition of categories of reasons for moving.

TABLE 11-5
Characteristics of Housing Occupied by Black Households in Selected SMSAs, by Residence and Mobility Status: 1974–1975[a]

Variables	Central city				Suburbs			
	Moved within central city	Moved from suburbs	Moved from outside SMSA	Nonmovers	Moved within suburbs	Moved from central city	Moved from outside SMSA	Nonmovers
Year structure built	1946	1948	1948	1943	1954	1955	1956	1949
Percentage of owner households	13.2	14.8	4.1	43.8	20.3	30.8	10.4	55.1
Value of property (owners)	$19,789	$25,069	$22,467	$19,609	$31,994	$32,220	$37,380	$26,285
Monthly gross rent	$173	$162	$134	$265	$325	$383	$318	$343
Total observations	1,663	103	133	8,728	273	175	83	1,636

[a] See footnote to Table 11-4 for list of SMSAs included in sample. All mean values are derived from a weighted sample.

192

simply too sharp to support the notion that movement to the suburbs among blacks represents mainly spillover effects.

By way of summary, it can be suggested that the results from the post-1960 sources give far greater cause for optimism than the results derived from the 1970 Census data suggest, at least with respect to future prospects for blacks upgrading their housing situation. One can speculate that the post-1960 trends in black suburbanization and housing are a twin result of the improved economic standing noted during the latter half of the 1960 decade and reductions in the extent of racial discrimination in housing brought on largely by the implementation of fair housing laws. I should point out, however, that the recent gains made by blacks, particularly those who have taken up residence in suburban areas, should not be used to argue that no further public policy initiatives are warranted. Blacks still have quite a distance to go before they reach parity with whites with respect to the character of their housing environment.

B. Black Suburbanization and Employment Opportunities

Increased suburban residence has been advanced as a possible solution not only to improving the residential environment of black households, but also as a means of providing greater access to employment opportunities. For example, some writers have maintained that the residential concentration of blacks in the core areas of central cities is in itself a major obstacle to improving their income-generating potential (Downs, 1973; Harrison, 1974b; von Furstenberg et al., 1974). In this view, the relatively stable residential distribution of blacks in the face of decentralization of economic activity contributes to high black unemployment, low black wages relative to skills, and high journey-to-work costs for blacks. Thus, it is argued, a major policy goal should be that of eliminating barriers that restrict black access to suburban housing where employment opportunity is growing.

As described in Chapters 9 and 10, recent studies have failed to support this view, concluding instead that black wages and unemployment levels are insensitive to residential location. Furthermore, James (1976) could find no evidence indicating an abundance of unfilled jobs in the suburbs. Thus it is unlikely that the suburban labor market would be able to accommodate all central city blacks seeking higher paying jobs in the suburbs. Indeed, as Harrison (1974b) noted, if all of the jobs currently held by white suburb-to-city commuters were vacated, there would be more jobs than blacks to fill them in the central city.

During the 1960s, the decentralization of employment paralleled rather closely the suburbanization of the white labor force, but approximately one-third of the labor force commutes to central city jobs, which suggests that there may be no cause and effect relationship between the co-occurring suburbanization of employment and white residence patterns. White workers' commuting, rather, shows the primacy of residential location factors in their decision making. In contrast, black workers' commuting seems to reflect *lack* of residential choice. Black workers (particularly blue collar) responded to the decentralization of employment by becoming city-to-suburb commuters but continued on as central city residents because their access to suburban housing was limited. The financial costs of commuting impose a relatively great burden on black workers, given the black–white wage gap, because these costs reduce their net take-home pay.

Results reported in this monograph do not directly bear on the issue of whether the decentralization of economic activities has increased black unemployment in the central city. They do, however, indicate that the wages paid to black central city workers are not substantially lower than suburban workers possessing equal skills. The higher wage level found for black suburban workers is associated with commuting from the central city and, in 1969, high black productivity accounts for somewhat more of the observed difference between central city and suburban workers than wage rate per se. Thus the average black who both lives and works in the central city would probably earn little more in wages by taking a suburban job, unless he or she upgraded his or her skills. However, the black central city resident who commutes to a suburban workplace would probably benefit financially from establishing residence in the suburbs, thereby cutting commuting costs. The problem in making such a move is that these city-to-suburb commuters may not earn enough to purchase housing in the suburbs, even if they found housing available to them (see Sternlieb and Lake, 1975).

While post-1970 trends in residential mobility do document an upsurge in the rate at which blacks are moving to the suburbs, it must be emphasized that suburban residence per se may not mean improved economic opportunity for blacks. Results reported in Chapter 6 and in the last section clearly indicate the primacy of housing and neighborhood over employment in residential decision making. The higher wages observed for suburb-to-city commuters, regardless of racial background, is certainly consistent with the point of view that economic opportunity leads to suburban residence rather than the reverse (see Tables 10–7 and 10–8). Eliminating barriers to black residence in the suburbs would probably have little or no effect on black–white wage differentials, since these differences stem from forces inherent in the labor market—such as racial discrimination. Thus residential decentralization for blacks would seem to be, on the whole, of dubious economic benefit to them.

I have already noted that differential treatment of blacks is a phenomenon that permeates the entire opportunity and reward structure of American society. Racial discrimination is one institutional sphere that does not occur in a vacuum, but is associated with and supported by discrimination in other institutional spheres. Labor market discrimination, for example, has an indirect but substantial effect on black consumption patterns, since it directly affects the amount of financial resources blacks bring to housing markets.

The wage differentials reported in Chapter 10 indicate that some significant progress toward racial parity was made during the 1960s, but the gap separating the income levels of black and white primary families remains substantial. (For example, in 1970 the average income of a white primary family of four was approximately $12,200, whereas that of blacks was approximately $8000—a difference of over $4000.) Further reductions in the income gap will depend on whether further reductions in labor market discrimination are made and whether there is a further upgrading of the marketable skills of blacks. Continued progress in these two areas would have a substantial impact on the residential consumption patterns of black households because of the potential each has for increasing average black wages.

References

Aaron, H.
   1970   Income taxes and housing. *American Economic Review* 60:791–793.

Aldrich, H.
   1974   Comment on Straszheim's racial discrimination in the urban housing market and its effects on black housing consumption. Pp. 185–188 in G. M. von Furstenberg, B. Harrison, and A. Horowitz (eds.), *Patterns of racial discrimination*. Vol. I: *Housing*. Lexington, Mass.: D. C. Heath and Company.

Alonso, W.
   1964a   *Location and land use: Toward a general theory of land rent*. Cambridge, Mass.: Harvard University Press.

Alonso, W.
   1964b   The historic and structural theories of urban form: Their implications for urban renewal. *Journal of Land Economics* 40:227–231.

Alwin, D. F. and Hauser, R. M.
   1975   The decomposition of effects in path analysis. *American Sociological Review* 40:37–47.

Apps, P. F.
   1973a   An approach to urban modelling and evaluation, a residential model: 1. Theory. *Environment and Planning A* 5:619–632.

Apps, P. F.
   1973b   An approach to urban modelling and evaluation, a residential model: 2. Implicit prices for housing services. *Environment and Planning B* 5:705–717.

Apps, P. F.
   1974   An approach to urban modelling and evaluation, a residential model: 3. Demand equations for housing services. *Environment and Planning A* 6:11–31.

Beesley, M. E.
  1965   The value of time spent in travelling: Some new evidence. *Economica 37*:174–185.
Beresford, J. C. and Rivlin, A. M.
  1964   Characteristics of other families. *Demography 1*:242–246.
Berry, B. J. L. and Cohen, Y. S.
  1973   Decentralization of commerce and industry: The restructuring of metropolitan
          America. Pp. 431–455 in L. H. Masotti and J. K. Hadden (eds.), *The urbanization of
          the suburbs*. Beverly Hills, Calif.: Sage Publications.
Berry, B. J. L. and Horton, F. E.
  1970   *Geographic perspectives in urban systems*. Englewood Cliffs, N.J.: Prentice-Hall.
Berry, B. J. L. and Rees, P. H.
  1969   The factorial ecology of Calcutta. *American Journal of Sociology 74*:445–491.
Bahl, R. W.
  1972   Metropolitan fiscal structures and the distribution of population within metropolitan
          areas, Part III. Pp. 423–440 in *U.S. Commission on Population Growth and the
          American Future*. Vol. 5. *Population distribution and policy*. Washington, D.C.: U.S.
          Government Printing Office.
Burt, R. S.
  1973   Confirmatory factor-analytic structures and the theory construction process. *Sociolog-
          ical Methods and Research 2*:131–190.
Butler, E. W. and Kaiser, E. J.
  1971   Prediction of residential movement and spatial allocation. *Urban Affairs Quarterly
          6*:477–494.
Cain, G. G.
  1976   The challenge of segmented labor market theories to orthodox theory. *Journal of
          Economic Literature*, December, 1215–1257.
Carroll, D. J., Jr.
  1949   Some aspects of the home–work relationships of industrial workers. *Land Economics
          25*:414–422.
Christian, C.
  1975   Emerging patterns of industrial activity within large metropolitan areas and their
          impact on the central city work force. Pp. 213–246 in G. Gappert and H. Rose (eds.),
          Urban affairs annual review. Vol. 9. *The social economy of cities*. Beverly Hills,
          Calif.: Sage Publications.
Clemente, F. and Summers, G. F.
  1975   The journey to work of rural industrial employees. *Social Forces 54*:212–219.
Colasanto, D. L.
  1977   The prospects for racial integration in neighborhoods: An analysis of residential
          preference in the Detroit metropolitan area. Unpublished doctoral dissertation, De-
          partment of Sociology, University of Michigan, Ann Arbor.
Connolly, H. X.
  1973   Black movement into the suburbs: Suburbs doubling their black populations during the
          1960s. *Urban Affairs Quarterly 9*:91–111.
Danziger, S. and Weinstein, M.
  1975   Employment locations and wage rates of poverty-area residents. *Institute for Research
          on Poverty Discussion Paper 243–75*. Madison: University of Wisconsin.
Darrock, G. A. and Winsborough, H. H.
  1972   Urban accessibility and residential densities: The impact of relative centrality and the
          journey to work. *The Center for Demography and Ecology Working Paper 72–2*.
          Madison: University of Wisconsin.

David, M. H.
1962 *Family composition and consumption.* Amsterdam: North Holland Publishing Company.

de Leeuw, F.
1971 The demand for housing: A review of cross-section evidence. *Review of Economics and Statistics 53:*1–10.

de Leeuw, F.
1973 The distribution of housing services. *The Urban Institute Working Paper 208/6.* Washington, D.C.: The Urban Institute.

de Leeuw, F. and Ekanem, N. F.
1971 The supply of rental housing. *The American Economic Review 61:*806–817.

de Leeuw, F., Schnare, A. B., and Struyk, R. J.
1976 Housing. Pp. 119–178 in W. Gorham and N. Glazer (eds.), *The urban predicament.* Washington, D.C.: The Urban Institute.

Downs, A.
1973 *Opening up the suburbs.* New Haven: Yale University Press.

Duncan, B.
1956 Factors in work–residence separation: Wage and salary workers, Chicago, 1951. *American Sociological Review 31:*48–63.

Duncan, B. and Duncan, O. D.
1970 The measurement of intra-city vocational and residential patterns. Pp. 243–255 in A. N. Page and W. R. Seyfried (eds.), *Urban analysis.* Glenview, Ill.: Scott, Foresman and Company.

Duncan, B. and Hauser, P. M.
1960 *Housing a metropolis.* Glencoe, Ill.: The Free Press.

Duncan, O. D.
1966 Path analysis: Sociological examples. *American Journal of Sociology 72:*1–16.

Duncan, O. D. and Duncan, B.
1955 Residential distribution and occupational stratification. *American Journal of Sociology 60:*483–503.

Erbe, B. M.
1975 Race and socioeconomic segregation. *American Sociological Review 40:*801–812.

Farley, R.
1976 Components of suburban population growth. Pp. 3–38 in B. Schwartz (ed.), *The changing face of the suburbs.* Chicago: University of Chicago Press.

Farley, R.
1977 Residential segregation in urbanized areas of the United States in 1970: An analysis of social class and racial differences. *Demography 14:*497–518.

Feagin, J. R. and Feagin, C. B.
1978 *Discrimination American style.* Englewood Cliffs, N.J.: Prentice-Hall.

Featherman, D. and Hauser, R. M.
1978 *Opportunity and change.* New York: Academic Press.

Featherman, D., Sobel, M., and Dickens, D.
1975 A manual for coding occupations and industries into detailed 1970 categories and a listing of 1970-basis Duncan socioeconomic and NORC prestige scores. *The Center for Demography and Ecology Working Paper 75–*1. Madison: University of Wisconsin.

Foley, D.
1973 Institutional and contextual factors affecting the housing choices of minority residents. Pp. 85–147 in A. H. Hawley and V. P. Rock (eds.), *Segregation in urban residential areas.* Washington, D.C.: National Academy of Sciences.

Foote, N., Abu-Lughal, J., Foley, M. M., and Winnick, L. (eds.)
  1960   *Housing choices and housing constraints.* New York: McGraw-Hill.
Freedman, D.
  1963   The relation of economic status to fertility. *American Economic Review 53*:414–426.
Gans, H. J.
  1962   Urbanism and suburbanism as ways of life: A reevaluation of definitions. In A. M.
         Rose (ed.), *Human behavior and social processes.* Boston: Houghton Mifflin.
Gans, H. J.
  1967   *The Levittowners.* New York: Random House.
Geisman, L. L.
  1973   *555 families.* New Brunswick, N.J.: Transaction Books.
Glazer, N.
  1974   On "opening up" the suburbs. *The Public Interest 37*:89–111.
Glenn, N.
  1973   Suburbanization in the United States since World War II. Pp. 51–78 in L. H. Masotti
         and J. K. Hadden (eds.), *The urbanization of the suburbs.* Beverly Hills, Calif.: Sage
         Publications.
Glick, P.
  1957   *American families.* New York: John Wiley.
Gold, N. N.
  1972   The mismatch of jobs and low-income people in metropolitan areas and its implications
         for the central city poor. In S. M. Mazie (ed.), *Population, distribution, and policy.*
         Vol. 5 of U.S. Commission on Population Growth and the American Future, Commis-
         sion Research Reports. Washington, D.C.: U.S. Government Printing Office.
Goldberg, M. A.
  1970   Transportation, urban land values, and rents: A synthesis. *Land Economics 46*:153–
         162.
Goodman, J.
  1974   Local residential mobility and family housing adjustments. Pp. 79–105 in J. N. Morgan
         (ed.), *Five thousand American families–Patterns of economic progress.* Vol. II. Ann
         Arbor: Institute for Social Research, University of Michigan.
Goodman, L. A.
  1972   A modified multiple regression approach to the analysis of dichotomous variables.
         American Sociological Review 37:28–46.
Greenbee, B. B.
  1969   New house or new neighborhood? A survey of priorities among home owners in
         Madison, Wisconsin. *Land Economics 45*:359–365.
Greer, A. L. and Greer, S.
  1976   Suburban political behavior: A matter of trust. Pp. 203–220 in B. Schwartz (ed.), *The
         changing face of the suburbs.* Chicago: University of Chicago Press.
Guest, A. M.
  1970   Families and housing in cities. Unpublished doctoral dissertation, University of Wis-
         consin, Madison.
Guest, A. M.
  1971   Retesting the Burgess zonal hypothesis: The location of white-collar workers. *Ameri-
         can Journal of Sociology 76*:1084–1093.
Guest, A. M.
  1972   Patterns of family location. *Demography 9*:159–172.
Guest, A. M.
  1975   Population suburbanization in American metropolitan areas, 1940–1970. *Geographic
         Analysis 7*:267–283.

Guest, A. M. and Weed, J. A.
    1977   Ethnic residential segregation: Patterns of change. *American Journal of Sociology*
           81:1088–1111.
Harris, B.
    1968   Quantitative models of urban development: Their role in metropolitan policy-making.
           In H. S. Perloff and L. Wingo, Jr. (eds.), *Issues in urban economics*. Baltimore: Johns
           Hopkins Press.
Harrison, B.
    1974a Ghetto economic development. *Journal of Economic Literature,* March, 1–37.
Harrison, B.
    1974b *Urban economic development*. Washington, D.C.: The Urban Institute.
Harvey, D.
    1972   *Society, the city, and the space-economy of urbanism*. Washington, D.C.:Association
           of American Geographers, Resource Paper 18.
Hawley, A.
    1950   *Human ecology: A theory of community structure*. New York: Roland Press.
Hawley, A.
    1971   *Urban society: An ecological approach*. New York: Roland Press.
Hermalin, A. I. and Farley, R.
    1973   The potential for residential integration in cities and suburbs: Implications for the
           busing controversy. *American Sociological Review 38*:595–610.
Hoover, E. M.
    1968   The evolving form and organization of the metropolis. Pp. 237–284 in H. S. Perloff and
           L. Wingo, Jr. (eds.), *Issues in urban economics*. Baltimore: The Johns Hopkins Press.
Hughes, J. W.
    1975   Dilemmas of suburbanization and growth controls. *The Annals 422*:61–76.
Hunter, A.
    1975   The loss of community: An empirical test through replication. *American Sociological*
           Review 40:537–552.
James, F. J.
    1976   Recession and recovery in urban economics: A summary of recent evidence. *An*
           Urban Institute Paper. Washington, D.C.: The Urban Institute.
Johnston, R. J.
    1971   *Urban residential patterns*. New York: Praeger.
Jöreskog, K. G.
    1973   A general method for estimating a linear structural equation system. Pp. 85–102 in A.
           S. Goldberger and O. D. Duncan (eds.), *Structural equation models in the social*
           sciences. New York: Seminar Press.
Kain, J. F.
    1968   Urban travel behavior. Pp. 161–192 in L. F. Schnore (ed.), *Social science and the city*:
           A survey of urban research. New York: Praeger.
Kain, J. F.
    1970   The journey-to-work as a determinant of residential location. Pp. 207–226 in A. N.
           Page and W. R. Seyfried (eds.), *Urban analysis*. Glenview, Ill.: Scott, Foresman and
           Company.
Kain, J. F. and Quigley, J. M.
    1970   Measuring the value of housing quality. *Journal of the American Statistical Associa-*
           tion 65:532–548.
Kain, J. F. and Quigley, J. M.
    1972   Housing market discrimination, home ownership, and savings behavior. *The American*
           Economic Review 62:263–277.

Kain, J. F. and Quigley, J. M.
  1975   *Housing markets and racial discrimination: Microeconomic analysis.* New York: National Bureau of Economic Research.
Kasarda, J. D.
  1976   The changing occupational structure of the American metropolis: Apropos the urban problem. Pp. 113–136 in B. Schwartz (ed.), *The changing face of the suburbs.* Chicago: University of Chicago Press.
Katzman, M. T.
  1977   *The quality of municipal services, central city decline, and middle class flight.* Boston: Department of City and Regional Planning, Harvard University.
Kaufman, I. R. and Schnore, L. F.
  1974   Municipal annexations and suburbanization: 1960–1970 *The Center for Demography and Ecology Working Paper 75–4.* Madison: University of Wisconsin.
Keller, S.
  1968   *The urban neighborhood.* New York: Random House.
King, A. T. and Mieszkowski, P.
  1973   Racial discrimination, segregation, and the price of housing. *Journal of Political Economy 81*:590–606.
Klaff, V.
  1978   Ethnic and racial residential segregation as an indicator of social integration: In search of a model. Paper presented at the Ninth World Congress of Sociology, Uppsala.
Lansing, J., Clifton, C. W., and Morgan, J. N.
  1969   *New homes and poor people.* Ann Arbor: Institute for Social Research, University of Michigan.
Lansing, J. B. and Hendricks, G.
  1967   *Automobile ownership and residential density.* Ann Arbor: Survey Research Center, Institute for Social Research, University of Michigan.
Lee, T. H.
  1968   Housing and permanent income: Tests based on a three-year re-interview survey. *The Review of Economics and Statistics 60*:480–490.
Leven, C. L.
  1972   Changing sizes, forms, and functions of urban areas. Pp. 395–421 in S. M. Mazie (ed.), *Population, distribution, and policy.* Vol. 5 of U.S. Commission on Population Growth and the American Future, Commission Research Reports, Part 3. Washington, D.C.: U. S. Government Printing Office.
Lieberson, S.
  1963   *Ethnic patterns in American cities.* New York: The Free Press of Glencoe.
Logan, J. R.
  1976   Industrialization and the stratification of cities in suburban regions. *American Journal of Sociology 82*:333–348.
Maisel, S. and Winnick, L.
  1960   Family housing expenditures: Elusive laws and intrusive variances. Pp. 359–435 in I. Friend and R. Jones (eds.), *Consumption and savings.* Vol. 1. Philadelphia: Wharton School of Finance and Commerce, University of Pennsylvania.
Marrett, C. B.
  1973   Social stratification in urban areas. Pp. 172–188 in A. H. Hawley and V. P. Rock (eds.), *Segregation in residential areas.* Washington, D.C.: National Academy of Sciences.
Marshall, H. and Jiobu, R.
  1975   Residential segregation in United States cities: A causal analysis. *Social Forces 53*:449–460.

Martin, P.
1966 Aggregate housing demand: Test model, southern California. *Land Economics* 62:503–513.
Masotti, L. H. and Hadden, J. K. (eds.)
1973 *The urbanization of the suburbs.* Beverly Hills, Calif.: Sage Publications.
Masters, S.
1975 *Black–white income differentials: Empirical studies and policy implications.* New York: Academic Press.
McAllister, R. J., Kaiser, E. L., and Butler, E. W.
1971 Residential mobility of blacks and whites: A national longitudinal survey. *American Journal of Sociology* 77:445–456.
Meyer, J., Kain, J., and Wohl, M.
1965 *The urban transportation problem.* Cambridge, Mass.: Harvard University Press.
Meyerson, M., Terrett, B., and Weaton, W. L. C. (eds.).
1962 *Housing, people, and cities.* New York: McGraw-Hill.
Michelson, W. H.
1970 *Man and his urban environment.* Reading, Mass.: Addison-Wesley Publishing Company.
Mills, E. S.
1967 An aggregative model of resource allocation in a metropolitan area. *American Economic Review* 57:197–210.
Morgan, J. (ed.).
1974 *Five thousand American families.* Vol. 2. Ann Arbor: Institute for Social Research, University of Michigan.
Morris, E. W. and Winters, M.
1975 A theory of family housing adjustment. *Journal of Marriage and the Family 37*:78–88.
Muth, R. F.
1969 *Cities and housing.* Chicago: University of Chicago Press.
Muth, R. F.
1970 The demand for non-farm housing. Pp. 146–165 in A. N. Page and W. R. Seyfreid (eds.), *Urban analysis.* Glenview, Ill.: Scott, Foresman and Company.
Muth, R. F.
1974 Residential segregation and discrimination. Pp. 108–119 in G. M. von Furstenberg *et al.*, *Patterns of social discrimination.* Vol. 1. Lexington, Mass.: D. C. Heath.
National Academy of Political and Social Sciences.
1975 *Toward and understanding of metropolitan America.* San Francisco: Canfield Press.
Nelson, R. H.
1973 Accessibility and rent: Applying Becker's "time price" concept to the theory of residential location. *Urban Studies 10*:83–86.
Oates, W. E.
1969 The effects of property taxes and local public spending on property values: An empirical study of tax capitalization and the Tiebout hypothesis. *Journal of Political Economy 77*:957–971.
Olsen, E. O.
1969 A competitive theory of the housing market. *The American Economic Review 59*:612–622.
Pascal, A. H.
1967 *The economics of housing segregation.* RM-5510-RC. Santa Monica, Calif.: The RAND Corporation.
Pearce, D.
1976 Black, white, and many shades of gray: Real estate brokers and their racial practices.

Unpublished doctoral dissertation, Department of Sociology, University of Michigan, Ann Arbor.

Pettigrew, T. F.
1973   Attitudes on race and housing: A social-psychological view. In A. H. Hawley and V. P. Rock (eds.), *Segregation in residential areas*. Washington, D.C.: National Academy of Sciences.

Pirenne, H.
1962   *Medieval cities*. Garden City, N.Y.: Anchor Books.

Popenoe, D.
1974   Urban residential differentiation: An overview of patterns, trends and problems. Pp. 35–56 in M. P. Effrat (ed.), *The community*. New York: The Free Press.

Poston, D. L., Jr.
1972   Socioeconomic status and work–residence separation in metropolitan America. *Pacific Sociological Review 5*:367–380.

Powers, M. G.
1964   Age and space as aspects of city and suburban housing. *Land Economics 40*:381–387.

Premus, R.
1976   Implications of the Tiebout hypothesis for residential property valuation within small metropolitan regions: An empirical analysis. *The Review of Regional Studies 5*:1–11.

Quante, W.
1976   *The exodus of corporate headquarters from New York City*. New York: Praeger.

Quigley, J. M.
1974   Racial discrimination and the housing consumption of black households. Pp. 121–137 in G. M. von Furstenberg *et al.* (eds.), *Patterns of racial discrimination*. Vol. 1. Lexington, Mass.: D. C. Heath.

Ray, P. H.
1973   Residential location, consumer demand and urban structure. Unpublished doctoral dissertation, University of Michigan.

Redding, J. L.
1977   The influence of functional specialization on residential patterns in six American cities. Unpublished doctoral dissertation, University of Wisconsin-Madison.

Reid, M. C.
1962   *Housing and income*. Chicago: The University of Chicago Press.

Richardson, H. W.
1971   *Regional economics*. New York: Praeger.

Roistacher, E.
1974   Residential mobility. Pp. 41–78 in J. A. Morgan (ed.), *Five thousand families*. Vol. 2. Ann Arbor: Survey Research Center, Institute for Social Research, University of Michigan.

Roof, W. C., Van Valey, T. L., and Spain, D.
1976   Residential segregation in Southern cities: 1970. *Social Forces 55*:59–72.

Rose, H. M.
1976   *Black suburbanization*. Cambridge, Mass.: Ballinger.

Rozeboom, W.
1965   Linear correlations between sets of variables. *Psychometrika 30*:57–71.

Rozeboom, W.
1968   The theory of abstract partials: An introduction. *Psychometrika 33*:133–167.

Sahagh, G., Van Arsdol, M. D., Jr., and Butler, E. W.
1969   Some determinants of intra-urban residential mobility: Conceptual considerations. *Social Forces 48*:186–200.

Schnare, A. B.
1977   *Residential segregation by race in U. S. metropolitan areas: An analysis across cities and over time*. Washington, D.C.: The Urban Institute, Contract No. 246-2.

Schnore, L. F.
1963 Urban form: The case of the metropolitan community. Pp. 167–197 in W. Z. Hirsch (ed.), *Urban life and form.* New York: Holt, Rinehart and Winston.

Schnore, L. F.
1965 *The urban scene: Human ecology and demography.* New York: The Free Press.

Shelton, J. P.
1968 The cost of renting versus owning a home. *Land Economics 44*:59–72.

Simkus, A. J.
1978 Residential segregation by occupation and race. *American Sociological Review 43*:81–93.

Sjoberg, G.
1960 *The pre-industrial city: Past and present.* New York: The Free Press.

Smith, D. E.
1971 Household space and family organization. *Pacific Sociological Review 14*:53–78.

Sorensen, A., Taeuber, K. E., and Hollingsworth, L. J., Jr.
1975 Indexes of racial residential segregation for 109 cities in the United States, 1940 to 1970. *Sociological Focus 8*:125–142.

Speare, A., Jr., Goldstein, S., and Frey, W. H.
1975 *Residential mobility, migration and metropolitan change.* Cambridge, Mass.: Bollinger.

Stanbock, T. M., Jr.
1974 Suburban labor markets. Pp. 51–70 in E. Ginzberg (ed.), *The future of the metropolis: People, jobs, income.* Salt Lake City, Utah: Olympus.

Sternlieb, G. and Lake, R. W.
1975 Aging suburbs and black homeownership. *Annals of the American Academy of Political and Social Science 422*:105–117.

Straszheim, M. R.
1974 Racial discrimination in the urban housing market and its effects on black housing consumption. Pp. 139–164 in G. M. von Furstenberg *et al.* (eds.), *Patterns of racial discrimination.* Vol. 1. Lexington, Mass.: D. C. Heath.

Strauss, A. L.
1961 *Images of the American city.* New York: The Free Press.

Suttles, G. D.
1968 *The social order of the slums.* Chicago: University of Chicago Press.

Suttles, G. D.
1972 *The social construction of communities.* Chicago: University of Chicago Press.

Sweet, J. A.
1972 The living arrangements of separated, widowed, and divorced mothers. *Demography 9*:143–158.

Taeuber, K. E.
1970 Patterns of Negro–white residential segregation. *Milbank Memorial Fund Quarterly 48*:69–84.

Taeuber, K. E.
1975 Demographic perspectives on housing and school segregation. *Wayne Law Review 21*:833–850.

Taeuber, K. E.
1976 *Demographic trends affecting the future labor force.* Special Report Series SR14, Institute for Research on Poverty. Madison: University of Wisconsin.

Taeuber, K. E. and Taeuber, A. F.
1965 *Negroes in cities.* Chicago: Aldine.

Thompson, W.
1974 Emerging issues in metropolitan economics. Pp. 7–30 in E. Ginzberg (ed.), *The future of the metropolis: People, jobs, income.* Salt Lake City, Utah: Olympus.

Tiebout, C. M.
  1956 A pure theory of local expenditures. *Journal of Political Economy 64*:416–424.
Tilly, C.
  1961 Occupational rank and grade of residence in a metropolis. *American Journal of Sociology 67*:323–330.
Timms, D.
  1971 *The urban mosaic: Towards a theory of residential differentiation.* Cambridge, England: Cambridge University Press.
U. S. Bureau of the Census.
  1972 *Public use samples of basic records from the 1970 Census: Description and technical documentation.* Washington, D.C.: U. S. Government Printing Office.
U. S. Bureau of the Census
  1975 *Current Population Reports,* Series P-20, No. 279, Table 15.
U. S. Bureau of the Census
  1975 *Current Population Reports,* Series P-23, No. 55, Tables G and H.
U. S. Bureau of the Census
  1978 *Current Population Reports,* Series P-20, No. 320, Table 39.
U. S. Bureau of the Census
  1978 *Current Population Reports,* Series P-20, No. 324, Table 18.
U. S. Department of Housing and Urban Development
  1968 *Housing surveys, Parts I and II: Occupants of new housing units, mobile homes, and the housing supply.* Washington, D.C.: U. S. Government Printing Office.
U. S. Department of Housing and Urban Development
  1978 *Preliminary findings of the 1977 housing market practices survey of forty cities.* Presented at the Tenth Anniversary Conference of Title VIII, April 17–18, Washington, D. C.
Uyeki, E. S.
  1964 Residential distribution and stratification, 1950–1960. *American Journal of Sociology 69*:491–498.
von Furstenberg, G. M., Harrison, B., and Horowitz, A. R.
  1974 *Patterns of racial discrimination.* Vol. 1. *Housing.* Lexington, Mass.: D. C. Heath.
Werts, C. E., Linn, R., and Jöreskog, K. G.
  1973 Identification and estimation in path analysis with unmeasured variables. *American Journal of Sociology 78*:1469–1484.
Wheeler, J. O.
  1967 Occupational status and work trips: A minimum distance approach. *Social Forces 45*:508–515.
Whitbread, M. and Bird, H.
  1973 Rent, surplus and the evaluation of residential environments. *Regional Studies 7*:193–223.
Wilson, F. D.
  1973 Dimensions of housing status. Unpublished doctoral dissertation, Washington State University, Pullman, Washington.
Wilson, F. D.
  1974 The cost of housing in black neighborhoods. *Institute for Research on Poverty Discussion Paper 241-74,* Madison: University of Wisconsin.
Wilson, F. D.
  1975 The ecology of a black business district: Sociological and historical analysis. *The Review of Black Political Economy 5*:353–375.
Wilson, F. D.
  1976 Journey to work: Metropolitan–nonmetropolitan comparisons. *The Center for Demography and Ecology Working Paper 76-12.* Madison: University of Wisconsin.

Wilson, F. D.
  1978 The organizational component of expanding metropolitan systems. Pp. 133–156 in K. E. Taeuber, L. L. Bumpass, and J. A. Sweet (eds.), *Social demography*. New York: Academic Press.
Wilson, F. D. and Taeuber, K. E.
  1978 Residential and school segregation: Some tests of their association. Pp. 51–77 in Frank Bean and W. Parker Frisbie (eds.), *Demography of racial and ethnic groups*. New York: Academic Press.
Winger, A. R.
  1968 Housing and income. *Western Economic Journal 6*:226–232.
Winger, A. R.
  1969 Trade-offs in housing. *Land Economics 45*:413–417.
Wingo, L.
  1961 *Transportation and urban land*. Washington, D.C.: Resources for the Future.
Winsborough, H. H.
  1972 Changes in mode of travel to work, 1934–1960. *The Center for Demography and Ecology Working Paper 72–12*. Madison: University of Wisconsin.
Wolfe, B.
  1977 Income measures in empirical work: Results with family size and value of home. *Institute for Research on Poverty Discussion Paper 428–77*. Madison, Wisc.: Institute for Research on Poverty.
Yeates, M. H. and Garner, B. J.
  1972 *The North American city*. New York: Harper & Row.
Yinger, J.
  1974 Three essays on the economics of discrimination in housing. Unpublished doctoral dissertation, Princeton University, Princeton, N.J.
Yinger, J.
  1975 The black–white price differential in housing: Some further evidence. *Institute for Research on Poverty Discussion Paper 308–75*. Madison, Wisc.: Institute for Research on Poverty.

Index

A

Accessibility, *see also* Intrametropolitan location; Commuting
  defined, 86
  as related to household activities, 86
  to work place, 86–87, 129
    assumptions about, 10, 27
    determinants of, 87, 104, 129
    distance, determinants of, 87–94, 95–97
    effect of spatial organization, 86, 95–96, 104, 129
      measurement of, 21, 27, 102, 104
    models of, 87–94
    time travel, determinants of, 97–98
Age of family head, *see also* Family status
  as an indicator of family status, 20–21, 41, 47–48
  and number of persons in household, 47–48

B

Black Americans, *see also* Racial differential; Wages
  improvement in residential environment, 132, 186
  and racial discrimination, *see also* Racial discrimination

  in housing markets, 13–14, 105–106, 130
    price differential, 107–108
    racial exclusion, 106–107, 108–120
  in labor markets, 13–14, 105, 107
  and racial differential in housing market, *see* Racial differential
  suburbanization of
    and housing characteristics, 190–193
    and location within suburb, 190
    and reason for moving to suburbs, 190
    and socioeconomic and family attributes, 188–190
    trends in, 153–154, 187–188
  suburbanization of employment, 14–15, 193–195
    and commuting, 139, 154–160
    effect on worker, 139–141, 161–165, 170–176
  and wages, 176–179

C

Central city–suburban differentials
  and employment, 13, 142–147, 161
  and family status, 76, 79, 87
  and fiscal structure, 79, 83, 128–129
  and housing quality, 83, 84

and housing space, 83
and neighborhood attributes, 70, 83
and perceptions of housing and neighbor-
    hood quality, 78
and population density, 83
and property tax, 79, 83, 128–129
and socioeconomic status, 76, 79, 83, 87
and socioeconomic status of neighbor-
    hoods, 83
and tenure of household, 79, 83, 84
value of single family units, 79
and wages, 165–166, 170–176
Commuting, see also Accessibility; Intramet-
    ropolitan location
differentials in, 154–160
and wages, 166–170

D
Data, source of
annual housing survey, 19, 77–78, 186–187
panel study of income dynamics, 19, 94
public use sample
    of neighborhood characteristics, 19–20
    of state, 141–142
Dwelling, characteristics of, see Housing
    space; Housing quality; Single fam-
    ily homes

E
Education, see Socioeconomic status
Employment, see Suburbanization of em-
    ployment
Estimation procedure
and canonical correlation analysis, 37
and component difference analysis, 170,
    172–175
and confirmatory factory analysis, 65
and LISREL, 41–45
and log-linear analysis, 147–149

F
Family life cycle, 5, see also Family status
Family status
and accessibility to workplace, 104
and housing consumption, 38
and housing quality, 39, 50–51
and housing space, 39, 50–51, 129
indicators of, 20–21, 41
    problems with, 47–48
and neighborhood attributes, 59, 109
and socioeconomic status, 38
and suburban location, 83
and tenure of household, 50, 51, 129

Financial institutions and residential choice,
    58–59, see also Housing markets

G
Governmental policies
effect on residential choice, 6, 58
and suburbanization of population, 75

H
Hedonic price index
and expected income, 22
and residential consumption
    owner households, 25
    renter households, 23–25
Housing markets
and constraints on residential behavior,
    6–7, see also Governmental policies;
    Racial discrimination; Realtors
Housing quality
and accessibility to workplace, 104
family status, 38, 39, 50–51, 52, 129
and housing space, 10, 38, 40, 71
measurement of, 21, 26, 41, 61–62
and neighborhood attributes, 69, 128
and relative income, 52
and socioeconomic status, 38, 51–52
and suburban location, 83
and tenure of household, 39, 48, 59, 127–
    128
Housing space
and accessibility, 104
and family status, 38, 39, 50–51, 52
and housing quality, 10, 39, 41, 62, 71
measurement of, 21, 26, 40–41, 61
and neighborhood attributes, 69, 71, 128
and relative income, 52
and socioeconomic status, 38, 51–52, 129
and suburban location, 83
and tenure of household, 39, 48, 50, 69,
    127–128
Housing services, see also Housing quality;
    Housing space
components of, 37
measurements of, 37

I
Income, see also Relative income; Wages
expected family income
    definition of, 21–22
    and racial differential in residential con-
        sumption, 113, 116, 118, 133–134
    and socioeconomic status, 21–22
neighborhood, median income of, and

socioeconomic status, 26
wife's contribution to family income
    measurement of, 21, 22
    and residential consumption, 110, 112–113
Intrametropolitan location, *see also* Suburbanization of employment; Suburbanization of population
    and employment, workplace, *see also* Accessibility; Residence–workplace mismatch
        industry, 142–143, 149, 150
        occupation, 143–147, 149, 150, 151
        racial differentials in, 153–154
        region of residence, 149
        residential location, 73
        size of place, 149–152
        wages, 165–166, 170–176
    and property taxation, 73, 128
    and property value, 79, 128
    and public service structure, 73, 128–129
    and residential consumption, 5, 73, 128

L
Life style, *see also* Residential differentiation
    and residential consumption, 110–120
    and socioeconomic status, 59

M
Metropolitan area
    spatial organization of, 137
    workplace, 86, 95–96, 104, 129

N
Neighborhoods
    defined, 2, 72
    and social contacts, 55–56
Neighborhood attributes
    and accessibility to employment, 104
    components of, 8
    and family status, 70–71, 129
    and housing quality, 69, 128
    and housing space, 69, 128
    measurement of, 21, 26–27
    residual correlations among, 10–11, 62
    and socioeconomic status
        of neighborhoods, 62
            problems in measurement of, 63–64
        of primary families, 70, 129
    and suburban location, 83
    and tenure of household, 69, 127–128
Neighborhood stability, *see* Neighborhood attributes

Number of persons in household, *see also* Family status
    and age of head, 47–48
    as an indicator of family status, 20–21, 47–48

O
Occupational status, *see* Socioeconomic status

P
Percentage black, *see* Neighborhood attributes
Percentage of units built after 1959, *see* Neighborhood attributes
Population density, *see* Neighborhood attributes
Primary family
    and residential consumption, 5–6, 13
    and sample selection, 20
    as unit of production and consumption, 3–4, 36, 126–127
    white, and suburbanization, 75–76
Public service structure, *see* Intrametropolitan location

R
Racial differentials, *see also* Black Americans
    and commuting, 39, 154–160
    and decentralization in employment, 154–160
    and decentralization in population, 154
    and housing price, 107–108
    and housing quality, 121, 122
    and housing supply, 108–109
    and neighborhood quality, 122
    and perception of housing and neighborhood quality, 109–110, 130
    and residential consumption, 105, 110–112, 121–122, 130
        residential expenditures, 116, 118–119, 130
        tenure of household, 113, 116, 119, 121–122, 130
    and socioeconomic status, 122, 133–134, 186
    and wage differentials, 170–179, *see also* Wages, differentials in
Racial discrimination
    in housing market, 14–15, 130
    in labor market, 14–15, 105, 107
    and racial residential segregation
        white motivation in, 132–133

and residential behavior, 13–14, 105–106
  price differential, 107–108
  racial exclusion, 108–120
Realtors and residential choice, 6, 59
Regional location
  and housing consumption, 38–39
  and suburbanization of employment, 147–
    149
Relative income
  definition of, 21, 22
  and housing quality, 52
  and housing space, 52
  and residential consumption, 52
  and tenure of household, 52
Residence–workplace mismatch
  adverse effects of, 139, 140, 193–194
  and decentralization of employment and
    population, 139
  race and sex differentials in commuting,
    153–160
  review of previous studies, 140–141
  and wages
    black and white, 166–176
    central city–suburb, 165–166
Residential consumption
  and housing price, 58
  measurement of, 21, 23–25
  and residential services, 8
  and workplace location, 10
Residential decisions
  and cross-sectional analysis, 6
  and utility maximization, 7, 11–12
Residential differentiation, see also Residen-
    tial segregation
  and accessibility, 54, 57
  and housing market actors, see also Gov-
    ernmental policies; Realtors, 54,
    58–59
  and housing supply, 54, 58
  and life-style, 54, 55–56
  and residential segregation, 54
  and social stratification, 55
  and urban growth pattern, 56–57
Residential goods, see Residential services
Residential mobility
  and employment location, 98–102
  and residential consumption, 5, 98–102
Residential segregation, see also Residential
    differentiation
  and ethnicity, 55
  and family status, 70–71
  and race, 55
    black and white attitudes, 133

discrimination, 14, 132–133
  level of, 132
  socioeconomic status, 133–134
  and socioeconomic status, 55, 76
Residential services
  component of, 8
  consumption of, 4
  demand, assumption related to, 8, 60–61,
    127
  as inputs into productive activities, 3–4, 36,
    59, 126–127
  and intrametropolitan location, 73
  and intrametropolitan mobility, 5, 98–102
  model of the demand for, 7–12

S
Single family homes, cost of, see also Dwell-
    ing, characteristics of
  and adjustment in purchasing patterns, 7,
    131
  and changes in housing production, 131–
    132
Socioeconomic status
  components of, 21–22, 41
  and family status, 38
  and housing consumption, 38
    housing quality, 39, 129
    housing space, 39, 129
  as an indicator of life-style, 59, 110, 112
  and neighborhood attributes, 21, 70, 129
  and suburban location, 83
  and tenure of household, 51–52, 129
Socioeconomic status of neighborhoods, see
    Neighborhood attributes
Suburbanization
  aggregate measure of, 27–28
  effects of, 52
  and neighborhood attributes, 70
Suburbanization of employment, see also In-
    trametropolitan location
  effects on central cities, 138–139
  historical patterns, 12–13, 137–138, 161
Suburbanization of population, see also Black
    Americans
  factors associated with
  historical growth, 74
  since World War II, 12–13, 74–75, 153–154
  and sources of growth, 75
  and suburban location, 83
    demand for single family homes, 75, 76
    and property taxation, 75, 76–77
    public service structure, 75, 76–77
Suburban location, see also Central city–

suburban differentials; Intrametropolitan location
and distance from the central city, 85
measurement of, 21, 27

T
Tenure of household
defined, 11, 21
and family life cycle, 5
and family status, 50–51, 52
and housing quality, 38, 48, 50, 127–128
and housing space, 38, 48, 50, 69, 127–128
and intrametropolitan location, 5, 128
and neighborhood attributes, 69, 71, 127–
128
and racial differential in, 113, 116, 119,
121–122
and relative income, 52
and residential consumption, 11
and socioeconomic status, 51–52
and suburban location, 83

U
Urbanized area
and housing consumption, 38–39
and suburbanization, 149–152

V
Valuation of neighborhood dwelling, *see*
Neighborhood attributes

W
Wages, *see also* Income
determinants of, 170, 172
differentials in
blacks and whites, 170–179, *see also*
Black Americans
central cities and suburbs, *see alo* Central
city–suburban differentials, 165–
166, 170–176